push the button

push the

Elizabeth Rodwell

button

INTERACTIVE TELEVISION
AND COLLABORATIVE
JOURNALISM IN JAPAN

DUKE UNIVERSITY PRESS
Durham and London
2024

Designed by A. Mattson Gallagher
Typeset in Minion Pro, Myriad Pro, and Helvetica Rounded
by Westchester Publishing Services

Library of Congress Cataloging-in-Publication Data
Names: Rodwell, Elizabeth, [date] author.
Title: Push the button : interactive television and collaborative
journalism in Japan / Elizabeth Rodwell.
Other titles: Interactive television and collaborative journalism
in Japan.
Description: Durham : Duke University Press, 2024. | Includes
bibliographical references and index.
Identifiers: LCCN 2023017403 (print)
LCCN 2023017404 (ebook)
ISBN 9781478025764 (paperback)
ISBN 9781478021025 (hardcover)
ISBN 9781478027898 (ebook)
Subjects: LCSH: Interactive television—Japan. | Interactive
television—Social aspects—Japan. | BISAC: SOCIAL SCIENCE /
Media Studies | SOCIAL SCIENCE / Anthropology / Cultural
& Social
Classification: LCC HE8700.95 .R369 2023 (print) |
LCC HE8700.95 (ebook) | DDC 384.550952—dc23/eng/20231120
LC record available at https://lccn.loc.gov/2023017403
LC ebook record available at https://lccn.loc.gov/2023017404

Cover art: Photo illustration based on a still from the
NHK-NTV collaborative broadcast event *60 Ban Shōbu*,
showing the use of a mobile interface for interactive television.
Illustration and title lettering by Martin Pepper, based on a
concept by A. Mattson Gallagher.

This book is dedicated to my father, Dr. John D. Rodwell, whose time in Japan when I was a child motivated me to do research there myself. To Martin and the boys, who buoy me up when I need it, you made space for me to finish this during a global pandemic and I love you. Finally, to all the journalists and hardworking media industry employees out there, your hustle and passion are models for my own.

CONTENTS

ACKNOWLEDGMENTS

First, thank you to the Duke University Press folks who made this happen. I had long dreamt of working with you before it became a reality. Special thanks to editing wizard Ken Wissoker and assistant supreme Ryan Kendall for replying to my emails filled with many !s and !!s along the way.

This book would not have happened if it weren't for grants from the National Science Foundation (EAPSI program), a Rice University Wagoner grant, and a Social Science Research Council/Japan Society for the Promotion of Science Postdoctoral Fellowship. It also would not have happened were it not for the space and support to work on it from the Department of Information Science Technology at the University of Houston. Thank you also to the inspiring scholars in the Comparative Cultural Studies program who have allowed me to pop in and out of their departmental space. To my UH colleagues, I am profoundly grateful.

I benefited from the support of gracious advisers, who have been patient with my incessant fretting over the years and let me find my way back to academia after a five-year detour working in UX. I am profoundly grateful to Anne Allison, Dominic Boyer, Jim Faubion, and Cymene Howe for being willing to help me out even when I wasn't their student anymore and never saying no to a single request for a letter of recommendation or some advice. Thank you also to Shin Mizukoshi for allowing me to be a part of your lab at the University of Tokyo, as well as for guiding me so expertly during my time in Tokyo—I hope Kansai University is treating you as well as you deserve. Thank you to William Mazzarella, who supervised my frenetic transition into the field of anthropology from media studies and has served as a role model for how to turn ethnography into elegant prose.

A special thank-you to the former interim president of the University of Houston–Downtown, Michael Olivas, who read something I wrote and bought me a plane ticket that changed everything. Dr. Olivas, you had no reason to believe in me when I was an adjunct at your university, but you did. I was in the middle of writing this paragraph when I learned of your passing, and you will be sorely missed.

A hearty cheer to the people of the University of South Carolina's Ann Johnson Institute for Science and Technology Studies for giving me a truly exceptional opportunity and for being people I'd choose to hang out with either way. Relatedly, a sincere thank-you to Ian Condry and Tanjev Schultz for taking so much time to thoughtfully review my manuscript.

A warm thank-you to everyone who helped support me in the field and contributed to my fieldwork in general, including Boku Masayoshi, Brian Berry, Jeremy Crawford, Muge Dane, Trevor Durbin, Alex Hambleton, Stefanie Holiman Durbin, Jenna Judge, Furukawa Ryuko, Kate Goldfarb, Hirata Makiko, Mutsuko Holiman, Iwakami Yasumi, Jinno Yoko, Kari-Hans Kommonen, Gabi Lukacs, Sarah Lyons-Padilla, Nishimura Mariko, Nomura Masamitsu, Ogawa Akiko, Kai Okura, Sakai Osamu, Glenda Roberts, Takahashi Hideki, Uesugi Takashi, Mikko Villi, Marcus Wellenski, Dan White, Yamashita Hiroshi, Russell Yost, the 2011 EAPSI cohort, the 2010 Middlebury Japanese cohort, and all of Bascule, the IWJ, GoHoo, the FPAJ/No Border, and Mizukoshi Sensei's lab. Thank you to the many other collaborators and friends who I am not naming here only to protect their confidentiality; I owe you so much and wish I could thank you by name.

Thank you to my colleagues at the University of Houston, which has truly been a lovely workplace thanks to the support of people like my department chair, Amaury Lendasse, and my former program director, Jerry Waite. Thank you to my diligent former research assistant Emiru Okada. And to my students—I owe thanks to you all too—especially the alumnae of my 2019 UX class. Extra thanks to the smart UH ladies I get to work with every day (even if only fleetingly on committees), including, but not limited to, Rachel Afi Quinn, Monika Alters, Nancy Beck Young, Pamara Chang, Peggy Lindner, Kristina Neumann, Debarati Sen, Leandra Zarnow, and Lauren Zentz. Your wit keeps me sane.

Special thanks to my grad school colleagues at Rice University, which was the most collegial, supportive department of my grad school career. And to Ellen, John, and Sarah Rodwell, who made sure I know that they believe in me and that I could finish this project, even when things got rough. Additional thanks to my father, Dr. John Rodwell, who motivated my interest in Japan through his trips and stories of Kyoto during my childhood, and who also encouraged me to have faith I could tackle a doctorate—no problem. Thank you also to the Peppers and Lutzes for the times you've supported my mental health and work by babysitting, providing company, and telling me I have a "big brain." And thank you to Kim Brims whose friendship got me through the hardest time I ever had in Houston.

Thank you to the kind people who run La Tartine on Dairy Ashford Road in Houston, Texas, for letting me work there when I got tired of my own four walls. And for the free encouragement croissants. It meant more than I told you.

Finally, I want to profoundly thank my partner, Martin Pepper, who listened to me when I got stuck, cheered me on as I revised this manuscript (sometimes with champagne around the fire pit), and helped me believe in adventure and a silver lining again. And to my four boys—August, Cyrus, Charlie, and Freddie—I love all of you. By the time you see this, I'll have (finally) taken you with me to Japan. But no matter where we go, there's nobody with whom I'd rather ride in a golf cart.

Introduction

Late one night on TV Tokyo, one of Japan's major networks, the latest project of one of Tokyo's most adventurous young companies is about to begin. The air is filled with tension of a sort both manufactured and autonomic. As with all live TV, and particularly the nascent genre of interactive television, there exists the potential for massive and spontaneous failure. As one employee later confessed, everyone's heart was racing, *dokidoki*. "We can't fail" (*Shippai dekinai*), he thought.

Bloody Tube, as the program is called, is an interactive game show allowing viewers to participate in a spacecraft race using smartphones as game controllers. Teams are divided according to blood type and directed by four guest hosts as the race unfolds within the simulated blood vessels of a female idol, Dan Mitsu. Several months earlier in 2013, *Bloody Tube* was still in pieces around the offices of a forty-one-person interaction design agency called Bascule.[1] Long before the summer evening when its staff gathered in a TV control room, Bascule's designers carefully plotted the position of cameras and fabricated a reproduction of Dan's body to test 3-D projection mapping. They storyboarded the animation sequences and sketched concepts for the program/game's animated *masukotto kyara* (mascots). Across many, many meetings they assembled a languid three-and-a-half-minute opening sequence for *Bloody Tube*, to entice audiences accustomed to conventional forms of passive pseudoresponse to join in a new kind of spectacle, within which technology was as much on display as Dan Mitsu's *utsukushii karada* ("beautiful body," in the words of the emcee). The final effect was part *The Matrix*, part *Tron* or even *Ghost in the Shell*, and it was also an attempt to create an immersive, interactive playground where viewers could come together as a public to experience television watching—or television using—as a communal activity.

Programs such as those constructed by agencies like Bascule, teamLab, and the in-house production teams of the major networks were, in the early 2010s, emergent. This is to say that just over a year earlier, there had been none. But in the immediate post-Fukushima era, the interest in and the effort to create interactive television increased dramatically. Driven by technology such as (television network) NTV's "Join TV" and Bascule's "Massive Interactive Entertainment System" (MIES), this kind of television raised provocative new issues for the theoretical apperception of what television means and what it is.

Television in Japan has been a contested medium since the 1950s, but this has especially been so since the 1964 Tokyo Olympics catalyzed rapid changes in broadcast infrastructure and a renewed focus on television's potential. One legacy of this field of media critique, TV Man Union (Terebiman Yunion, or TVU), was founded in 1970 by former Tokyo Broadcasting Service (TBS) network directors Hagimoto Haruhiko, Konno Tsutomu, and Muraki Yoshihiko as an independent and mutually owned creative group. Influenced by an earlier twentieth-century discourse on documentary cinema's role and artistic potential, this "union" challenged the (still) dominant model wherein production companies served as subcontractors to the TV stations and established TV Man Union as Japan's first independent production company.[2] Foreshadowing the media self-enquiry discussed in this book, this effort also arose out of a tension between media professionals and conservative Japanese politicians over what kinds of political commentary can be broadcast. Like many thought leaders featured in the subsequent chapters, TV Man Union's founders established their legacy through an enduring manifesto, titled "You Are Just the Present," within which they argued for the capacity of television to celebrate the everyday and to divest documentary video from a need for artfulness over authenticity.[3]

Echoes of the TVU venture also exist in the numerous experimental and innovative media-related groups found in contemporary Tokyo, and in the precedent that some of the most prescient mass media critiques would come from those who once worked for the major networks (e.g., Hori Jun, Shiraishi Hajime). They also reflect a historic schism between those who believe change can come from within the TV system and those who wish to demolish it in favor of something more democratic.[4] I highlight TV Man Union here within the history of Japanese media theory, because of the empathy between its specific provocations and those of the interactive media experiments in this book. Konno Tsutomu writes about ownership over the present (*genzai*) as something "difficult for power to allow,"[5] which we see challenged by programs like *The Compass* (chapter 2) and by the activities of the Free Press Association of Japan and Independent Web Journal (chapter 3).

TV Man Union's arguments arose within an ongoing tradition of media industry insiders and critics alike scrutinizing the interplay between presentation strategies, capitalism, and audiences. In 1957, influential social critic Ōya Sōichi famously referred to television as turning the Japanese public into a nation of "100 million idiots" (*ichioku sō hakuchi-ka*).[6] Media critic Uesugi Takashi later appropriated this phrase in the "100 million brainwashed" subtitle of his own 2011 book, to underscore his perception of a public that blindly accepts media narratives.[7] But what if these "brainwashed" audiences could have a direct hand in shaping the contents of the programs themselves? And if this strategy could align the medium with the ethos of other contemporary media forms?

Despite Japan's embrace of its reputation for technological innovation, the country's use of a sophisticated interactive TV infrastructure has generally gone unnoticed, even domestically. If the questions often posed to me by Americans are any indication, Japanese TV has a transnational reputation for wacky and extreme stunts or placing foreign celebrities in awkward situations (the *Lost in Translation* effect[8]), by contrast with the documented conservatism of its mass media. But significantly for this project, television in 2010s Japan was characterized by long-standing tensions for which the massive 2011 earthquake and Fukushima nuclear plant disasters merely acted as an accelerant. The burden of declining ratings and advertising revenue, combined with a crisis of faith in television's capacity to provide essential information during that disaster, led mainstream TV professionals to seek novel ways to maintain television's slipping dominance in the media sector. Historically speaking, interactive TV seems a logical progression from the problem that "young people aren't watching television," to the cause, "because they are spending their 'media time' engaged with interactive technology," to the solution, that "we should create programming that combines the platform of television with the interactivity of these devices, appropriating them directly as part of the viewing experience."

Born out of ethnographic fieldwork conducted in Tokyo in the two years immediately following the Fukushima nuclear disaster, *Push the Button* explores how interactive television and audiovisual media producers—both in the mainstream television industry and the nascent independent news media sector—conceived of ways to marry interactivity to a mass medium that has long been critiqued for its monodirectional approach to transmission. Against the chronic ambiguity of these terms, some of the core questions posed by this book are the following: What constitutes interactivity, and how do interactive media authors envision audiences and publics as coproducers? How do producers build programming around opportunities for interaction as they seek to bridge audience participation to television content? While I initially conceived of my fieldwork as being about the contrast between open versus closed systems of knowledge production, I have largely moved away from the limitations of this framing. But the interactive projects I describe can still be divided according to their resources, production facilities, and the legitimizing framing of institutions. This insider/outsider divergence remains one of the core binaries operating in this book.

I chose to study Japanese television because of a cosmonaut reporter. When I learned that the first Japanese citizen in space was TBS journalist Akiyama Toyohiro, sent by his employer aboard a Soviet rocket to document his experience on TV (for an impressive 36 percent audience share), I was curious about how the medium's public significance and authority had evolved since then.[9] The broadcast conglomerates (*media konguromaritto*) seemed both powerful and perilous—and essential to consider if one wished to write about Japan. As sociologist John Clammer has observed, "The sheer size and power of the Japanese media, and of advertising within the media, make it central to understanding cultural processes in contemporary Japan."[10] But what happens to these cultural processes when technology facilitates the dissemination of competing narratives about nationalism, public safety, and even community? And what if television is tested by a national disaster just as audiences have begun to look elsewhere for news and entertainment?

The Meanings of Interactivity

In Japan, a renewed interest in adapting networked interactivity to television came after 2011, when the Fukushima nuclear disaster triggered a political and media crisis that collided with mounting worries among Japanese television professionals about the loss of audiences to the internet. Consequently, much industry dialog began to revolve around how television content, including news, could be made more responsive to public reaction and input by expanding the capacity of social media–enhanced television. At the same time, a galvanized independent news media sector emerged with several new startups interested in developing alternative televisual news sources by harnessing the interactive and participatory capacity of live streaming video services and websites. What these two bodies had in common was a belief that better TV could be made by interpolating audiences into both the production and output of television content.

In this book, interaction is defined as audiences taking an active role in the development of programming, but it occurs at varying degrees of depth within the featured case studies—from television shows that allow viewers to push a few buttons and play an instrument along with a popular musical group (the *Arashi feat. You* special in chapter 4) to content solely in the hands of audience-authors (Our Planet-TV in chapter 5). Each of these complicates and challenges the categories of mass media producer/consumer by proposing to allow audiences to occupy both categories at the same time, in a way that serves the mainstream media system itself (and social media companies) in inconsistent ways.[11] Contributing an additional layer of complexity is the evolving nature of *interactivity* as a concept and accompanying uncertainty about what it means for audiences in terms of control over process and outcome. Whose needs would it meet? Would interactive programming merely serve to comfort producers that they had made every effort to engage audiences on their terms? Would it check off a box on the technological advancement timeline, if it even was an advance? Or would it allow them to make a meaningful contribution to the public sphere and fulfill some of the iconic fantasies of the internet age?

The relationship between interactivity and publics has been of interest to media producers and theoreticians since the earliest days of television. Experiments with interactivity have taken many different forms, frequently by allowing audiences to participate as contestants in programming like the American game show *Twenty-One* (1956–58), sometimes called the first reality TV contest.[12] Or it has meant subjecting audiences to ostensibly unwitting participation in pranks as in the Japanese *Nandemo Yarimashō* (1953–59) or the American *Candid Camera* (1948–2014). Additional overtures toward audience participation can be found in the ubiquitous shows that allow audiences to participate by submitting votes (e.g., the international *Got Talent, X-Factor,* and *Idol* franchises, or Japan's *Kōhaku Uta Gassen*), taking part in social media polls, or tweeting at live television (e.g., sports, the news).

In Japan, television producers' grander ambitions for interactivity had long been stymied by technological limitations. Producers for Japan's public television network NHK (Nippon Hōsō Kyōkai) spoke to me of their 1990s vision of participation that could sculpt media content rather than just reacting to it, such as the 1993 *Kinmirai Terebi SIM,* described in chapter 2. Unlike participation that required physical presence in studios or the accompaniment of a roving camera, proposals for a contemporary adaptation of this vision captured the imaginations of Japanese media producers in the 2010s. Therein, producers hoped to marry the simultaneous collective participation made possible by the internet to a broader, more representative national public than was accessible to variety shows or "person on the street" interviews (*gaitō intabyū,* discussed in chapter 5).

This stage of evolution in the Japanese television industry was significant on a few fronts. A common assertion that television companies had, as of 2013, already appropriated social media in productive ways—essentially eliminating the tension between the two mediums—overestimated the transformative effects of program-related websites and tweeting.[13] Rather, these efforts seemed little different from early efforts to extend television to the internet via home pages providing supplemental content in the form of resources, background information, and merchandise.[14] Indeed, there was only token interactivity to be found in such efforts, as television used the web mainly as a means by which to transmit announcements and maintain its monodirectional format.

The many targeted surveys that circulated among media professionals during my fieldwork seemingly supported the move to interactive television by promoting methods to track internet use habits and formulate marketing strategies around them. One frequently invoked study emphasized several points that have become common industry knowledge since then: 1. Japanese iPhone and Android users accessed YouTube more frequently (measured both daily and weekly) than the official websites of television companies. 2. Social media use among smartphone users was dominated by the circulation of images (photographs or videos), but also the reposting of content via sharing or retweeting. 3. Men continued to represent the largest number of cell phone users, but women, young people (in general), and—most importantly—television viewers were well represented.[15] These data were offered up either in defense of various strategies to increase viewership, or simply pro forma, following any number of NHK Research Institute talks. "Social TV" was born of such studies, which showed that desirable young audiences were spending most of their cell phone time interacting with friends, via SMS, Line, Instagram, MIXI, email, and so forth.[16] If 81 percent of smartphone users did not use their phones to watch television,[17] television would insinuate itself into their established behaviors.

The move toward interactive TV experimentation was therefore significant because it represented the most serious acknowledgment thus far that Japanese television considered its hegemony to be threatened by the internet. As an oligarchical system dominated by five major national broadcast networks, Japanese television was reliant on a share of the national audience that it seemed to be losing (see figure I.1). According to NHK's report, in the funding year 2009, the commercial networks entered into a decline in advertising revenue ranging from 8 to 16 percent (10 percent within five years)—a downward trajectory that has continued since then, with the exception of 2010.[18] Despite the introduction of mobile phone–viewable live TV back in 2006, television consumption outside of the home could not compensate for what was lost during home viewing.[19] These seemingly small shifts were uncomfortable for the industry—particularly as ratings were largely being buoyed up by senior citizens, whose consumer spending was insufficient to maintain comfortable and consistent advertising revenue for the networks.

The threat to TV viewership represented by social media notwithstanding, broadcast professionals working on interactive programming found hope in data from one of Japan's biggest advertising companies, Hakuhodo, which reported that during 2010–2013, consumers in the Tokyo metropolitan region maintained a steady amount of overall media "contact time" (*sesshoku jikan*)—and only 29.4 percent of audience members did not use their cell phones at all while watching TV.[20] In this, broadcast professionals perceived an opening: the potential to redirect the individual already holding their phone to a form of television that used both. Despite the finding by the same survey that in 2013, 69.7 percent of television viewers neither read nor wrote about programs while watching them, and only 50.8 percent had ever talked about TV on social media at all,[21] the basic profile of Japanese

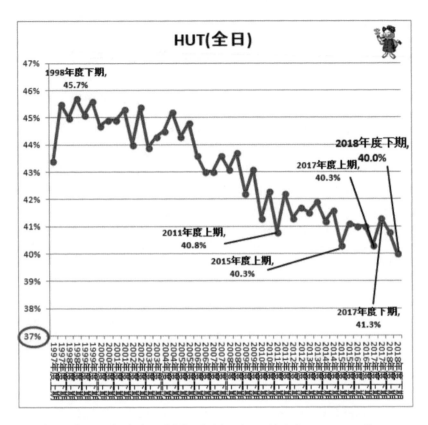

I.1 A chart indicating the decline of daily television viewership in Japan, measured by household.

social TV was conceived: it would involve users directly acting on TV content in real time using a second-screen device (smartphone, tablet, laptop/ desktop computer)—or even a remote control due to Japan's data transmission infrastructure (*dēta hōsō*).[22] It would use social media to enable audiences to interact with broadcast content in a way that determined the final qualities of that content.

The new interactivity proposed, in its ideal form, to change the nature of authorship and respond to the most basic critiques of television as invested in audiences as passive and uncritical consumers. With his "100 million idiots" rhetoric, Ōya was in good company among intellectuals critical of television—a medium to which Frankfurt School theorists Max Horkheimer and Theodor W. Adorno easily applied their critique of the culture industry.[23] Echoed in recent arguments made by my fieldwork collaborators, theoreticians have blamed both capitalism and a limited number of media conglomerates for the inherent conservatism of mass media content. Essays linking television to social decline (including, famously, Neil Postman's work[24]) have been abundant and frequently described the nature of TV content as inevitable/intrinsic to the medium, while neglecting to explore the professional praxis of media professionals and the agency of audiences. The project of marrying interactivity to live broadcast was promoted by media producers using some of the same arguments as intellectuals who have considered the medium harmful for encouraging passive consumption.[25] Producers framed the notion of involving audiences in coconstituted content as harnessing the pleasure of social media and enhancing it through connection to the single stage of television. As they appropriated the language of early internet development, Japanese TV networks delighted in the idea that the passive viewer could become the active coauthor, rendering television a democratic medium after all. That editorial control remained central to these projects was subsumed by idealistic discourse about a new, progressive kind of media subjectivity and reenergized audiences.

Those who wished to go beyond the limited interactivity of the past by more closely combining internet and TV content found themselves in a new experimental category with the potential to reconcile seemingly divergent modes of interacting with media content and increase ratings accordingly. But the emergent nature of these projects made it difficult to define "interactive television" and necessary to clarify the objectives behind the term "interactive" (usually anglicized as *intarakutibu*). Further ambiguating matters, media professionals also referred to their experiments as "social TV" (*sosharu terebi*), and I have used the terms interchangeably myself at times.[26] Reflecting earlier practices mentioned above, these names formerly either suggested television shows that allow viewers to call in and register votes or news programs that display Twitter comments along the bottom of their screens. But the new 2010s interactive television in Japan was different. New experiments were able to leap forward into allowing audiences to participate in content generation and "play along" with the programs.

Finally, concern about interactivity occurred during a significant moment of tension for both the news and entertainment sectors of the television industry as they fought to retain their role as chief architects of national publics. Compared to the greater capacity of online forums and social media to capture a range of national moods and concerns (and simply to function more democratically), television promoted a manicured, well-mannered version of nationhood that many media makers outside the big conglomerates found increasingly irrelevant, if not harmful.

Historically, the TV industry had been protected from competition by a national requirement for broadcast licenses, which limited the total number of television channels. Thus, the internet represented a form of competition for audiences that TV was, in a sense, not accustomed to. In Ujiie Natsuhiko's phrasing, the privileged (*tokkenteki*) space of television infantilized it, allowing it to ignore the development of other media until "*terebi no kabe ga hōkaishi hajimete iru noda*" (the wall surrounding television is beginning to collapse).[27] That moment of collapse appeared imminent in the wake of the Fukushima disaster.

Publics and the News in Post-Fukushima Japan

On March 11, 2011, a magnitude 9.0 earthquake near East Japan triggered a tsunami and subsequently caused a massive nuclear accident at the Fukushima Daiichi Nuclear Power Plant. The human impact as well as the historical significance of these events was enormous—the earthquake was the strongest ever recorded in Japan, and the nuclear disaster was categorized alongside Chernobyl as the worst to have ever occurred in the world.[28]

In the months after the Fukushima disaster, domestic news coverage highlighted order-in-chaos, focusing on the choice of individuals to reinforce and restore social order as efficiently as possible through mass cooperation, self-restraint (from looting and theft), etc. At the same time, lateral communications allowed individuals to bypass official news, which tended to be both too general and too cautious, in order to exchange information of immediate importance (e.g., open supermarkets and places to bathe).[29] This diversion of normal information flows was significant because Japan's TV news landscape is dominated by five major national networks.[30] The five major broadcasters in Japan (TV Asahi, Fuji TV, NTV, TBS, and public broadcaster NHK) operate "key" stations in Tokyo and provide content to regional channels, with the identity of those stations conventionally determined by the network whose news broadcast they use. Broadcast law prohibits local channels from having an exclusive relationship with any one key station (i.e., establishing affiliates), but partner stations generally source 80 percent of their content from a single Tokyo key station.[31] As Palestinian-Japanese journalist Shigenobu May wrote, "3/11" and the Arab Spring of 2010 contained some basic parallels, insofar as citizens bypassed or supplemented mass media in favor of social media–driven information exchange. In both cases, the major media outlets largely sought to manage and contain the crises and were accordingly considered untrustworthy—too proximate to a coercive governmental infrastructure.[32]

The disruption that occurred in the early 2010s cannot be properly appreciated without understanding how political journalism, and specifically TV news journalism, functions in Japan. Political scientist Laurie Freeman has noted, "The reality in Japan . . . is that the mass media have frequently worked together with, or on behalf of the political core—capturing, subverting, misleading, or alternately ignoring the political periphery represented by the public sphere."[33] This is endemic to Japan's oft-critiqued *kisha kurabu* (reporter's club) system. As has been well documented, reporters from all the major newspapers and television networks who are assigned to a particular post work within one shared office/room in the government/corporate buildings, are subjected to reductive official sources of information at periodic intervals, often exclude the foreign and independent press, and punish deviation from the official story.[34] In other words, rather than ostensibly serving audiences in the traditionally monodirectional sense, journalism, particularly under the Abe Shinzo administration, strove to meet the needs and expectations politicians had for its platform.[35]

Following 3/11, tensions between political parties and the mass media in Japan heightened, and the Japanese political system increasingly indulged in performances of power over television and newspapers. Among several such incidents, in 2013 the Liberal Democratic Party (LDP) announced that it would boycott TBS after one of its programs aired a clean energy activist's critical report on the party's energy policies. While the party claimed to have no issues with the factual content of the report, it commented that the "editorial presentation" was problematic and that the party could not allow TBS to "cunningly highlight a negative image of our party."[36] TV Asahi and NHK have endured similar friction and meddling from the government.[37]

Post-Fukushima, journalistic circles acknowledged that (then) prime minister Abe Shinzo's second administration was determined to foster a hostile relationship with the Japanese media.[38] This relationship only worsened in the years after the disaster, with the administration encouraging reporters to neutralize their work for fear of losing access to sources—or their job.[39] Requests made of television broadcasters—for example, to cover the party fairly—were taken as veiled threats that they must do so, and journalists who critiqued the Abe administration faced institutional repercussions, including transfers and personal blacklisting. As Abe's appointee to the chairmanship of Japan's public broadcaster NHK pronounced during his first press conference in 2015: "[The media] cannot say left when the government says right."[40]

Thus, when I arrived in the immediate post-Fukushima era to begin preliminary fieldwork, the word "crisis" (*kuraishisu*) was frequently invoked to describe the condition of journalism, which many people told me had finally crossed over from a "system in need of reform" to a "system putting citizens at risk." In parallel, it was of great interest to self-proclaimed "media activist" Tsuda Daisuke that while an estimated one-third to one-half of Japanese computer users engaged with any form of social media, Twitter use had expanded dramatically between 2010 and 2012 as individuals sought alternative means by which to exchange written and visual information.[41] (Japan has remained one of the strongest Twitter markets in the world.[42]) As a result, throughout the 2010s, media activists perceived social media in Japan as entering a period of great potential as a tool for social reform. What media activists considered mass media's unconscionable habit of information withholding inspired them to go beyond their usual punditry to form media watchdog organizations and to provide alternate information channels for others who felt they could no longer trust the mass media.[43] This acted as the rallying cry around which several online news organizations formed and initially generated a pool of sympathetic donors. These independent media startups would try to serve the public with news content more worthy of their attention, and their approach sought to interpolate the public, via internet-based communications technologies, as citizens in a democratic process of political dialog and engagement.

The Interactive Public Will Save Television

Meanwhile, long before the 3/11 disasters, television industry professionals were sounding the death knell for their medium. As early as 2001, former Fuji TV producer Ōta Tōru had identified one of the main tensions surrounding the medium, stating that Fuji TV and networks like NTV and TBS had been repeatedly doing the same thing for ten years—and within his genre ("trendy" dramas), the formula had already been exploited to exhaustion.[44] Television, he argued, is a medium that "sleeps with the times," meaning that it surrenders itself to contemporary trends rather than leading them.[45] During my fieldwork, people in the industry whispered conspiratorially to me that average citizens would never see the collapse coming, and society would carry on until—as in the case of the 2008 global banking crisis—its inevitability exceeded the industry's capacity for containment.

Such theories were born of television's declining advertising revenue, and of an increasing amount of time spent by audiences using social media at the expense of TV time.[46] As previously described, many decided that a solution was to marry the interactivity made possible with social media to the flatness of TV—to reengage internet audiences in television content. But the pursuit of interactivity was also seen as an antidote to another significant transformation of television watching after the 1990s: the disappearance of national publics unified by consuming the same content.

Although Japan is globally known as a leader in the development of broadcast technology, the nuances of how broadcasting works domestically and the historical culture surrounding television are less widely known. The idea of television as something consumed collectively and ritualistically dominated Japan's thinking about the medium during the early days of television technology. A philosophy of television emerged not just from the equipment being too expensive for most consumers but from a related notion of ideal consumption patterns revolving around total numbers of viewers rather than individual TV sets. As such, Shoriki Matsutaro, the president of the *Yomiuri Shinbun* (newspaper) and Japan's first commercial television network (NTV), focused on installing televisions in public places (so-called *gaito terebi*), from street corners to train stations.[47] Bars, restaurants, and barber shops gradually followed suit as spaces of television consumption, and the Japanese press celebrated the public embrace of this mode of viewing when more than twenty thousand people gathered to publicly consume a single sumo match in 1953. It was between 1956 and 1960 that television viewing relocated from the public to the private sphere, largely in response to the fledgling industry's sensationalism about Crown Prince Akihito's engagement and frenetic promotion of his 1959 wedding as a massive broadcast event. Their campaign ultimately succeeded, as two million people hurriedly purchased television sets at newly lowered prices and established an estimated at-home market of fifteen million viewers for the fifty-minute wedding parade.

The 1960s set a rapid pace for ongoing technological experimentation and development, as Japanese television anticipated the 1964 Tokyo Olympics by importing American hardware and then independently developing color and satellite broadcasts.[48] A massively communal home viewing experience, the resultant broadcast was a performance of miraculous postwar recovery and sophisticated technological development, which has ostensibly been sustained in the still-potent connection between Japanese national pride and global performances of technological innovation.

Yet my interlocutors inside and outside of the broadcast corporations found it frustrating that despite this continuing emphasis on technological prowess, the Japanese television industry has remained conservative about content development. For decades, producers created programming to appeal to entire families who gathered around a single TV set in the medium's *cha no ma* heyday (see chapter 1). But individual ownership of mobile devices with fast data transmission and streaming content had broken the family into siloed viewing units with greater choice over what they watched and less dependence on television. And yet, Japanese television remained hesitant to change its formulas. In the area of news programming, one reason was that television networks, which are also newspaper and radio station owners, have been consistently challenged to protect the interests of both their print and broadcast journalism markets. As summarized by behavioral scientist Eleanor Westney, this has meant that the broadcast divisions of these conglomerates are dependent on the journalistic efforts and resources of their print counterparts and deliberately retard their broadcast divisions to avoid competition between the two for audiences.[49] The second source of recalcitrance for the TV industry can be found in its emphasis on broadcasting to a national body, for which it has struggled to translate legacy forms of content to contemporary viewing habits.[50] One might expect the country's experiments with interactive TV to follow reliable patterns, to overlay conventional taxonomies onto new technologies—and indeed, this is what happened.

Besides formal news programs, the oligarchical broadcast system remains dominated by a combination of morning shows (*jōhō bangumi*), variety shows (*waido shō*), dramas, and special events. Given widespread perceptions of repetitive and undesirable content dominating the country's mass media, I was not surprised when a former employee of Hakuhodo (the second-largest advertising firm in Japan and eighth in the world) mused during my interview with him:

> "There is NHK, there is TBS, TV Asahi, there is Fuji TV, there is NTV. Five stations is probably too many . . . too many.[51] And so they all make inane (*kudaranai*) programs, so I'm thinking that maybe two or three will disappear or become specialty channels. Like one for variety, one for sports. Maybe they can change in that way . . . [Japan has] BS channels, cable, and on-demand viewing, and I think people are going to increasingly move to watching those. I admit that I want a news-only channel. It's weird that Japan has five networks, eh?"[52]

Attempts to keep costs down while appealing to the most desirable consumer demographics raised their own set of tensions. During my preliminary fieldwork, long-standing tensions between Japan and Korea and perceptions of Fuji TV's increasing reliance on imported Korean dramas led to protests involving thousands of people outside the network's Odaiba headquarters, which I waded through on my way into the offices.[53] Although content decisions like these were generally made for budget reasons during this era of "TV recession" (*terebi fukyō*), some audiences were unsympathetic to financial arguments.

The methods by which Japanese television and media producers heralded the interactivity of experimental 2010s programming highlighted the recalcitrance of the industry there. The closer that diverse audience voices came to the threshold of gatekeeping, the more marginalized a broadcast was. This meant that the shows featuring the coolest tech and encouraging active participation confined that participation to a very limited number of actions and restricted commenting to a dedicated app or mobile responsive website. However, the ambitions of producers generally exceeded the outcomes of these programs. What they were permitted to accomplish within the context of media conglomerates, or the smaller platforms of independent media groups, was heavily compromised. The most compelling experimentalism was therefore often found less in these outcomes of professional labor than in the conversations held behind the scenes—at networking events, in production meetings, on filming trips, and in studios during a broadcast.

Open and Closed Systems: Independent vs. Mainstream Broadcast

Two very different media sectors—mainstream broadcast television and independent news media agencies—were therefore seeking new publics at the same time, but to serve different ends. For TV, it was to secure the role of the industry (and its financial health) into the future, but for news journalism, it was to generate an engaged political citizenry. Nonetheless, both considered their efforts a radical shift away from a media system intent on prescribing content, to one that engages audiences' participation in customizing and curating their own media experiences. Experiments with interactivity in both sectors had in common their goal of reforming the content and media practices of conventional broadcast TV and reframing the role of audiences. This book ultimately chronicles ad hoc interventions by my interlocutors rather than a comprehensive policy of change within the industry. Indeed, the resource-intensiveness of interactive programming and limited motivation to normalize it relegated the technology to "special events" and/or alternative media outlets rather than representing a new direction for mass media. Yet its authors remained ambitious, and at the heart of their labor was an idealistic desire to transcend the stifling monodirectionality of the producer-audience relationship.

It is this tension between a willingness to readily experiment with new kinds of television technology and a disinclination to depart from proven formats of programming that makes television in Japan especially interesting. Within the immediate post-3/11 climate, some in Japan feared that theirs was a system that would always favor displays of technical innovation over meaningful reform of problematic institutions like the long-standing *kisha kurabu* system. Yet as the media activists who emerged during this time argued, the transformation of problematic institutions and conventions required rethinking the interaction between mass media producers and publics. In particular, Ujiie Natsuhiko, a frequent contributor to one of the blogs written for and by industry insiders, commented that television companies must evolve from media companies to media *service* companies and update their conceptualization of viewers to the category of users.[54] Although this process was often conceived by media producers in terms of economics or technological affordances, it also could not help but be thoroughly social and cultural—and these competing needs often worked at cross-purposes with what they sought to achieve.

If studying the production processes taught me anything, it was that experiments in interactive broadcast rarely fell into neatly defined theoretical or aspirational categories. Japan, like other countries that have attempted to bring TV into the internet age, has experienced incongruent development of technological, economic, political, and creative infrastructures and ideologies, leading to projects that were low-tech but conceptually ambitious and vice versa. Fieldwork also taught me that perceptions of Japanese mass media were remarkably consistent among those holding positions of power in TV companies, contractors working for them, and self-labeled "independent" journalists. Apart from cynicism, there was a combination of giddy exhilaration and anxiety among interactive TV advocates and media reformers alike, with the Fukushima disaster reviving sentiments that something should change. Although Henry Jenkins once wrote that, "despite the rhetoric about 'democratizing television,' [the shift toward participatory media] is being driven by economic calculations and

I.2 A doodle posted on a wall in the Free Press Association of Japan's office, showing a cat ripping up a newspaper. Photo by author.

not by some broad mission to empower the public,"[55] this was not necessarily how individual Japanese TV producers and journalists saw it.

This book is an attempt to understand the stakes of work within Japanese mass media (television and journalism) during a critical time in its development, by exploring how idealistic stakeholders attempted to force fundamental changes in the way their news and entertainment divisions produced content and engaged audiences. Some of these stakeholders are the industry insiders—a cross section of business and creative players who are working to construct and introduce provocative new television technology within the mainstream TV industry, to fulfill the promise of interactivity suggested by early experiments in symbiotic content and inspired by the rise of internet use in the 1990s. Their projects, which frequently draw on traditional Japanese programmatic themes and formats, are using cutting-edge technology to "turn viewers into users," to allow audiences to cocreate content and narratives as this new genre of television unfolds live. The other stakeholders are the independent media activists and media startups composed predominantly of disaffected former industry employees, as well as some media industry hopefuls who could not (for reasons that frequently amount to insufficient educational credentials in status-conscious Japan) gain employment by the companies and corporations represented by the technologically minded first category. For this group, technological transformation is an issue of lesser concern than their project of comprehensive ethical reform, and their efforts are largely based on a strategy of creating alternate media spaces in which audiences are encouraged to become content creators—or at least participants in nonmainstream production spaces—to increase the diversity of voices represented in the public sphere(s). What emerges from these two overlapping spaces of media practice is a portrait of interactivity in television as less of a breakthrough of technology than one of social and cultural connection, latently centered on the relationship between media creator and audience.

The Fieldwork That Made This Book

Push the Button is the outcome of eighteen months of fieldwork conducted within several categories of Tokyo-based sites (with some detours to Aomori, Nagoya, and Osaka) and using a full arsenal of ethnographic tools to track media makers across their many sites of professional activity. My field sites included all the major broadcast networks (although I spent the most time at two of them), one radio station, two affiliated television production companies, and the offices of five independent media startups (the Free Press Association of Japan aka *Jiyū Hōdō Kyōkai*, No Border, Independent Web Journal [IWJ], Our Planet-TV, and GoHoo aka *Masukomi Gohō Kenshō*).[56] I also held an internship at the company responsible for most of the interactive and social television programming that aired during my fieldwork (Bascule) and visited the offices of the other for interviews. Further, I made myself a regular at as many media research presentations as I could attend and at many independent media events that were supported by those at my startup field sites or involved members of these. Indeed, to echo a fellow anthropologist of Japan, Ian Condry, "the number of potential field sites was daunting."[57] To follow the activities of freelance journalists and TV insiders pushing for experimentation with interactive broadcast, I attempted to spend an equivalent amount of time each week embedded in the offices and production sites of both categories of media, dividing my time in half whenever events schedules and interviews allowed it. I also had to engage in digital ethnography, following the communications of media stakeholders and the contributions of anonymous web users on 2chan and NicoNico,[58] but I viewed this process as secondary to understanding the production culture of different kinds of interactive media authors through participation in their work-worlds.

This project, therefore, represents "polymorphous engagement" of the type envisioned by anthropologist Hugh Gusterson, who understood through experience how creative researchers must be when approaching fieldwork in restricted corporate environments.[59] Competition between networks meant that management at each tended to be extremely sensitive to the idea that I was doing fieldwork with their competitors, and they consistently asked me to refrain from directly comparing institutional climates and resources. In other words, a scarcity mindset informed the way networks appraised one another. And mass media is always a moving target; as Mark Deuze notes, "The key challenge of communication and media studies in the 21st century is, or will be, the disappearance of media."[60] Indeed, this book chronicles attempts to push back against the extinction of media forms by coaxing them into a new hybrid form that conventional, monodirectional television has since outlived.

I focus on media producers to examine how the communities responsible for broadcast content experience their work as a social process, part of an ongoing conversation with and about audiences and themselves.[61] While textual analysis of media products and audience surveys/reception studies are relatively commonplace, there remains even now a paucity of lengthy workplace studies involving the media makers themselves—particularly in East Asian countries. Criticism by parties not privy to internal media industry dialog has rendered TV professionals either caricatures lacking the sophistication to understand the ramifications of formulaic programming, or sinister actors plotting the obfuscation of politically sensitive information. While early media research focused on consumption and circulation, the practices of institutions themselves remained black boxes that "menace[d] democracy and local individual autonomy."[62] It is easier, when one excludes the voices of broadcast professionals, to assess television as a coherent body with a uniform set of values and messages—to write about it as a sophisticated and even Orwellian behemoth slyly coaxing citizens into desired political positions or lulling them into indifference. The reality is, of course, much messier. If media scholarship allows audiences to act as opinion-having bodies for whom dis/pleasure is a viable response, it must also allow broadcasters to engage emotionally with their work and recognize the institutional limitations compromising their vision. Just as reception studies have granted us access to the worlds of audiences and permitted us to understand them as active decoders of media messages, ethnographic accounts of media workplaces have taught us that the world of production is no less negotiated.[63] An accurate and three-dimensional theory of mass media must account for the messiness of being a viewer, as well as what it means to be a producer under similar circumstances, *and* acknowledge that audiences are shaped both by producers' conceptualizations of them and their self-perception relative to interactive technologies.

Fieldwork for this project has generally been a collaborative endeavor involving interlocutors with educational backgrounds that resembled my own and who periodically invoked canonical media theory to explain their decision-making. (Favorites included the Frankfurt School theorists and Marshall McLuhan, whom some deployed self-deprecatingly to illustrate the compromises inherent to their work.) Following Laura Nader's canonical treatise on "studying up," through which she illuminated the tensions inherent in conducting fieldwork among those with greater social power, Ulf Hannerz characterized research on media professionals as "studying sideways." Under such conditions, the ethnographer is among subjects who often possess similar credentials and (sometimes greater) cultural capital than the anthropologist and are accustomed to critically assessing and reproducing culture themselves.[64] Studying educated elites introduces particular anxiety; by anthropologist Maureen Mahon's account, such subjects are complicated targets, not easily fixed spatiotemporally or theoretically due to their self-awareness, mobility, and mediation.[65] As such, I have sometimes engaged in subsequent chapters with the arguments of classic theorists invoked by my interlocutors, as a way of thinking with them as collaborators and to better represent their perspectives on what they may have been trying to achieve. References to Western models (infrastructural, or of content) as ideals of media practice also came up often in my conversations with Japanese interactive TV and news media producers, although it was not always clear the extent to which my presence elicited these references or to what extent such references were a part of everyday praxis.

A tendency for Japanese TV producers to invoke the US industry as a foil for their systems has therefore informed my juxtaposition of the two markets, though there are many countries whose infrastructure more closely approximates Japan's. The American broadcast model was held up as an ideal by my collaborators, as the United States moved toward high-budget cinematic shows in the *Game of Thrones* era and embraced smart TVs with on-demand streaming apps. Differences in broadcast infrastructure have contributed to the divergence between the US and Japanese industries. For one, an American cable TV model that never gained traction in Japan prompted the US industry to segment audiences into niches early on and target them accordingly.[66] While networks in Japan may not have to compete with as many rivals, they also lack the budgets of their American counterparts or the expectation that their shows are destined for global consumption. Japanese television was also engaged in ongoing collaboration with its American counterpart that surpassed its relationships with the media of any other country and contributed to a transnational negotiation about versions of interactivity that could appropriate and integrate American social media platforms. Thus, when I do bring the United States into the conversation, it is an attempt to connect to a dialog I began during my fieldwork and have maintained from afar since then.

Matters of theory and structure, therefore, motivate my engagement with the 1980s–90s debates in anthropology regarding the benefits of reconstituting ethnography as more "discourse" than "text"—as "postmodern" ethnography meant to function as a dialog rather than a monolog and as a product of collaboration with the individuals whose lifeworlds we visit[67]— were especially salient in my work with critical theory–savvy media professionals. Approached in this way, the resultant project is cooperative, with the anthropologist's impressions of another culture complicated by those of its most mediated representatives.

How to Use This Book

This is ultimately a book about the meaning of interactivity and the ways that different Japanese business/cultural sites of production and television/journalistic modes of practice informed the ways that interactive content fulfilled its potential (positive and negative) or laid the groundwork for a more participatory, inclusive mass media in the future. It is also a book about the catalysts for such efforts, ranging from anxiety over young audiences' lack of engagement with TV content in Japan to a feeling that television would never choose audience interests over those of sponsors when curating the news. What each of the projects and organizations in this book sought, even more than opportunities for technological innovation, was a chance to build spaces of social and cultural connection for audiences (and latently, between audiences and media producers).

Push the Button as a title refers to a few different concepts. Chiefly, it is the mediated moment between the media author, user, and platform captured within each of the projects described here. These broadcasts employed mobile responsive user interfaces that solicited repeat touch in different ways: to keep time to a beat, race a spaceship, vote in a game, or tap a Like button. Indeed, interaction design revolves around such "button moments," to the extent that they are a topic of significant user experience–related commentary.[68] Buttons as a component of technology occupy a particular space in our imaginations, as the final catalysts allowing a tool to carry out its function. Buttons sit at a crossroads between kinetic and potential energy for those who will use them and act as a point of intersection between the authors and users of tools. They are the locus of the connection sought by media creators and are subject to as many negotiations as the programs themselves. While this book places media makers at the forefront of its examination, the imperative "push the button" represents hope as much as a command. The semiotic power of buttons is such that they serve as conduits for users' needs and expressions of their behavior within systems.

The projects described here represent a metaphorical "pushing of buttons" for those who saw only risk in allowing greater participation in the flow of broadcast. Further, the phrase "push the button" points to the convergence of media users, mediating technology, and media makers and evokes the feelings of apprehension and instability introduced by such buttons. All the interactive broadcast events described in this book were indeed anxiously unpredictable in their unfolding and represented attempts to strike a balance between intimacy and collective effervescence, to harness the different kinds of affective experiences possible for members of a virtual crowd. Several underlying questions seemed to drive these anxieties: Would new kinds of publics emerge from these experiments? Would these publics save television from its financial difficulties or rescue democracy from a stifling journalistic environment? Or would they produce other kinds of publics entirely?

The experiments addressed here account for the ways that participation is negotiated by audiences and producers of mass media—as creators and cocreators alike. Each chapter tracks the development and execution of a specific interactive project, locates it within the context of Japan's mass media history, and examines the outcomes of its production and its implication for the future of participatory, community media. Chapter 1 discusses the media industry reception of one famously ambitious interactive TV experiment, a joint NHK-NTV special titled *60 Ban Shōbu* (60-year battle), held in honor of Japanese TV broadcast's sixtieth anniversary. Based on my participation in trade events around Tokyo, the conversations I document show how the Japanese TV industry continues to contend with issues of ratings and profitability, even as media producers seek to align with audiences' current media practices in ways that could revolutionize the television industry. Chapter 2 follows by examining an experimental interactive news talk show on Fuji TV called *The Compass*, which allowed audiences to make live contributions to its discussions. Despite the idealistic orientation of many TV producers about the benefits of introducing more diverse voices into news commentary, the show's potential was handicapped by traditional forms of gatekeeping, even as the informality facilitated by some of its information channels promised to create intimacy between media maker and audience, and between audience members themselves.

In chapter 3, I move to a discussion of independent news startups to examine the ways that interactivity as an ideal extended beyond the television studios to a form of self-described "media activism" deployed to revitalize the body politic. In this chapter we see what happens when media producers' gatekeeping is restrained on public platforms that strive to be truly interactive, the consequences of which included the migration of an aggressive internet right-wing (*netto uyoku*) presence to these participatory channels. Independent journalists using interactivity to promote more equitable journalism are shown in this chapter to occupy a liminal position between media maker, audience, and technology. Chapter 4 traces some of the most ambitious interactive TV experiences in the major broadcast networks: interactive game shows. Focused on using interactivity to create community around a sense of national belonging, these experiments were surprisingly successful at introducing familiar concepts of national homogeneity into innovative contexts, but in so doing they treated audiences reductively and deprived them of meaningful intimacy within interactive spaces.

Finally, in chapter 5 I follow Our Planet-TV, an organization devoted to citizen journalism, as a participant in one of its training workshops. Based on my experiences with our group documentary project, I explore the perspectives held by both producers and audience members about media production and the shared vocabulary they use to communicate their goals.

I also evaluate Our Planet-TV's efforts to teach authorship to media audiences and describe how participants in its workshops draw substantially on their own past media exposure to create content that feels authentic. As the final body chapter of the book, this chapter shows that interactivity is ultimately a dialectic between media makers as creators and audiences as receivers. In the practice of citizen journalism, media maker and audience member engage as parts of a single self.

1

The Interactive Consumer-Viewer

THE SOCIAL TV PROMOTION COLLECTIVE, RATINGS, AND ADVERTISING

It is the sixtieth anniversary of television broadcast in Japan, and the country's oldest broadcasters, NHK and NTV, want to do something big, something to usher in the next sixty years of television history. Their plan is rather ambitious: a two-day, live interactive television broadcast on February 2–3, 2013, representing a collaboration between the networks and an ambitious Tokyo agency called Bascule. The program is designed as a contest, with one day's two-hour special hosted at NHK studios, the next at NTV, and both networks mobilizing their most compelling historical footage to win the most *ii*'s (likes) from audiences. The show as a contest makes a game out of the usual cutthroat competition for ratings and talent that characterizes the relationship between TV networks. That it is a collaboration is more exceptional.

60 Ban Shōbu (60-year battle), as the program is dubbed, is heavily promoted—a large banner announcing its broadcast hangs over the famously frenetic Shibuya "scramble" intersection in the heart of Tokyo. Studio tension exceeds that of a standard live television broadcast, with viewer interactivity both possible and essential, but little prior experience in the execution of such systems. Staff upload giddy cell phone shots of the behind-the-scenes vigil, tagging each other in images documenting their patient attention to the necessary infrastructure of this new television experiment. Given the celebratory nature of this broadcast, it is imperative that this, the current pinnacle of Japanese televisual technology, function correctly, and that it successfully transfer audience admiration of broadcast technology in its heyday to an equally ambitious future. The content of the program itself represents a narrative of technology's becoming through time. As viewers screen the historical footage curated by NHK and NTV for the *Shōbu*, we are reminded of how Japan announced its post–World War II techno-infrastructural rebirth to the world in part through the unveiling of revolutionary new broadcast technology during the 1964 Tokyo Olympics.[1] The narrative that emerges is that of a nation for whom technology, especially television technology, has been critical to national pride.

The interactive system that accompanies this narrative is simple: viewers access a mobile-responsive page containing a single button: *ii* (like).[2] When so inspired by the content onscreen, they can press this button, and in-studio graphs behind the program's hosts consistently update to show audience responses in real time (see figure 1.1). *Tarento* (TV personalities) both instruct on and participate in the use of this technology, which can be accessed via smartphone, tablet, computer, and even remote control. And viewers do engage, hitting their *ii* buttons almost twenty million times during the two days of broadcast.[3]

During our meeting soon after the *60 Ban Shōbu*, staff of Japan's major ratings aggregator, Video Research Ltd., expressed delight at the "*ii* button" concept. While traditional ratings measured the state of a television set (on or off, and which channel), they had never curated real-time enjoyment. The collective effervescence of the historic street-corner crowd was technologically unreachable despite the arrival of practices like live tweeting and live streaming via websites like NicoNico (discussed in chapter 2). Rather, the echo chamber of public opinion about programming was generally time shifted and steered by formal reviews, while extemporaneous reactions still unfolded privately as individual social networks processed TV together.[4] By contrast, during *60 Ban Shōbu*, viewers' enjoyment could be mapped in real time to specific moments in the show. And it was as much the gap between how accurately television and social media could measure audiences as it was any interest in technological advancement that drove TV's anxious pursuit of interactivity.

As the live broadcast choreography begins, the number of app users climbs and the program narrates a history of broadcast technology itself—from

1.1 The mobile responsive interface for the *60 Ban Shōbu* collaboration between NHK and NTV.

the 1953 emergence of NHK, to the construction of the Tokyo Tower in Roppongi, to highly rated moments in TV history presumed to be beloved, programs from the 1950s dissecting American culture, the 1973 series *Mokuyō Supesharu*, a twenty-four-hour television marathon from the 1980s, and—by far the most entertaining to the in-studio and home audiences, as measured by their "likes"—an episode of the 1994 NHK program *Shumi Hyakka*, featuring a man slowly contorting himself into jaw-dropping yoga poses. This historical bricolage serves dual purposes for the network; apart from its entertainment value, it secondarily performs NHK's public value as a curator of educational content. More so than NTV, its commercial broadcast partner for this program, NHK is charged as Japan's publicly funded station with "elevating the level of civilization" and must therefore perform its worth by displaying its history.[5]

Given the pioneering nature of the *60 Ban Shōbu*, it was immediately appropriated by the *terebi no mirai* (future of television) research set; over the next eight months I would see its telltale primary-colored stills reproduced on PowerPoint screens across Tokyo, its system evaluated and dissected by researchers and industry insiders alike. Prominent among them was the Sōsharu Terebi Suishin Kaigi (Social TV Promotion Collective, or STSK), dominated by senior-level television professionals with the agency to engage in thought leadership.[6]

Meetings of the STSK had the ambiance of a collegial academic roundtable, with demonstrations of new technologies and analysis of social TV experiments preceding introspective philosophical discourse on broadcast's future. During the time of my entry into the group in early 2013, the *60 Ban Shōbu* was a subject of ongoing scrutiny for its potential to modulate the representation of viewers on television and advance their capacity to act on TV content. Presentations about this program also took the form of dissecting the technologies used by NHK and NTV to produce the *Shōbu* but chiefly focused on the broader implications of increased audience engagement, including its potential benefits to advertisers and the contribution to ratings.

A March STSK postmortem on this program by NHK, NTV, and Bascule representatives begins with the usual overview quantifying and correlating smartphone use among young audiences (with graphs, Venn diagrams, and tables marshaled to show evidence). An NHK producer talks specifically about the tendency of young viewers to use smartphones while watching TV; this is a trend they might be able to appropriate: 22 percent of viewers engage with social media while watching TV every week, 14 percent daily.

But 74 percent firmly denied the habit.[7] I look around, awaiting the dismayed reactions of the TV professionals, but find only pleased or neutral expressions on the faces of those around me. They experience these data as potential, as suggestive of a brand-new mode of television consumption. A member raises his hand and asks, "So, does connecting television and social networking (like SNS) have any effect on ratings?"[8] This, unfortunately, nobody can answer. Although STSK members can quantify ratings and the unreliable number of times viewers report engaging with social media while watching television, they cannot yet determine whether tweeting or Facebooking about a program encourages others to tune in. How social TV can be used to disambiguate ratings will be one of the group's most enduring themes during my time with it. (And it still is.)

This chapter examines how the STSK appropriated interactive television as a potential solution to the industry's ongoing economic tensions and dissects the tension between its members' aspirations, the technological limitations of new programming, and the critical roles of audience participation and virtual community building. Meetings of this group were also spaces for industry leaders, inspired by earlier waves of TV experimentation, to test theories about what drives national audiences. Their themes converged on television's mandate to attract younger viewers to television, connect their viewing to newer forms of technology, and update ratings measurement to account for contemporary viewing habits. These dialogs raised questions about the existence of publics as the TV industry had conceived of them so far and contested historic approaches to theorizing audiences as crude demographic categories (if not a single national body). To a large extent, the conversations held within the STSK predicted the direction taken by the industry since then, toward expanding how it tracks audiences and writes about ratings.[9] And although this chapter discusses the evolving relationship between audiences and television, my approach here is to focus on the internal dialog of industry professionals, mirroring the conventional orientation of the communications industry in some of the media theory they most frequently invoke.

Happiness Is Essential to Television

On a day so windy in mid-March 2013 that it stopped a couple of Tokyo's train lines, public television broadcaster NHK's Hōsō Bunka Kenkyūjo (Broadcast Culture Research Group) is holding one of its regular symposia to discuss the future of television. These presentations, which rely heavily on both survey and ethnographic data, are essentially academic in nature—indistinguishable from a social scientific conference apart from their comparatively large audience size. With a focus on youth markets and contextualization of their (lack of) television viewing, today's presentations incorporate findings from surveys indicating that kids claim to increasingly be enjoying school, and a related survey claiming that 90 percent of middle and high school kids consider themselves happy (*ima shiawase*).

Most of the presented data suggested that happiness and regard for Japanese society decreased with age and were grounded in the assumption that maintaining television audiences required mass media professionals to consider fostering positive social connections as critical to their success. Essentially, with image sharing across social media services taking up a lion's share of its audience's leisure time, the industry has become invested in not just insinuating itself into this practice, but in keeping audiences sufficiently invested in maintaining social contact with one another to share media content at all. Indeed, the alternative is to keep losing out to social media, or whatever comes next—even in the case of young audience members who both own a television set and turn it on. Following these internal conversations, NHK aired a 2013 special in which the network ethnographically tracked individual viewers—watching them watch TV, the camera positioned so that the television appeared to return their gaze.[10] And the program's archetypical teenage subject performed the fears and expectations of many a media producer. Even with the television turned on, the girl's eyes remain overwhelmingly on her phone. To make light of this, and perhaps to underscore it as well, a comedic sound is triggered each time the girl looks up to face us. The scene becomes a commentary on a contemporary unwillingness to detach from one kind of technology in favor of another, with the audience in the position of the televisual apparatus—watching her *not* watch us.

A subsequent researcher continues the NHK event with a survey asking audiences why they might choose to view programs with their family; the majority answer is amusingly pragmatic: the best household television set is in the living room. The man sitting next to me with his arms crossed clears his throat and mumbles, "Is mass media okay?" ("*Masukomi wa daijōbu?*")

Contemporary Japan is frequently appraised in both scholarly and media production circles as one of fragmented and mobile connections (that is, when connections are even made) and characterized as a society in which media consumption is both mobile and solitary.[11] Clip art and stock photographs of cell phones inevitably make an appearance in presentations about contemporary TV viewers. At the Symposium "Mobile '13," during a well-attended presentation by representatives of the massively popular Korean chat app Line, company representatives argued that we had already moved from the eras of the newspaper, the radio, the television, and the PC to arrive in the smartphone's historical moment.[12] But while technology is represented here in terms of a Hegelian succession of stages, with television already two steps in the evolutionary past, presentations crafted by those among the body of Japanese communications researchers studying television locate handheld devices (including laptops) in a synergistic relationship with television. In their presentations, arrows, transmission lines, and presumably data are bidirectional. The possible use of interactive television and other new technologies to bridge the gap between the two represents the Sōsharu Terebi Suishin Kaigi's entry point.

I am invited to attend a meeting of the STSK after this presentation when Sakai Osamu approaches me and introduces himself. He is a walking snowball effect, seeming to know most of the people in the NHK auditorium already—and he knows my name and biographical information before I have a chance to recite them. Talking to him means a flurry of business card exchanges as prominent media industry professionals greet him and then turn to acknowledge me. During the first STSK meeting mentioned above, Sakai reminds the group of some of his research findings: following the 2011 Fukushima nuclear disaster, young people frequently chose to stop watching television; they reported being motivated by participation in a nationwide campaign to save electricity, but a substantial number were already indifferent to the medium in general.[13] Further, when Sakai first began research on television, VOD (video on demand) services belonged to the United States, with Netflix, Hulu, iTunes, and Amazon offering downloadable TV content and an already rising number of American households choosing to pull the plug on live television.[14] During the early 2010s, Japan was still struggling to come to terms with the idea of losing DVD sales by emulating this model, and companies had pursued different investment strategies. Massive media chain Tsutaya dug in its heels by launching a Netflixesque disc-by-mail service. Conversely, and in a portent of things to come, the pay service Gyao allowed viewers to buy individual episodes of programs to watch on demand (in a model reminiscent of iTunes or Amazon Prime streaming).[15] Hulu had only just arrived and had not yet been purchased by NTV.

Often romanticized as a relic of the past in Japan, as well as in the United States, the notion of families gathered around a single TV watching programs together (the "*cha no ma*" heyday) still informed goals for the medium. (*Cha no ma* generally referred to the living room of a home, next to a kitchen, where families gathered to eat, watch TV, and relax.) Updated for the twenty-first century, however, the *cha no ma* collective viewing experience was conceived as inefficiency, a process of imposing on others rather than strengthening ties by inviting others to share a viewing experience. Moreover, when younger family members can take smartphones to their bedrooms, the need for household viewing lessens—as does the utility of measuring ratings by that standard.

During the STSK meetings I attended throughout 2013, members casually discussed their research indicating that individuals not living alone considered time-shifted content to be inconsiderate or awkward to view on the family TV. Besides the drawbacks of a DVD rental model that some other countries had already outgrown—for example, the time commitment involved in traveling to obtain rental material, and the less portable nature of its consumption—viewing recorded or DVD content also required monopolizing household goods and sacrificing privacy. While kids in the Shōwa era (1926–1989) might have known the television schedule, Sakai argued in one essay that the medium could not compete with rival technologies in the Heisei (1989–2019) and Reiwa (2019–) eras unless it evolved and adapted quickly.[16]

Television also began in 2013 to dismantle entrenched systems of ratings calculation, as outlined in the introduction. What started in the 1950s as a means of capturing audiences simply by placing television sets in such locations as restaurants, train stations, and barbershops (*gaito terebi*) and equating ratings with public crowds became the simultaneous collective family viewing of the 1960s living room, and then the increasingly isolated, demographically targeted viewing of the present.[17] Sakai, born in 1962, remembers fondly a consumer era in Japan driven by more uniform fantasies—the era categorized by the 3 C's: a car, cooler (air conditioner), and color TV (none of which begin with "C" in Japanese, incidentally). In those days, the audience came to commercials willingly and TV advertising presented less of an engineering problem. Even in the 1990s, Sakai noted, television was "the king of media."[18] In the early 2010s, however, ratings aggregators could not electronically and immediately account for the viewing habits of Japanese audiences, many of whom used DVRs to record television or consumed it in some alternative manner, such as by phone or online.[19] The consequences are reflected on by Yamamoto Eiji, a broadcast "salaryman" formerly in charge of his network's ratings surveys: stations have held onto household ratings over individual ratings because they fear that they will have to abandon programming for all but the demographics most sought after by sponsors, and that household ratings will fall if programs aren't targeted to elderly viewers.[20] The system of calculating live TV ratings, as explained to me by staff at Japan's major ratings aggregator, Video Research Ltd., "need[ed] to change."[21]

The Role of Advertising

The interconnectedness and codependence of powerful players in the media were commented on frequently by my interlocutors, who identified the major advertising firms as particularly culpable for the nature of television content. This system, as described by those who have worked in or on Japanese advertising, is one of collaboration and cronyism.[22] I first met Honma Ryū, a vocal critic and former employee of Japanese advertising agency Hakuhodo, at a Foreign Correspondents' Club press conference arranged to promote his new book, *Dentsu and Nuclear Coverage: How Big Advertisers and Big Advertising Firms Control the Media*.[23] According to Honma and others, the Japanese media relies on the goodwill of major advertisers (frequently represented by Dentsu and Hakuhodo, two of the largest firms in the world) for a plurality of its revenue. Accordingly, the content of mass media in Japan is crippled by a web of social pressures and implied threats. Though pointedly ignored by the Japanese media itself, Honma's claims were supported by the *New York Times*' Tokyo bureau chief Martin Fackler, who simultaneously published a personal account and identified in the coverage of the Fukushima crisis symptoms of a mass media infrastructure with major procedural flaws.[24]

In December 2012, over tea in Tokyo's Ikebukuro neighborhood, Honma described the relationship between advertisers and mass journalism: Typically, agencies monitor the news for coverage of their clients, ever prepared to do damage control. This practice also involves calling the sales departments of mass media corporations to feel out any developing stories. After those sales departments make internal inquiries and report back, the advertising agency representative might request that a story be moved, diminished, or otherwise altered on behalf of a client/sponsor that has been a reliable supporter of the network's programs in the past.[25] Honma mimicked a prototypical reaction if a network resists pressure to alter a story:

"It might be difficult for my client to continue the same level of advertising as in the past."[26] Conversely, hints will be made that clients could be willing to spend more on advertising in the future if their needs are met.

When I later probed my contacts in the TV industry and at Dentsu, they confirmed how advertising industry staff come to heavily identify with the clients they represent and to feel personally responsible for their well-being and protection. Within the major Japanese advertising firms, there are service levels, so the more a client spends, the more comprehensive its protection against negative media coverage. Among the power clients, nuclear energy interest groups (such as TEPCO, aka Tokyo Electric Power Company, which ran the Fukushima nuclear plant) have the largest budgets.[27] While one of anthropologist William Mazzarella's Indian advertising interlocutors quipped that a PR man could not control the news but only manipulate impressions, Japanese agents of PR are often able to either act on the impressions created by a story or erase it altogether.[28] The meaning of damage control under these conditions is thus more draconian, if not entirely foolproof. Honma pointed to historic cases of manipulation at TV Asahi: a Hōdō (News) station anchor mentioned on air that he was reprimanded for even the suggestion that he might put together a program critical of nuclear energy for the anniversary of March 11. Further, during a late-night talk show immediately following the disasters, a panel discussion on nuclear reactors was composed only of Dentsu-arranged pronuclear commentators. Typical of the cronyism endemic among global elites, Dentsu is known to be the agency responsible for the conservative Liberal Democratic Party (LDP)'s advertising and seeks to hire those with influential connections in government, industry, or media to serve in its own offices.[29]

In television programming more generally the process remains consistent with the profile constructed by anthropologist Brian Moeran: the advertising framing a particular show is assembled from sponsors without product rivalries (ideally) and appears in the form of commercials, product placements, and voice-over announcements.[30] Tantamount to the early 1990s, when Moeran's fieldwork was conducted, programs are generally sponsored by around six companies, whose allotted commercial time correlates with their capital investment. My fieldwork conversations and related observations at networks, production companies, and affiliated agencies uphold his account that program fabrication universally revolves around corporate sponsorship. Whether networks come to sponsors with a particular concept or agencies approach networks with the same, it is the willingness of advertisers to support a program that makes it happen, as part of an intricate *kashikari* (lend-and-borrow) system of mutual obligation.[31] Networks typically find themselves indebted to the big ad firms when ratings are low, or during particularly unprofitable periods in the annual programming cycle; firms perform their formidable powers of negotiation during downturns by coaxing clients into sponsorship in exchange for future favors.[32] Thus, the relationship between TV networks and advertising agencies is the primary author of the industry's anxieties and molds industry decision-making more than almost anything else. For this reason, Dutch journalist Karel van Wolferen once labeled Dentsu the "hidden media boss" and argued that it plays a greater role in controlling the conversation and forging national culture than any other advertising agency in the world.[33] It is an ad agency with an internal PR firm, forever monitoring the Japanese news landscape and ready to take the offensive if a client missteps.

The bridge between television production and advertising revenue is the ratings system, currently dominated in Japan by Video Research Ltd. Still considered quasi-scientific, despite their small sample sizes and the inevitable introduction of human error and/or deception, traditional ratings are the data by which a highly lucrative industry still assigns value.[34] Shin'ichiro, a prominent midcareer television producer who himself has written and presented on the future of Japanese television, observes, "In the case of Japan, the old model for measuring ratings is large scale, and we're still figuring out what of that system to keep. This is the biggest problem confronting television stations . . . since the concept of 'television ratings' defined by the television set alone has become suspect, we need to extend this notion to the smartphone and computer."[35] Despite its development of methods to track time-shifted and second-screen viewing,[36] consistent uncertainty about how best to measure ratings and reassure sponsors has fed the TV industry's self-consciousness and compelled robust self-defense before Dentsu and Hakuhodo. Accordingly, networks sought a new way of encountering audiences, through transmedia interaction.

The New Interactive Advertising

With a hidden Facebook group and an invite-only policy, the meetings of the STSK have an air of exclusivity. Therefore, I make a point of attending the next one on April 4, 2013, walking eleven minutes from Tokyo's Shibuya station to an entirely anonymous office building. Inside, I find the offices of a quirky marketing design agency, whose rooms each represent a different visual theme, and the STSK assembled in a speakeasy-style salon containing black crystal chandeliers and ornate shaded lamps. Roll is taken at meetings, each name answered with *hai* (yes), *yoroshiku onegai shimasu* (thank you), and in some cases, a self-introduction. On first entering, I note the faces of several people I have met during my television studio fieldwork and interviews; high-ranking producers who have generally spent their entire careers in television and are known for their experimentalism—in at least one case, internationally.

The first presentation of the night walks newcomers through the basics of the "second screen" as a concept—the idea that television as the first screen can become part of a chain of synchronous use that includes all other screen-based technologies. A young female presenter, a rarity among this group of mostly midcareer men, holds a phone up to a television broadcast and shows how a prototype iPhone application can pick up the audio of the program and immediately display additional information about related content. Her example appropriates a prime-time drama, and as the app listens to the audio it shows the viewer/user where she can buy a handbag and other accessories seen onscreen—product placement without the need for active viewer research.

That the example invokes a young female consumer audience is unsurprising; during one of my visits to a television production company near Shinjuku Station an HR representative told me, "Young women own the market." And indeed, Gabriella Lukács and Moeran have described a market for media advertising that has fragmented substantially since the 1980s, with new consumer demographics consistently being defined by marketers to test novel approaches to selling.[37] An increasing tendency for young women to work outside the home and to have disposable income has prompted companies to invent new ways for them to spend it. Therein lies the justification for the variations on bottled tea in the marketplace, for example, or the number of cosmetic lines. This sets up a clash between the conventional practice of household ratings measurement described above, wherein the members of the resultant family unit had to be marketed to simultaneously, and the lure of more precise forms of measurement and targeted advertising.

Picking up the discussion of the potential for advertising and data collection through interactive programming, another STSK presenter announces a venture intended to entice consumers back to live television. The "Saturday Drama App" that he unveils to the room rewards audiences with points and prizes if they consume commercials (a common category of incentive). Moreover, in a nostalgic gesture to the visions of call-in television's choose-your-own adventurism of decades past, the user is also able to indicate midway through a commercial what kind of ending she'd like to see executed. The presenter shows an example of this working, via a Nissan commercial: "You press A or B," he explains, to direct the video to one of two alternate endings, and the most popular wins. As he points out that it also ties into Twitter and Facebook, audience members are smiling and nodding.

By promising rewards, or even by simply making the program sufficiently engaging, television has developed a means by which to track not the *viewer*, but the *user* of television content. By registering to participate in such programs, such users voluntarily provide basic demographic data: age, gender, location, and even blood type. If rewards are offered as part of the campaign, they connect to national store-agnostic loyalty cards such as Ponta,[38] which follow a common model for such cards by trading accumulated points for consumer data on spending habits and preferences. A tendency for sponsor-driven mass media to subsume (Japanese) differences into the idea of a monolithic national public or define and promote specific ways of group belonging is innately compatible with its need to define broadcast consumers as demographic personae with manageable preferences. However, the golden age of television in Japan did not always propagate community—whether on the street, as in the case of *gaito terebi*, or in the home. Historian Jayson Chun challenges the notion of *cha no ma* viewing as actually bringing individuals together; in some cases, it became an excuse for families to ignore one another, lose themselves in separate programs, or even engage in violence over programming disputes.[39] Or as media theoretician Sean Cubitt writes, "Mediation is not representation: media serve to mediate, not between subjects and objects, but between subjects."[40] In other words, television ultimately sought to replace the relationship between viewers with many parallel relationships between individual viewers and the apparatus. These descriptions characterize interactive television as much as they did early internet communication; interactive television similarly creates relationships between users of a space constructed, in many cases, by a corporate entity. The transformation of mass media forms over time, therefore, does not necessarily mean the destruction of subjectivity, but its appropriation.

Some theorists also fear that by introducing fragmentation into the marketplace, one creates conditions best compared to the perceived risks of allowing transnational programming to enter the Japanese sphere.[41] Just as anthropologist Purnima Mankekar observes of India, Japanese culture has proven itself a battleground, with issues of national identity and ethnic purity dominating the rhetoric, and the semiotic tools used to describe the television-watching experience shifting over time from a Japanese to an American model.[42] This transition is exemplified by the process of gradual individuation described above, wherein viewing became progressively less communal, then segmented into narrower demographics, and eventually saw much of the audience moving to online and on-demand viewing.[43]

However, rhetoric from the early days of television did silo users into groups and target them separately, as indicated by Sakai's nostalgic reflections on family television dynamics. Their examples, while gesturing to a rose-colored vision of the 1960s, are suggestive of earlier market fragmentation than is generally acknowledged—and articles by Japanese researchers about women's television consumption beginning in the 1950s further support the argument.[44] Women, owing to new social pressure to withdraw from the workplace, were said to watch much more television than their male counterparts, and marketing targeted them accordingly by focusing on labor-saving devices for the home (washers, vacuums, etc.). The genders were further divided by their news medium of choice; women, it was observed, learned 60 percent of their news from television by 1958, but only 35 percent of men did so. This was because television purportedly fit more easily than newspapers into the multitasking routine of a busy housewife.[45] And while the ubiquitous (even then) sports programming targeted the men in a household, entertainment kept its sights on women and helped to constitute the category of housewife.

An International Effort

On a sunny April 2013 day in Tokyo's Shibuya neighborhood, Gracenote is holding an event for media industry insiders.[46] For the occasion of this presentation, it has flown out some of its Los Angeles technical support staff, who wander around the cafe checking wires and ensuring that iPads and televisions function correctly. Members of Gracenote's Tokyo office function as the front line, explaining the TV and poster board content to the assembled individuals—among them members of the STSK. According to its staff, just as Gracenote's existing technology can be used to identify music based on its digital footprint, the technology it is seeking to embed in the televisions of the future will identify members of a household and target advertising to them based on gender, income level, and past purchases. For example, a Ford commercial featuring a different vehicle is shown to viewers in the category "Female 35–39, Household Income $50k–100k, Honda LeaseHolder," and another to viewers in the category "Family, HH (Head of Household) Income $25–50k, Los Angeles Designated Market Area," based on statistical indications about the car to which they're likely to be most receptive. Until now, programs and time slots have been assigned demographic information rather crudely, with no room for particulars (or any departure from the "Nielsen family"–style individual household).[47] Describing this challenge, Yamamoto observes, "A private car is a household item if it can transport the whole family, even if it is in the name of the father. A washing machine is a household good if you use it to wash the clothes of the whole family . . . television is a household good if the children spend time in the living room watching TV with the whole family. However, with that time decreasing considerably, the characteristics of television as a household good are being lost."[48] For an industry that belatedly trades in aggregates, systems such as Gracenote's offered another means to retrofit existing systems.[49]

Despite these signs of the potential—even desire—for change, the ratings system has historically served to quantify the successes of television professionals and to passively disclose what audiences like. Therefore, the many ways that Video Research Ltd. has developed to track audiences in Japan notwithstanding, the system represents a collective will-to-believe on the part of industry professionals.[50] For industry insiders, ratings are the parlance of daily speech about the medium, treated as factual enough by the mass media industry. The walls of television network offices and their hallways are covered in pieces of paper announcing individual TV episodes with dates and exceptional ratings, as a reminder of what drives the past, present, and future of programming.

While the networks focus on the idea of social television to live up to those ratings printouts, members of Video Research Ltd. explained to me that it still measures household percentages using a Nielsenesque model and relies on random sampling surveys to track individual viewing habits in greater depth. Additionally, it offers more complex pay-for services that can be harnessed to probe deeper into the nature of audiences if required by clients.[51] Research on children's programming audiences, for example, is a pay-for service, but it is the advertising firms instead that will eventually go deepest on demographics and viewing habits.[52] In March 2013, as we sit around a conference table in its Sanbanchō office, the topic of

Video Research's new system of "assigning ratings through Twitter comments" comes up—a concept that has attracted the attention of the English-language press but is still considered too new to opine on. It's "in the testing stage," they tell me. The company is consistently reinventing ways to measure user behavior, including its new "es XMP" system, which allows it to index the ways people use smartphones.[53] But the space between smartphone use and TV viewership remains elusive and hard to disambiguate.

Given this effort to track socially networked viewers, the smartest part of interactive TV might be its capacity to collect microscale feedback on what pleases audiences—no longer measured in terms of "I watched x program" but instead "at three minutes and twenty seconds, I was enjoying myself." This, combined with social TV's capacity to directly tie engaged and known-to-be-watching individual consumers to their lucrative spending and profile data, forms the television industry's new approach to audience quantification. The conventional ratings for the *60 Ban Shōbu* (2.3 percent on the first night, and 2.7 percent on the second), although not bad for a program that aired at 12:58 a.m. and 12:50 a.m., respectively, were rather beside the point.[54]

Television as Social Theory

Members of the STSK, and broadcast professionals in general, routinely mentioned Frankfurt School theory in both formal and informal settings as they worked through the theoretical implications of their work and embraced a certain humor about the constraints of mass media production. As John Caldwell has noted, media industries and media professionals individually spend a substantial amount of time unpacking the critical implications of their product and engaging in self-study—which, indeed, was the purpose of the STSK.[55] And although Frankfurt School theory may seem a model at odds with the perspectives of media professionals (apart from its top-down representation of image dissemination), its use suggests resonance with the cynical pragmatism of many, and its influence represents the era in which many senior industry leaders came of age intellectually (the 1960s). Many of the people now steering industry conversations were part of the so-called "McLuhan boom" in Japan of the 1960s (and again in the 1980s); contrary to a widespread Western interpretation of theory as belonging to Europe and North America, Walter Benjamin's work was translated into Japanese before English.[56] The children of the TV age, influenced by the Marxian media theory of the 1960s, are now running

Tokyo's broadcast system and have retained and passed on their intellectual orientation to subsequent generations.

Although the concept of publics has had a tumultuous history in Japanese media theory,[57] Adorno and Horkheimer's assessment resonates with the self-critique expressed by some members of the STSK—including a sense that publics subjected to the output of the culture industries essentially lose their capacity for reasoned choice and become involuntarily and rapidly subject to the logics of simulated decision-making. It was partially a lack of active audience participation in mass media products that Adorno and Horkheimer found so troubling, the *mindlessness* of its consumption, and the systematicity of the mass media in general. The influence of Marxism on their work was perhaps most apparent in their discernment of categories of art, with those produced by a profit-minded mass industry compromising a Kantian vision of ideal aesthetic reception.

Conversely, Japanese producers of social TV aspire to more than the reproduction of such systematicity. Cynicism aside,[58] STSK meetings could be considered theoretically provocative, as they largely pertained to discussions about how to reinscribe citizens who had broken from one of the most troubled tools of the culture industry. In his commentary on the *60 Ban Shōbu*, Sakai Osamu wrote that one of its major themes was the breaking of taboos, from welcoming comedian Akashiya Sanma to appear on NHK for the first time after his unofficial ban from the network thirty years previously (the most *ii*'ed moment of the show), to the collaboration between two networks on a cross-channel program, the behind-the-scenes exploration of the way television is made, and the twenty-four-hour production competition between the two networks to see who could put together the most successful short segment.[59] As Sakai commented, by extending beyond the boundedness of the television set, "They are literally breaking down the frame of television [with this program]."[60] By pushing a button, the user can act on the screen, and users' actions directly formulate the reactions of the program's hosts.

In the present climate of knowledge production, the ecology of new media forces expertise into a bidirectional exchange and a constant state of self-defense as publics debate the validity of its findings. Relatedly, anthropologists Dominic Boyer and Cymene Howe write about a "lateralist revolution" in anthropological knowledge production, influenced by the bidirectional aspirations of newer forms of media.[61] This is to say that academia itself has attempted to move past its "broadcast era," when knowledge was able to rest on a kind of authority born of inaccessibility. Similarly,

Japanese TV embraced lateralism in different ways, some of which overlap with efforts made in the United States. But aside from their shared use of hashtags to corral discourse, the two countries differ insofar as the official channels for engagement in Japan often direct users to dedicated apps or mobile-responsive websites within which they can comment in truncated form or directly manipulate live TV content—an approach that is less common in the United States.

Nonetheless, in both countries, television in the early 2010s was scrambling to figure out how to appropriate the technologies perceived to function as its saboteurs, just as other forms of historically successful mass media are struggling to adapt to evolving modes of consumption. This is the point made by Naohiro,[62] the first presenter on another night at the STSK in May 2013, who introduces himself by his Twitter handle and refers to himself as a "VJ" (video jockey, in English). He introduces a new application made by one of the television networks that is supposed to work in tandem with television shows to allow users to receive bonus content about programs—including directions to and coupons for restaurants as they are being reviewed by presenters. But then Naohiro stops, and says abruptly, in an affectless voice, "TV could die, right?" (*"Terebi wa shinu, deshō?"*)

This, he blames on the rise of "CGM" (consumer-generated media), and at the utterance of this anglicized acronym, a few of the suited audience members frown and sigh audibly. The answer is not more television, he argues, and several more people look up—among them some of the auteurs of the most provocative recent social television. "The solution is AR (augmented reality)," he proclaims.[63] We need to find a way to integrate television into physical space, he tells us. Into the everyday lives of people so that it *crawls into their bodies* in much the same way that user-controlled spaceships entered Mitsu Dan's bloodstream during *Bloody Tube*. If his projects work, we will at some point be able to click on designated places within an application's television listings to view a holographic clip related to the show. "Check out the app for *Dokidoki Precure*," he instructs.[64] "AR is now."

The reading of consumers as passively subject to the authority of a concept like the culture industry has long since been debunked in its totalitarian form.[65] Nonetheless, interactive television has the capacity to both challenge Adorno and Horkheimer's fears about the inevitable outcome of culture industry projects and to support it—depending on the program. Indeed, the production of social media challenges the notions of disconnection as Adorno described it, and distraction, as did Walter Benjamin.

Although there has been much effort to argue the use of social media also leads to less real-world connection (and thus, disconnection is its essence), there remains disagreement about this correlation.[66] And if distraction, as written by Benjamin, describes a state of approaching one's environment without the full engagement of the senses, the television of the future might be at least less so.

Conclusion

Considering the powerhouse of influential television professionals in attendance, the conversations of STSK members accurately capture a strong and ongoing drive within Japanese television companies to further disambiguate audiences and appropriate their interactions. The appeal is nearly overwhelming considering the potential increase in the scope of consumer feedback it represents. Audience subjectivity has, since the early days of television, been constructed around the idea of consumer-viewers, who might purchase the goods to which they are subjected via various forms of advertising. Where that subjectivity has changed is that the new forms proposed by the members of the STSK and others require greater proximity between moments of television and material consumption. Side by side with applications that allow viewer-consumers to learn more information about material goods featured in television programs (certainly a boon to the audiences of evening "trendy" dramas, which are as much about conspicuous consumption as any storyline) are applications that attempt to persuade users to generate content on behalf of a company, or to check in to an application while watching TV to earn points that can be traded for goods.[67] The thread connecting each of the strategies mentioned herein is to invite audiences to, if not cocreate media, participate in its direction and provide real-time feedback. From the *60 Ban Shōbu* and its use of the *ii* button to responsive commercials, the subject to-be-advertised-to in the future will be able to choose the nature of her advertising experience—that is, if she becomes willing to return to a model of television that forces ads, or if television becomes willing to risk further alienating skittish audiences by foregrounding the scaffold of viewer data exchange that supports it.

On this topic, the industry exists in a state of nervous suspension—it holds its breath as it tests new technology, awkwardly shares space with older interactive media, and nervously monitors the ratings. With the suspension of disbelief in the relevance of ratings practiced by all parties, the industry has no immediate need to reinvent its system, to threaten its

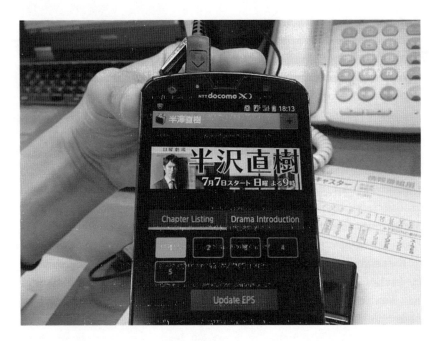

1.2 A website, called up onto a television industry employee's phone, that allows free streaming of Japanese television.

application of the audience concept. If anything, it is the associated physical instruments (*pīpurumētā* or "people meters") that generally bear the brunt of criticism rather than the underlying sampling or surveying methodologies. As a result, if audiences were in 1991 being "desperately sought," to borrow Ien Ang's canonical phrase, by 2014 the industry was nearly begging.[68] Industry chatter during much of my fieldwork still revolved around the constant influx of ratings data—particularly considering the astounding success of TBS's drama *Hanzawa Naoki*.[69] Indeed, when I asked Shin'ichiro, himself a TBS employee, to take a photo for me that represents the future of Japanese television, this is the one he sent back (see figure 1.2): It is of a Taiwanese website where users can stream Japanese television for free. No commercials. No ratings. No DVRs. "*Yabaissu*" (Dangerous), he says.[70]

Despite the intricate technology required by social TV, it feels as though television is catching up more than it is pioneering. While social media and the internet have already leapt ahead with much more sophisticated algorithms for tracking user interests,[71] TV has hesitated to embrace that model wholesale as it wrestles with the question of how to configure a dialog between media professionals and audiences to honor a vision of cocreation—even in seemingly exploitative cases like interactive advertising or in such a basic expression of engagement as "likes." Producers view interactive projects as a means of creating a public motivated by consumption (of media and goods), or that is interested in coevolving television to be more dialogic. Even now, producers remain frustrated by limitations on the kinds of interactions that are possible, which largely result in users trading personal data for content.

Nonetheless, innovation within the context of a bureaucracy as labyrinthian as network broadcast is celebrated by the STSK whenever it happens. Tonight, at the April 2013 STSK meeting, one of my most frequent interlocutors and a producer on *The Compass* (the interactive news discussion show that is the subject of chapter 2), is giving a talk about that program. He leads with a photograph of the program's stage set identical to one I've used in my own presentations. Insofar as this content differs from the substance of his on-the-job commentary, with a focus on the theoretical implications of this program rather than the production details, I find myself learning more about its polemical characteristics than I have in any other setting. Nonetheless, he also explains the program's logistics: the staff sourced topic ideas from its audiences and carefully tracked the correlation of activity on Twitter, Facebook, and NicoNico with the on-set discussions. Sakai, acting as emcee, takes questions from fellow producers, who are hungry for details on the mechanics of such programming and a chance to vent about the network's decision to cancel it. One of the STSK members reassures everyone that TV programs come and go, and a discontinued series makes space for future innovation. Those around him nod and grunt in resignation. The next chapter looks at how this complicated experiment in social news TV played out.

2

Interactivity and Gatekeeping

THE COMPASS AND THE LIMITS OF
CONSERVATIVE CORPORATE CULTURE

March 23, 2013, is the final broadcast of Fuji TV's interactive news discussion program BS *Fuji LIVE Social TV The Compass* (BS *Fuji Raivu Sōsharu TV Za Konpasu*), and its multiple spaces of production feel charged. Many more people than usual mill about in the shadows of the cavernous studio space, some of whom are Fuji TV staff generally interested in social media and television who wish to bear witness to the end of this experiment. Tonight's internet audience is also larger than usual; before the television broadcast even begins, 11,707 NicoNico users have already tuned in online.[1] They banter about the prime minister and the underfunding of interesting television programs (such as *The Compass*) as well as tonight's theme: the political advantages of being media/tech savvy.

The Compass was the project of a small group of ambitious idealists hoping to expand live participation in television content. And having been given neither the resources nor the time slot necessary to succeed, it was finally canceled after nearly eleven months. Airing on Fuji TV's secondary BS Channel and the NicoNico NamaHōsō (NN) live streaming platform simultaneously,[2] the television program ran from 9:00 p.m. to 10:25 p.m., while its parallel internet broadcast ran longer, from 8:00 to 11:00 p.m. At 8:50 p.m., the NN live stream is therefore well underway while the television broadcast hosts are still in hair and makeup.

On the third floor of Fuji Television's labyrinth-like headquarters, staff mingle around a dimly lit, gray-carpeted television control room—typical but for the Apple laptops scattered on ledges around the switchboards. Two glass-walled rooms off to the side hold the technology and people responsible for the NN portion of the broadcast; presently, the male-female internet hosts sit behind its desk and their laptops discussing North Korea's threat to Japan with the internet audiences. In the main studio below, another pair of hosts arrange their bodies in preparation for live television broadcast. As an assistant counts down to broadcast, chatter in the main studio slows while the internet broadcast in the room above continues unaffected. "*Ippun!*" (one minute!) calls the assistant director.

Multiple input and output channels mean that *The Compass* has a lot going on: while guest experts discuss current events, audiences weigh in via Twitter (#compassTV), Facebook, or NN. The two broadcasts converge periodically as the NN hosts descend from their glass box during commercial breaks to join the TV broadcast in the main studio, stay until the next break, and eventually return to their separate transmission. In the main studio, a ticker behind the hosts' table displays aggregated Twitter comments, while assistant directors offstage periodically run live polls of NN users' opinions and feature the results on both broadcasts. Hosts choose Tweets to read as part of the discussion, posing viewers' questions and the points they raise to the usual news magazine program parade of commentators. The NN viewing experience is especially unique; as a feature of the NN platform, users' real-time comments stream directly over the live-streamed image (see figure 2.1). More so than on other social media, NN allows audiences to act on the program directly, responding to the hosts' questions and each other in such a way that their words become part of the broadcast itself.

Partly in conversation with the recent amendment of Japan's laws allowing politicians to use social media, and partly in a nod to its format, the finale of *The Compass* addresses the construction of political messaging and identity through social media. The TV broadcast begins with a famous set of images from the television debate of former US presidents Richard Nixon and John F. Kennedy in 1960, another recurring theoretical trope of American media scholars and Japanese television producers alike, who have appropriated it to argue that media savvy is more important to politics

2.1 A typical screen on the website NicoNico (https://www.nicovideo.jp/), shown as a recording after the live stream has ended and commenting is disabled. This broadcast featured Tsuda Daisuke and Hori Jun, both of whom are mentioned in this book.

than policy know-how.[3] They scrutinize (then) South Korean prime minister Chung Hong-won and president Park Geun-hye's social media use, but their incredulity is reserved for (then) Japanese prime minister Abe Shinzo's use of Facebook to discuss his workout routine and post selfies in jogging clothes.[4] This form of insight into the personal lives of Japanese politicians, historically known for their rigid self-presentation, was titillating to the panelists as a more exaggerated version of the way that *The Compass'* NN hosts relaxed their framing when "merely" appearing online.

The 9:55 p.m. commercial break ushers in the routine scramble to touch up makeup and hastily curate comments from Twitter and NN. Two assistant directors (ADs) peer into laptops and select several comments from Twitter user @ray_luno. Of the 35,967 individuals in the NN chatroom, most are now typing emphatic missives about the state of mass media, or about how the program ought to continue:

"It's said that mass media came to an end fifteen years ago." (*Masu ga owari o tsugeta to iwarete, mō 15-nen darō.*)

"It's the era of making mass media online." (*Netto de masukomi o kaku jidai.*)

"There's still a wall between the net and TV." (*Kono jiten de terebi to netto ni kabe o tsukutteru kan aru na.*)

"Television has no future. (Laugh)" (*Terebi no mirai wa naitte koto ja ne? W*)

"TV already doesn't have a bright future." (*Iya, mō terebi ni akarui mirai wa nai desu yo.*)

"[It had] good contents." (*Ii kontentsu datta no ni.*)[5]

In response to a user question about why it got canceled:

"Pressure from the top?" (*Ue kara no atsuryoku?*)

"More people watched online than on TV?" (*Terebi de miru yori netto de miru hito ga ōkattan ja ne?*)

"Money." (*Okane da ne.*)

"So, what's next week? Just uncut NN broadcast?" (*De raishū wa? Niko-nama dake demo iin da ze?*)

While the broadcast enters its last segment, the scholars and staff on-stage engage in a metaconversation about the necessity and importance of programs such as *The Compass*, and their collective instinct that such bidirectionality (*sōhōkō-sei*) is, at the very least, the future of television. Several of Fuji TV's most prominent innovators join the hosts on stage to close the evening with a discussion of the network's intention to pursue this kind of programming as part of an overall modernization project.[6]

As the program moves again to a commercial break, the last television broadcast of *The Compass* approaches its finale and the NN transmission simply goes black even as users are still joining the chat, their comments appearing as white text marching rapidly across the terminalesque screen from right to left. While the live stream continues, imageless, those around the U-shaped studio desk congratulate and thank one another. Off camera, the department chief brings presenters and production staff together in the hall connecting the upstairs control rooms and downstairs studio. Flowers are brought in for those who played critical roles, and those assembled take turns making warm speeches to the in-studio crowd about their enjoyment of the experience and the collective hard work that made it possible. This prolonged session of mutual appreciation is followed by a return to the studio stage, where those who worked on the show sit before the TV-quality broadcast cameras, turned back on and uploading only to NN, to take questions from the chat room.

Because the Japanese television industry does not syndicate shows, most of what airs is either live or temporally contingent. To keep costs down, it also relies heavily on expert discussion panels. Interestingly, this limitation—the liveness—of much Japanese programming is extremely well suited to integration with interactive features like online chat rooms. There is an enduring impression among scholars of mass media in Japan (and globally) that young people in the twenty-first century are more receptive to media that permit them to cocreate content through active participation, in contrast with what is often labeled "passive" media (and its accompanying theoretical baggage). What constitutes liveness in the twenty-first century, however, is evolving from a definition centered around individuals—the holder of the camera, a reporter—who function as surrogates for the audience at an event unfolding in the present moment, into a mode that allows viewers to engage with the liveness of the program itself. Or as media scholar Philip Auslander summarizes it, "The idea of what counts culturally as live experience changes over time in relation to technological change."[7] The "spatial co-presence" he describes has similarly evolved to include co-presence in the virtual spaces constructed by programs like *The Compass*, where liveness is unfolding as much on NN as it is in the studio.

Though arguments about interactivity are often made by invoking more recent technological innovation, the basic scaffolding for theories of its potential emerged in response to the expansion of internet access at the turn of the century. On April 24, 2000, the cover of *Variety* heralded the arrival of "Television 2.0" and added, "The next generation of television is here. interactive.personal.internet," juxtaposing television's interactive future with a passive past.[8] In media scholar Lisa Parks's assessment, this pronouncement not only reified categories of participation in mass media but did so by introducing class- and nationality-contingent discourses of access and connection speed.[9] Though the capacity to interact with mass media remains socioeconomically contingent, access has opened significantly since 2000, and the increasing habituation of users to virtual social interaction, combined with the saturation of cell phones in Japan, has made social TV increasingly possible.

Typically, news discussion shows like *The Compass* have operated with indifference to extramural input, preferring the manageable drama of approved guests debating current events. Throughout May 2013 I attended the taping of a second show whose scale and topical focus were comparable to those of *The Compass*, minus the ambition (and pressure) of social TV. *Crossfire* (*Gekiron! Kurosufaia*, on TV Asahi) shared topical overlap—during one of my visits, the program similarly addressed Japanese anxieties about conflict with North Korea—but its exclusion of the affordances of NN and social media rendered its messaging easier to manipulate and contain. Like most news discussion programs *Crossfire* was prerecorded, which granted staff considerable leeway to sculpt panelists' commentary on the episode's topic. Producers gave the hosts advance lectures on recent news, supported by lists of talking points and offstage signboards to guide their reactions. During this research, I asked myself whether being able to deliver a more accurate message and deny misinformation (and racism) a platform were worth the narrowing of opportunity for all but familiar TV personalities to opine on the news. Was it the conventional format of programs like *Crossfire* that has led global audiences to seek out a more diverse range of news sources and commentary online? And would the liveness of shows like *The Compass*, which was referred to in internal documents as *The Compass x NicoNico Live*, constitute a discursive flow different enough to help remake news-consuming publics in Japan?

This chapter focuses on *The Compass* as a case study of how one network experimented with social TV in a news discussion format to attract audiences and introduce more diverse commentary without the risk of departing from the narrow range of standard Japanese political discourse. *The Compass* represents a significant case study, both because it was the first of its kind, and because it served as a touchstone for the community leading social TV development in Japan, who dissected and referred to it in meetings as much as it did the *60 Ban Shōbu* from the previous chapter. It was also among a few that were attempting to test the boundaries of acceptable experimentation within the bounded infrastructure of conservative mass broadcast. Others, which included *Crossfire* and another low-budget program called *Nyūsu no Shinsō* (Truth in the news), experimented with pushing boundaries by integrating more diverse guest panelists into the discussion. They were permitted this latitude as programs assigned to non-prime-time slots on the networks' secondary BS channels and were assigned to such undesirable spots because of this latitude. The production budgets of such shows were accordingly limited, to the extent that the crew almost always joked about the cheapness of their glitter- and paint-covered sets during my visits and compared them to primary school projects. The efforts of both categories of experimental broadcast, then, signified a desire to expand what was permitted in TV news commentary, and the number of participants who found *The Compass* indicated the need was felt by producers and audiences alike.

Defining Preferred Liveness: TV vs. Internet

Streaming sites such as YouTube, with which television has a perpetually jealous relationship, have acknowledged the effervescent potential of disembodied collective viewing by their support of group viewing technologies (e.g., Watch2Gether and Facebook's Watch Party). The key to this ostensibly more profound connection lies in the spatiotemporal synchronicity introduced by live television and the intimacy made possible by consuming the same media moment at the same time. NicoNico was a global pioneer in its attempts to combine the strengths of interactive television with internet broadcast by integrating uncensored user/viewer comments into the live broadcasts themselves.

Originally developed as a YouTube aggregator, NN evolved into a forum for users to comment on live streaming content in real time. Not just relegated to a sidebar, users' comments are overlaid onto the screen of the program, an interpolation of the audience that differs from their marginal framing in most programs. There is a feeling of titillation that comes with the opportunity to essentially write graffiti across a live broadcast and a degree of boldness that accompanies its forced anonymity.

Despite the tendency of many people with whom I spoke to taxonomically relegate NN's user base to the category of the nerdy/antisocial *otaku* and/or the online alt-right *netto uyoku*, the site's traffic, composed 72 percent of individuals ages 10–39 (34.5 million active monthly users as of March 2023), is extremely desirable to marketers for whom this *mūbumento* (movement, to use their term) represents a body that is crucial to classify and appropriate for marketing purposes.[10] This is true even though its membership is predominantly male (68 percent vs. 32 percent female in 2019),[11] while advertisers across platforms primarily seek access to female consumers. Active commenters on NN (and therefore participants in interactive TV that connects to it) are more likely to be male as well, specifically men in their thirties, even though more men in their twenties are site members.[12] Of the approximately one-third of Japan's population who have a NN account, many are the *datsu terebi* (removed from TV) generation, or the generation about whose experience it has been written, "In the era of bidirectional media, television feels [to them] 'pushy' somehow."[13] As prominent (self-described) "media activist" Tsuda Daisuke writes about NN, its strength lies in its capacity to allow viewers to interact with presenters, and with one another, simultaneously.[14] Always seated behind his laptop during broadcasts, Tsuda, who appears regularly on both television and radio as well as NN, practices what he preaches by engaging fluidly with both embodied and virtual interlocutors simultaneously during his media appearances. Tsuda's frequent commentary resembles media scholar Kitada Akihiro's theorization of participation in these rapid-fire online communities as being more about the "pleasure of the social communication itself" than the topics being discussed.[15] Such participants learn to perform the form and the style of places like NN (and 2chan, mentioned in the next chapter), and the content of their posts should not necessarily be interpreted as reflective of genuinely held beliefs so much as models of conventional intercommunity discourse, a display of the participant's literacy of form.

Until 2016, NN's growth was mostly in premium memberships, a major appeal of which is the capacity to escape the temporal limitations of a live broadcast–only system. The success of this on-demand model predicted the individualization of television and the process by which Japanese viewers increasingly consume video content. According to many industry commentators, what started with TiVo in select countries ushered in what Parks calls the "post-broadcasting" era (in places with comprehensive high-speed internet access), wherein content is tailored to narrower demographics and consumed asynchronously.[16] In a nod to the two major characteristics of this form of broadcast, and by contrast with the scope and reach of conventional television, she labels it "flexible microcasting."[17] But to choose to view NN content at one's convenience is always a trade-off. Commenting on videos can only be done as they are transmitted live, and indeed liveness is part of the appeal of the service. Rather than belonging to an impression of liveness deriving from the technology itself, as in a connection to the outside world permitted by the machine, it is the "social co-presence," to borrow Nick Couldry's term, that creates the feeling of liveness.[18]

When one views a NN event posthumously, one can consume only the input of others that becomes flattened, like that of any other online video to be consumed passively and as purely visual. Liveness as an essential component of the viewing experience is insisted on by media scholar Jostein Gripsrud, who in 2004 predicted a growing resemblance between cell phones, computers, and television, and the conversion of characteristics of the internet and television.[19] Nonetheless, different technologies, even as they assume characteristics of one another, constitute different ontological conditions. The divergence in energy between synchronous cocreation and viewership of live broadcast transcends the specificity of the technologies used to facilitate it. While different modes of presentation may, to paraphrase Auslander's discussion of both Steve Dixon and Margaret Morse, trigger different modes of attention, I am most interested here in the agglomerate social energy produced when live audiences communicate with one another through technology rather than how they interact with the technology itself.[20]

News shows often already benefit from the uneasy intimacy of live broadcast and are therein well suited to become interactive TV experiments. As a television producer named Takashi who was active in the social TV community told me, conspiratorially, "It started with Kume Hiroshi. *He was the first social television.*"[21] This was a point made by a few television professionals—that the inauguration of TV Asahi's groundbreaking news talk show *News Station* in the late 1980s had introduced a feeling of intimacy with its audience that TV producers have sought to replicate with "reality" TV since then. In those days, with low news ratings and therefore little at stake, TV Asahi broke with established formulae by appointing former quiz show host Kume Hiroshi as the program's news anchor and granting him license to experiment with modes of address. Kume distinguished himself from the then top-rated NHK news program anchors by his refusal to use a teleprompter, and by his self-consciously colloquial language (using the casually masculine *boku* rather than the formal and conventional *watakushi* to refer to himself, for example).[22] In so doing, he made the news a living object about which even a comedian could speak extemporaneously, and to a massive public. The climate or "*fun'iki*" of *News Station*, therefore, approximated that of a talk show rather than a newscast and foretold versions like *The Daily Show* in the United States—without the overt satire. By offering his opinion on the stories he covered, Kume broke with existing models of TV news and, through conversational discourse, introduced intimacy between himself and the audience and transcended the role of a newsreader to become, or maintain his role as, a television personality.

During the final broadcast of *The Compass* the informality governing the internet live stream more sharply than usual contrasts with that of the main television broadcast, and while a lack of commercial breaks has always encouraged internet-streaming hosts to engage in corporeal gestures before the cameras such as putting in eyedrops, *The Compass'* imminent demise grants a certain permissiveness in which even the relaxed rules of internet broadcast may be broken. High-ranking production staff wander in and out of the NN transmission room, briefly sharing space and bantering with the program's official internet hosts in front of the camera. Although the two sets are separated physically only by a staircase, their semiotic value is much less proximate even on an average day, and what might be considered a breach for television is unremarkable for its comparatively informal internet counterpart. The live stream has accordingly been approached with less formality throughout the show's run.

Television has long induced flatness and erased authentic physicality in favor of appearances. But the narrow intimacy of so much TV programming has nothing on the act of (for example) putting in eyedrops on camera—an act that violates the directive that television refrain from gesturing to bodily demands. The excess inherent in such a tiny breach extends the image beyond image and into embodied physical space, disrupting a mode of viewing that never really managed to become the detached aesthetic observation of so much philosophical discourse. More so than for the majority of television broadcast, this category of action erases some of television's formality and reinforces the intentions of interactive TV producers to create a comparatively intimate broadcast-mediated conversation.

Publics and Engagement in the Minds of Producers

The producers appearing before the camera in the NN broadcast postlude of *The Compass'* finale represent some of Japanese television production's classic archetypes—one slim and black clad, another square jawed and gruff. Both men are chain-smokers. Their appearance calls to mind John Caldwell's description of a specific habitus, a mimesis of costume for screenwriters and directors, and a Bourdieusian taxonomy of media work's most stalwart incumbents.[23] The hosts join them in this outro, although as television "personalities" they receive another round of makeup and hair touch-ups before returning to the stage. Here, before cameras transmitting only to the internet, this impromptu panel takes turns discussing the gap between "TV people" (*terebi no katagata*, rather than *geinōjin*— "entertainers") and "audiences" (*shichōsha*). The difference, according to one producer, is that internet comments are "straight" (*sutorēto*), while those of TV people are often slanted. Speaking to the more than thirty thousand people gathered in the NN chat room by this time, another producer boldly claims that TV culture is contrary to freedom of the press, while connection to spaces like this chat room is the future of broadcast. This bold comment passes without further elaboration by the others; instead, they turn to invite most of the program's affiliated staff to appear on camera and bid their farewells.

After a lengthy wrap-up, we adjourn to a nearby American Western–themed restaurant for drinks, food, and a postmortem on the program. Between speeches by those who have worked on *The Compass*, one of the producers laments that he wants to make more programs of this sort, but that they aren't valued by the networks. He invokes Marshall McLuhan by name, emphasizing loudly to be heard over the din: "*Media wa messēji de aru!*" (the *media* is the message!). This translation of the phrase, the use of the word *media* over the word *medium* (*baitai*), initially startles me. I ask about it, and he holds up a hand and insists that it is always translated into Japanese in this way to remain consistent with McLuhan's intentionality.[24] It is the *media* that are the message, and in this case television as a collection of individuals, rather than a technological infrastructure, is sending a very strong message by integrating with internet content. The interpretation of McLuhan echoes an inquiry raised concurrently by TV Man Union founders Hagimoto Haruhiko, Muraki Yoshihiko, and Konno Tsutomu: "How can we create true dialogue and solidarity, not within the relationship of 'sender/receiver', but in the relationship between equal human beings."[25] These arguments represent a pivot from focusing on the technology to focusing on the individuals using it—not as people with greater access to the platform and tools of mass media production, but as potential collaborators seeking accountability to their fellow humans.

Noncontradictorily, technology is the mediator in Kitada and Zahlten's discussion: "Technology . . . is rather a (physical) thing that initiates the trial-and-error process of interaction between the human and nature, as well as, within this process, the transformation of its own functions/abilities. Technology is not a tool enabling the human manipulation of nature, but rather a medium that enforces both reflection on and renewal of the very relationship of humanity and nature."[26] So, which is foregrounded in the creation of shows like *The Compass*, or its more traditional noninteractive counterparts? Hagimoto, Muraki, and Konno were not denying the power of technology in their manifesto—if anything they were acknowledging its power by acknowledging its obligations. And Kitada and Zahlten here land on technology's capacity to enhance relationships, ultimately reinforcing Hagimoto, Muraki, and Konno's best hopes. But does technology in these specific cases facilitate the connection between sender and receiver, or is it still getting in its own way? Is the Media (people) or the Medium (television) the driver?

Recalling the on-set conversation from earlier, I ask if the "straightness" of internet commenting is part of this, whether by this producer's interpretation the media or *baitai* constitute the message. Would television always be considered slanted, even if its objective in news contexts is to insist on its own neutrality?[27] His clarification is consistent with my observations: Isn't coercive neutrality a kind of slanting? Indeed, television's self-conscious refusal to take a position, even during a discussion of positions in a program such as *The Compass*, is notable. Official commentators on *The Compass* are careful to mention arguments without identifying with them, using the passive voice and speaking indirectly about current events. But how is neutrality (*chūritsu*) different from objectivity (*kyakukansei*) or balance in journalism? How does it manifest differently, and which term best describes the conditions of television and print journalism in Japan? As media scholar Sandrine Boudana argues, neutrality and objectivity can no longer be considered synonyms.[28] My work with journalists in Japan leads me to a similar conclusion and—riffing on Boudana—to define objectivity as a kind of journalistic performance, and neutrality as a measured individual stance.[29] To complicate matters further, however, recent journalism under conservative governance in Japan seems to me to be about neither objectivity nor neutrality. Although it functions to relay information from powerful channels in a way that pretends to be either or both, it chiefly strives to protect the messenger.

A 2017 survey of 747 Japanese journalists reveals that their self-conceptualization revolves around a sense that they must "report things as they are" (65.1 percent said this was extremely or very important to their job) and only 44.1 percent said the same about "be[ing] a detached observer."[30] This survey reveals that, against public perceptions of their work, Japanese journalists do not view their role as one of advocacy but as one of "monitoring and scrutinizing political leaders" (90.8 percent). This appears consistent with the notion of uncovering and reporting objective truths but raises the question of why "reporting things as they are" is perceived to conflict with "detached observation." It seems likely that the concept of detachment conflicts with an overall finding of strong identification with and commitment to professional codes of conduct or ethics learned primarily on the job in Japan (versus through university training), whereas reporting things "as they are" implies adherence to an ideal of truth-telling that concedes the impossibility of true neutrality. The overall importance of such surveys is that they reveal a discrepancy between external perceptions of mainstream journalists' autonomy and journalists' self-perception—even as all parties acknowledge the impact of various internal and external pressures on news content. This survey signals how much everyday structural/institutional limitations preoccupied most mass media professionals, and indeed this was a common theme in our discussions.

Another producer, Eki, has been listening silently to our discussion of "slanting." He changes the subject to the economic conditions of television labor, pointing out to me that the individuals drinking together are mostly not employees of Fuji TV, but contingent labor belonging to various production companies—and they will be scattered to different programs soon. He later writes to me in an email: "*The Compass* and [another program he worked on], BS Fuji Live were experimental, interesting programs that allowed professionals and the general public to discuss the news and social phenomena to exchange opinions. The style of the program was not fully realized, even immature—the program was cancelled before it could mature. But I think programming like this will become ubiquitous in the future."[31] Eki identified sports as the genre most likely to facilitate interactivity, as individuals were already habituated to consuming the highly rated genre live and to want to talk about it with others. "People already want to share the 'now' of sports viewing," he noted.

Nonetheless, Eki was clear that he didn't necessarily see the future of television as being coincident with that of "social TV," predicting that "the devices on which television can be watched in the future will increase, and the content consumed on viewing platforms will include TV without being limited to it. The likelihood that social TV will spread in the future is high, but the future of television has no relation to social TV, and social TV has no relation to the future of television." Eki's prediction here contradicts the tone of so many scholars mentioned above, whose enthusiasm and expectation for developments in interactive technology of the late twentieth century led to a kind of euphoria about the potential for a massive transformation of television. The uncertainty reflected in the commentary of TV professionals like Eki is more accurately captured by William Uricchio and other media theorists, who describe TV as having always been a highly unstable medium (despite being driven by a consistent underlying logic until the twenty-first century) and emphasize the need for new language with which to discuss what has become an evolving and hybridized technology.[32] For producers like Eki, technology could reliably be counted on to march forward,[33] but whether the content would be permitted to march alongside it, to evolve commensurately, was less certain. "The future of television depends on our capacity to produce content," he asserted.[34] In the end, he rearticulated a divide between audiences and producers, stating that TV currently panders to audiences and must be willing to transcend this practice.[35]

Indeed, it was not uncommon for the television professionals with whom I worked to openly critique their medium in this way, lamenting a need to appeal to unsophisticated and often-meddlesome viewers and corral them into mutual self-identification. As one producer confided, "This is terrible to say but . . . the great majority of programs are made for old people, the stupid, and the poor. Programs that are stimulating for smarter, younger, and wealthier audiences are very few."[36] In his work on Indian cinema, William Mazzarella noted comparable speech acts: when articulating the necessity of censorship, his interlocutors invoked the notion of the "common man" in the third person as a means of transferring the liability for punitive action onto an ill-defined public body whose characteristics were a bricolage of media consumption data.[37] Such categories are commonly deployed in mass media work as a means of divorcing the speaker from publics classified as receivers of media content, less intellectually sophisticated than producers or regulators themselves. Television content is always a text with many authors and therein diverges from models of creative output found in much of the literary and art worlds by sidelining individual contributions. In television, as in film, creative expression is as likely to originate in the conceptualization of a program as from individual directors, editors, and (more transparently) actors. And in the case of mass media, content is predominantly composed of hidden labor subsumed by large corporations and acknowledged in the televisual equivalent of footnotes. Thus, what individual creative laborers lacked in agency, they often projected onto the notion of a powerless audience.

Yet, well before the current era of "deep fakes," the obfuscation of boundaries between image and reality limited the expression of viewer agency,[38] and interactive TV has so far retained many of the formations of conventional television. In both cases, the choice of where to look and when is decided on behalf of the viewer; their individual experience is ideally unified with that of a hundred thousand others. Gesturing to this ultimate form of control in mass media broadcast—the selection of camera angle—Jostein Gripsrud, therefore, theorized that the television of the future would allow users to take over decision-making about looking.[39] Indeed, during my conversations with NHK TV producers I discovered that this was one of the first concepts for interactive television that they envisioned in the 1990s, along with a 1993 program that introduced such possibilities—SIM TV (*Kinmirai Terebi SIM*, or as Nishida translated the name, "Simulating the Future with Technology"). In an early example of television that allowed audiences to act directly on the appearance of mass broadcast, viewers could call in with analog phones and change the graphics displayed on an on-set screen. But Nishida sought specifically to create the possibility for viewers to control camera angles as well, imagining that audiences could take over the role of the broadcast technicians in the control room whose job it was to signal and execute camera changes. And indeed, viewers would have plenty of opportunities: during one of my control room visits, a single technician called 134 camera changes in the first twenty minutes of a news discussion program that included an extended commercial break. Yet, complicating Nishida's vision was the fact that 1990s technology only permitted viewers to change the camera once every twenty seconds by phone and, considering the audience size anticipated by even a low-rated program, the process seemed guaranteed to generate a frustrated queue of audience members who never made it past a busy signal to take their turn with the camera.

The NHK group had subsequently experimented with allowing viewers to control the outcome of television dramas by voting, and Nishida sighed, "It seemed to take the punch out of the drama. It took people out of the immersion in the story that made watching pleasurable." In his reflection on this category of interactivity, he underscored the maintenance of immersion as especially critical; by permitting audience members to assume the authorial voice (albeit by choosing between a limited set of options), the story's constructed status was foregrounded and the audience forced to disengage from a position of viewing to act. That this has been tried again in later interactive programming such as TBS's 2013 *Jinrōrian* (which resembled dinner theater) is not a testament to television's failure to learn from its history. Indeed, if accounts such as Caldwell's teach us anything it is that media production workers are self-reflexive and generally engage in *strategic* mimesis.[40] Thus, in newer experiments, networks have removed the capacity to act on narrative and divorced the goal of immersion from that of participation. In cases of successful interactive television, the content is inseparable from audience intervention—the entire product a game that must be played in order to exist. *The Compass* too offered the capacity for viewers to integrate their opinions into the show under controlled conditions, and it did so without breaching the space of television, by adapting conventional gatekeeping strategies.

Techniques for managing both the interactive viewing public and *The Compass'* miscellaneous onstage participants are evident from the beginning of the show's final broadcast. In front of the TV cameras, one of the main announcers launches into the weekly run-through of the program's mechanics, while off camera the mostly middle-aged male staff gathered in the big studio gaze in the direction of the stage with their arms crossed and intermittently glance at the monitors in the assurance that home audiences are seeing what is intended. When the first commercial break arrives, the NN announcers dash down the stairs to join the others on the main stage, while an assistant counts down the time remaining: "Twenty-three seconds!" It is 9:13 p.m., and the program's additional political commentators are being connected via Skype to the in-studio hosts. Official guests on this program often joined the discussion via Skype, while those present in the studios sat before laptops equipped with webcams and appeared in similar windows on the television/computer screen. Another assistant stations herself near the edge of the stage with large whiteboards bearing the names and titles of the remote experts. There are now 20,437 users chatting freely on the NN application.

The delicacy of managing the interactive viewing public adds a layer to the already complicated dance of live news roundtable programming: to distribute airtime equitably among those seated on stage, an assistant holds up signs indicating whose turn it is to speak. The TV broadcast hosts guide programmatic flow through carefully timed questions posed simultaneously for debate among the panelists and posted on NN. Observing staff in the studio cannot hear the commentary of the Skype experts (generally professors at one of Japan's major research universities); their microphones are fed directly into the earpieces of the hosts and out into the broadcast itself. The only nonmuted sound in this room is an errant beep from a computer in the corner of the studio (quickly silenced by a staff member) and the "hmmms" of the hosts as they listen to these comments. The program requires careful choreographing to balance the voices from each platform; following the closing of a poll on NN, the results are conveyed on TV as part of the broadcast before it moves on to comments from the *nama koe* (literally "raw voices") of Twitter. Now 25,812 people are in the NN chat room, a lively and opinionated bunch whose observations often differ from those of the named commentators solely by the manner of their mediation.

Even within this carefully structured workflow, however, there is a great deal of tension in the room of any social TV production, redolent of this loss of control to the mechanics and social complexities of live interactivity. Will people participate? Will too many people participate? Could the system "go down," forcing television into the excruciating position of being both live and unscripted? Could something entirely unforeseen happen?[41] Though massive amounts of contingency testing do occur, resembling nothing if not the (natural) disaster preparedness drills that are commonly held throughout Japan, early forays into this genre represented a massive unknown that could be perceived in the bodily comportment of their creators.

Conclusion

Since the 2010s, television has broken with a model of detached artistic engagement envisioned by classical philosophy; now it "indicates the implicit presence of the outside within the inside."[42] Where before viewers were thanked for watching, in the aftermath of interactive television programs, they are thanked for participating. Such programs cannot be rerun; resolutely live, they conscript audiences bodily, seeping from the two-dimensional screen into the third dimension of embodied action. Nonetheless, Niklas Luhmann's "second-order observation" remains a relevant concept;[43] audiences are fundamentally beholden to the vision of producers, directors, and artists, their creative agency contained by the choices of media professionals. While the collaboration represented by *The Compass* and more high-tech interactive TV programs has complicated the relationship between audiences and expert producers of media content by relinquishing partial control over programmatic narrative to an unpredictable and unknown body, these programs remain subject to the traditional gatekeeping structure of mass media.[44] Participants must be *permitted* to appear within the framing of the TV screen itself, their comments selected based on compliance with established norms and standards, while the forced anonymity of *The Compass*' NN stream denies them even voluntary accountability.

The *shichōsha*, a term that in Japanese colloquially refers to TV audiences but technically means "[those] who look and listen," recalls a viewer once conceptualized as submissive, whose experience has continued to evolve to become, at times, a less vicarious version of itself.[45] Participants in the NN broadcast stream were privy to a less formal construction of the relationship between audience and presenter, and the highly controlled comportment expected of TV news program hosts was relaxed somewhat to allow for this reframing. Not just webcast, not quite formal broadcast, the live stream component of this show breaks ground for its willingness to genuinely ad-lib, for the feeling one gets in watching that they are experimenting with and through viewers. Publics, in this participatory but curated format, are shaped by the tension between two different data flows, one orchestrating controls (from media producers to audiences), and the other representing displays of engagement (from the audience to media producer). For now, these flows represent implicit acceptance of the convergence of competing (and sometimes overlapping) priorities. As is true on any platform, at least until audiences retrofit it to their specific needs, the terms of use are to accept a limited range of affordances in addition to the professional management of their contributions. This may be standard practice for technology companies, but having never done this before, television is willing to play, keeping audiences at arm's length even as it conscripts them bodily.

In her classic account, Ien Ang wrote of audiences that they represent an unknowable category, merely a discourse object useful for indicating something that cannot fully be measured or seen. And indeed, in the conversations between television producers, the slipperiness of audiences, and the inadequacy of the antiquated means by which we still sometimes categorize and account for them, remain a primary concern despite an increase in the volume of quantitative data now obtainable by tracking audiences online.[46] In chapter 3, I turn to the independent news organizations that emerged in response to the Fukushima media crisis and examine how they attempted to create spaces for interactive content and participation that could bypass these traditional forms of gatekeeping.

3

Cultures of Independent Journalism

THE FREE PRESS ASSOCIATION OF JAPAN, INDEPENDENT WEB JOURNAL, AND GOHOO

On the second floor of a nondescript building in Tokyo's Kojimachi neighborhood in August 2012, the cohort of interns and volunteers of the Free Press Association of Japan (FPAJ, or Jiyū hōdō kyōkai) is setting up for a press conference. The room is a bureaucratic white and gray, lit by fluorescent lighting and dotted with cameramen setting up their equipment. It is both cleaner and emptier than the press club (*kisha kurabu*) conference rooms (see figure 3.1), and the wall behind the speakers' table is papered with the FPAJ's cerulean logo (see figure 3.2).[1] Interns and volunteers take names at the registration table, set up the chairs, and prepare tea for the speakers "backstage." The space consists of a lobby in which volunteers run metal detectors over journalists, a formal tatami-matted tearoom/greenroom, kitchens, a more intimate greenroom, and a rear fire escape from which speakers can furtively arrive and depart. The building is owned by Dwango, the parent company of NicoNico (NN), and is occupied alternately by Dwango's events and the FPAJ's.[2] Press conferences held in this space are live-streamed on both NicoNico Namahōsō and UStream,[3] allowing

3.1 A press conference at the Liberal Democratic Party headquarters. In the background, Abe Shinzo celebrates his reelection. Photo by author.

internet viewers unedited and immediate access to the entirety of the press conference proceedings.

Nearby in Nibanchō, on a cold and rainy October night, a diverse assortment of volunteers gradually trickles into the Social Entrepreneur School (Shakai Kigyō Daigaku) building, shaking off their umbrellas and coats as they enter. The group is here to work on a start-up project named GoHoo (Misinformation),[4] a website run by the umbrella group Nihon Hōdō Kenshō Kikō (The Watchdog for Accuracy in News Reporting, Japan). Inspired by American websites such as Politifact and Factcheck.org, GoHoo proposed, in the words of its founder, to "fact-check the information provided in the [Japanese] mass media."[5] Still in the early stage of web

3.2 The speakers' table at a Free Press Association of Japan press conference. Photo by author.

development and resource acquisition, the group's primary focus tonight and during its other monthly meetings is on user interface concepts, site features, and promotional strategies. Tonight's main presentation is therefore given by a professional social media manager who stands at a whiteboard and draws arrows and boxes with a red marker, explaining to us how Japanese users conduct research online, and why (according to Dentsu public relations research) they decide to seek more information about a topic.

Both the FPAJ and GoHoo were independent media start-ups established in the wake of the Fukushima disaster as part of a burgeoning interest in media activism, and both engaged the bidirectional, interactive (if not egalitarian) nature of blogs and other social media to achieve their goals. In so doing, they followed a growing international model for "journalism as activism," within which "activists use and create new communication tools and take up the work traditionally ascribed to journalists, expanding what it means to be involved in the production of news and, in the process, gaining influence over how traditional news stories and genres are constructed and circulated."[6] In statements like this, the FPAJ frequently followed the model of TV producers by foregrounding the capacity of new technology to introduce ways to improve public discourse and "expanding what it means to be involved in the production of news" through interactive tools by inviting audiences to take on the more active role of citizen journalist.

Diverging from the TV professionals I studied, the FPAJ was conceived of in reaction to the *kisha* (reporters') clubs by one of its most vocal critics, Uesugi Takashi, a controversial public figure who sought to formulate an alternative space to produce news content, accessible to anyone with an interest in "practicing journalism," or really anyone at all.[7] During the winter of 2012, Uesugi explained why he founded the FPAJ:

> Along with Iwakami-san and Shiraiishi-san ['s organizations][8] the FPAJ is fighting the Japanese press club system which does not allow freelance, magazine and online journalists, foreign media, etc. to enter its conferences. To put it simply, employees of the major TV and newspaper companies have spaces with specialized access, wherein the freelance journalists can't actually collect data.[9] Since 1990, I myself have been working on this issue . . . after I became involved in working with the *New York Times* and Koizumi Junichiro became prime minister the issue became even more urgent.

He continued, "[Our] model was the FCCJ (Foreign Correspondents' Club of Japan). [Founding member] Jimbo [Tetsuo]-san and I, we thought: 'Let's us Japanese make a version of this as well.'"[10]

The FPAJ's one-room office was located up the street from its press conference space and conveniently positioned within the daily beats of many reporters. And indeed, reporters wandered in and out regularly, checking in on FPAJ business, chatting with the office manager, interns, and volunteers, or indulging in a respite from the weather. Organizational routine was contingent on the day's schedule: press conferences, association meetings, and the comings and goings of various affiliates. On press conference days, nearly everyone but Mariko, the office manager, wandered over to the Dwango building early to set up chairs, test the table mics, and prepare the check-in table or metal detectors (in the case of high-profile guests). By maintaining its own space, the FPAJ sought to liberate itself from mainstream news media—not just through all-access press conferences held far away from the *kisha* club desks found in government buildings, but by following a new model of political activism in Japan and streaming these conferences online, making information directly accessible by the public.[11] Its press conferences mostly featured politicians, both famous and fringe, and nearly everyone involved in Tokyo-based media reform, literacy, and citizen journalism seemed to hold an FPAJ event during the group's tenure.

Media fact-checker GoHoo had a similarly critical stance toward mainstream news. During our initial meeting, GoHoo's founder, Hitofumi Yanai, explained his organization's governing principles: American newspapers, when they make a mistake, print a retraction or an apology in a particular place, he said, using the *New York Times* as an example: "In the US, corrections are printed on a designated page each day.[12] Such revisions are easy to find in newspapers if one looks for them—and online, American journalists generally acknowledge at the bottom of an article that factual updates were made. Japanese newspapers do not do this. Although a culture of online news influenced by Western models has begun to take hold in Japan, the media is not in the habit of admitting mistakes."[13] GoHoo therefore attempted to function as mediator between the infrastructure of mass media and its publics, by selecting stories to verify, posting "warnings" (*chūihō*) and "misinformation reports" (*gohō repōto*) on its website, and promoting its findings through social media.

Both the FPAJ and GoHoo shared a mission to transcend the limitations of a conservative national press by exploiting democratic fantasies about the internet.[14] Using audiences as fact-checkers, witnesses, and even authors, the organizations conceived of their websites as means to crowdsource greater accountability for mass media. But neither foresaw the challenge of raising public support in a country without a "donation culture,"[15] the intensity of mainstream journalism's resistance, the greater visibility of right-wing positions online, and the labor-intensiveness of their endeavors.

Journalism in Japan

Ethnographic studies of journalism have historically embedded journalists in a web of institutional constraint and marginalized their professional agency; for this reason, former journalist Mark Allen Peterson took exception to much of the work on journalistic praxis in the twentieth century, and more recent ethnography has refrained from classifying journalists according to uniform structural limitations, social capital, and agency.[16] Moreover, frequently invoked Bourdieusian taxonomies must be applied carefully in Japan, as "doxa" in that country is generally associated with institutional belonging rather than journalistic habitus. Specifically, independent Japanese journalists identify with orthodoxies frequently invoked in Western studies of incumbent journalists, while incumbents' attachment to power very much represents that described by Gregory P. Perreault, Patrick Ferrucci, and Scott A. Eldridge.[17] Although Roger Dickinson and Bashir Memon have argued that "journalism's history, wherever it is located, is always one of an evolving, developing occupation which, in the process of its formation, is always in pursuit of collective autonomy," this does not seem to be consistently true in Japan.[18] In other words, to fully understand the hurdles facing organizations like the FPAJ and GoHoo, we must understand the extent to which autonomy is not a universal, or even mainstream, journalistic goal in Japan and therefore complicates Bourdieusian theory.

The limitations of structure, and the tension between interpersonal and institutional constraints, cannot be overstated in the case of Japan's *kisha* club system—described to me by a former NHK bureau chief as still "[the nation's] biggest problem." That the Japanese press has been in a state of repression, and even crisis, since 2011 has been widely argued.[19] By 2022, Japan was ranked seventy-first in the World Press Freedom Index, down from a high of eleventh before Abe Shinzo took office again.[20] The organization responsible for these rankings, Reporters without Borders, explained its original 2014 demotion of Japan in the rankings with a series of warnings:

> Arrests, home searches, interrogation by the domestic intelligence agency and threats of judicial proceedings—who would have thought that covering the aftermath of the 2011 Fukushima nuclear disaster would have involved so many risks for Japan's freelance journalists? The discrimination against freelance and foreign reporters resulting from Japan's unique system of kisha clubs, whose members are the only journalists to be granted government accreditation, has increased since Fukushima.
>
> Often barred from press conferences given by the government and TEPCO (the Fukushima nuclear plant's owner), denied access to the information available to the mainstream media (which censor themselves), freelancers have their hands tied in their fight to cover Japan's nuclear industrial complex, known as the "nuclear village." Now that Prime Minister Shinzo Abe's government has tightened the legislation on "state secrets," their fight will get even more dangerous."[21]

The parochialism of Japanese *kisha* clubs has been mentioned earlier in this book, but it is worth briefly revisiting their structure and the public perception of them in the post-Fukushima era—a time when journalism emerged as a serious "topic of national debate," primarily due to its failure to relay timely information about the Fukushima nuclear disaster (but before the Abe administration's crackdown on journalistic freedom largely took hold).[22] In Japan, where formal journalistic training is uncommon and reporters, who are typically recruited from among the country's elite universities and learn on the job from their *senpai* (more senior journalists, in this context), an absence of polemical engagement with "credentialed facts" is the normative model.[23] The advantage of *kisha* club membership primarily has to do with the access to metalevel information that it provides, as members are often informed about the scheduling of press conferences up to a month in advance, so they might fix the schedules of their camera crews or collectively agree not to pursue extracurricular reporting about designated topics.[24] Moreover, the clubs are attached not just to each outpost of governmental news generation but also to major corporations and agencies (most significantly during my fieldwork Tokyo Electric, the Japan Atomic Energy Headquarters, and even NHK itself). By focusing on direct transmission of information delivered by official sources in official settings, journalists seek to dictate national consensus and construct a "we," with the nature of that body managed by formal institutions. Although these clubs can insulate their members from retaliatory activity by governmental agents, the practice of "pack journalism," where individuals from various news companies engage in daily contact and cover identical events, has historically resulted in rampant press conformity.[25] The ritual of regular and controlled news dissemination means that members have the same story, and peer/governmental pressure ensures that in most cases, they stick to it. Much in the world of the *kisha* club functions in terms of implicit agreement regarding what can and cannot be said, with allegiance to one's colleagues and employer a better long-term strategy than gaining an exclusive scoop.[26] The nature of this system discourages investigative journalism in general, as reporters working in close quarters and in the same press club space day after day coordinate questions and even collaborate to rehearse the process of question asking in general.[27] Their routines are also occupied by the sorting of frequent press releases and attentiveness to the public routines of the officials they are assigned to cover.[28] In short, rather than the clubs protecting journalistic freedom, they encourage members to engage in fundamentally conservative journalism to prevent retaliation against the group.

In a news landscape where the model of journalism differs radically from that of the intrepid and radically individualistic news correspondent romanticized by Western culture, it means something different and arguably more revolutionary for even a faction of journalists to attempt radical transparency. By providing direct access to moments of news dissemination and fact-checking those who were supposed to be fact-checkers, the FPAJ and GoHoo created a provocative challenge to the integrity of professional journalists in Japan. Like many transnational media startups before and after them, they sought to redefine news as a conversation—not in the manner of a TV talk show (except maybe *The Compass*), but by bypassing conventional limits on what may be said in the Japanese public sphere and inscribing a more diverse range of voices. Their contribution lay in their potential to provide people a space within which to comment on TV and newspaper information, and therein to complicate their narratives.[29]

The Struggles of Post-Fukushima Media Activism

Even during the period of heightened support for independent journalists during the immediate post-Fukushima years, individuals attempting to organize outside of the major Japanese news conglomerates faced significant challenges. Despite a common appraisal of the internet as the more democratic but diffuse other to mass media's privileged platform, a din of overlapping voices means internet audience share can be unpredictable and comparatively diminutive—particularly in a country where cable television adoption never established dominance and the number of television channels accessed by most residents is limited. As mainstream journalism in Japan relies extensively on "credentialed facts," or information gleaned from official sources,[30] alternative news sources can be considered either untrustworthy or *more* trustworthy (depending on who you ask), based on the same lack of accountability. Although the FPAJ, GoHoo, Independent Web Journal (IWJ, discussed later), and other independent news groups promoted the societal benefits of direct access to news materials, information circulated online even now can possess an aura of "unofficial facts" that renders it suspicious.[31] Moreover, despite the influence of social media and streaming content, one 2019 survey found that a majority of eighteen-year-olds in Japan still trust television news more than information consumed online.[32]

In reflecting on the ideal position of journalism within a national body, the Japanese media activists with whom I worked frequently drew on the United States for inspiration, perceiving within the American landscape a symbiosis between traditional mass media and watchdog punditry found on blogs and social media.[33] The American model of funding alternative news sources by fundraising among sympathetic audiences was something these organizations hoped to replicate during what seemed to be a turning point in Japanese public sentiment toward journalism. But for the FPAJ and others, the barriers to newsgathering frequently took the form of literal walls, as they petitioned for access to the press club spaces. A major site of contestation was the National Diet Press Club building, which housed approximately 159 media companies but excluded freelance, magazine, and foreign reporters. The FPAJ issued a formal petition for office space in July 2012, following similar unsuccessful appeals from fellow independent media organization Our Planet-TV. Our Planet-TV had repeatedly requested to film ongoing anti–nuclear energy protests in front of the prime minister's house from atop the building and was denied each time.[34] It eventually petitioned in Tokyo's lower and higher courts to gain access (denied), and subsequently brought an unsuccessful lawsuit against the National Diet Press Club for discrimination.[35] Its petitions were followed by similar efforts involving three other independent journalists—one a prominent FPAJ member—to use, if not office space within the building, at least its privileged rooftop vantage point. The FPAJ's own petition in July 2012 was therefore framed by this ongoing agitation of the journalistic status quo by those excluded from it.

I joined the FPAJ for its first in-person meeting with the building's director (*jimukyokuchō*) on September 12, 2012. As the group waited in the lobby, Sekimoto pointed out the empty, usable desk space visible from where we stood. The group nodded grimly. The meeting began formulaically with an exchange of business cards and polite greetings as the FPAJ members seated themselves quietly before cups of tea. The *jimukyokuchō* slid on his glasses and examined the letter. He began to read it out loud, while the group looked down at their hands and laps. The news wasn't good.

UESUGI: May I make my case again?
JIMUKYOKUCHŌ: There is no point.

A series of dueling monologs followed, and the tension between the two rose with each exchange. Uesugi stood up to pace and glance at his flip phone, opening and snapping it shut in a nervous rhythm.

JIMUKYOKUCHŌ: I have already answered all relevant questions.
SEKIMOTO: Might there be any conditions under which the FPAJ could hold space in the building?

JIMUKYOKUCHŌ: Membership is contingent on a few characteristics your organization lacks—scale, and funding.

Uesugi had begun making sounds of disgust in response to the *jimukyokuchō*'s words, snorting and snickering, and stepping outside the room to leave the occasional voice mail in pursuit of advice and support from his allies. He returned to the table.

UESUGI: The FPAJ will have to go over your head and talk to the club's political director.
JIMUKYOKUCHŌ: The director is very busy.
UESUGI: He is not. You could call him right now if you wanted to.

With the meeting at a standstill and Uesugi's temper irrevocably lost, the group rose to leave. After a quiet ride back to the offices in Uesugi's car, Mariko (the office manager) and I climbed the stairs to return to the FPAJ's office. Mariko said quietly, sadly, "This is my least favorite part of the job.[36]

If insufficient funding prevented the FPAJ from signifying legitimacy, GoHoo's funds were even more limited. Involvement in GoHoo therefore remained a side project for nearly everyone attending its monthly meetings—that is, its staff generally had to maintain their day jobs. Among the volunteers were lawyers (including the founder, an ex-journalist turned lawyer), students, retired journalists, and social media marketers. But fact-checking the news requires substantial personnel; pursuant to the twenty-four-hour news cycle, comprehensive news monitoring would require a robust infrastructure like that of the Associated Press, wherein an ever-attentive body of individuals tracks news in real time.[37] But even if the news could be effectively monitored round the clock by GoHoo volunteers, fact-checking requires additional resources. Focusing only on newspaper content still left the organization with a massive labor shortage.[38]

Interactivity and Objectivity in Guerrilla Journalism

Given their lack of access to mainstream media platforms and resources, technologies promoting interactivity on a budget have been among the Japanese independent media's most critical tools and provided the sole means of content distribution for several small media start-ups. Interactivity generally meant encouraging audiences to synthesize raw news information in real time, with this commentary becoming a visible barrier between events and the audience on NicoNico's live stream. As GoHoo struggled with the resource demands of its fact-checking operation, other groups wrestled with the infrastructure necessary to make live streaming a viable challenge to mainstream journalism.

The Independent Web Journal (IWJ) is one of numerous independent media organizations in Tokyo that has grown in prominence and refined its mission since the March 2011 disasters in Eastern Japan. Founded in December 2010, its primary objective is to provide unedited streaming access to important events—from press conferences to protests—and its mission is overwhelmingly defined as one of supplement rather than comprehensive alternative to the mass media. Where the mainstream media refuses to go or offers a truncated and filtered version of events, IWJ streams live, relying on its network of regional reporters and a sizable Tokyo staff to provide such exhaustive and resource-intensive coverage.[39] "It's really difficult to do" (*Taihen tsukuridzurai*), founder Iwakami Yasumi explains.[40]

Over the course of several months in 2012–13 I watched them work; as members of a small media production company their tasks are comparable to those of network television employees, and yet necessarily less specialized. Next to me, Ai reviews video from a previous day's recorded broadcast, pausing occasionally to answer the phone or to make a call to coordinate press conference attendance by the organization's sizable staff. She switches screens to the IWJ's elaborate scheduling spreadsheet to enter an event, and then a name. With 184 UStream channels spanning both the country and the world, scheduling for the IWJ is a slot game requiring the cooperation and coordination of many actors—and Ai is not the only one editing or accessing this schedule.

Ai's daily routine is a dance involving many simultaneous bids for her attention, her workflow part air traffic controller, part control room technician. She continues to stream press conference audio in the background while calling up Google Maps to relay directions to a lost and frantic staffer. He won't need any ID, she insists, glancing at the clock, but he's about to be late and needs to immediately locate the event within the labyrinth of bureaucratic government spaces. Flipping to the spreadsheet containing details for this press conference, Ai cradles the phone between cheek and shoulder and reassures him again that *kisha* club credentials are unnecessary for this press conference. As she hangs up, Ai brings the IWJ UStream feeds up on her screen to check that staff members are in place and the tech is working correctly. Tabbing quickly, she updates the corresponding Twitter feeds for those channels. In the background another staffer, Kaori, moves from assembling IWJ mailings to monitoring the consistent influx of faxes, cataloging equipment, and phoning the other office to sync up. "This is the boring office," she informs me without irony. Turning away from her computer monitors for a moment, Ai agrees. She offers to take me to the IWJ's second location on the west side of Azabu Juban Station where, she assures me, I can get a better feel for how they *really* work. The journalists will all be over there.

In Iwakami's account of its founding, the IWJ was an extension of his work as a journalist and motivated (similarly to the Free Press Association of Japan) by a desire to provide an alternative to *kisha* club journalism in Japan. Iwakami writes that it was the sheer number of politically significant topics he wished to address and events that seemed worthy of diligent coverage that inspired his creation of a news organization: the Trans-Pacific Partnership and USA-Japan alliance controversies, the consumption tax increase, the issue of nuclear power, and others. His vision was of a more "nimble" (*migaru*) journalistic mobility, in which he could orchestrate the coverage of many significant political events simultaneously while remaining outside of the major mass media infrastructure, replicating the resources of the major networks under the ethos of "independent journalism."[41] And it was only three months after the IWJ's founding that the 2011 disasters occurred, before Iwakami and his fledgling staff of two had attained the necessary technical literacy to build the infrastructure that he envisioned. In the early days of the IWJ, he was nonetheless able to introduce coverage of two generally restricted press conference spaces: the TEPCO (Tokyo Electric, or Tōkyō Denryoku) and NISA (Nuclear and Industrial Safety Agency, or Hoanin) and subsequently mobilize a network of fifty-five relay points around the country, all streaming live to his website.

The hope of groups like IWJ, FPAJ, and GoHoo is that this more comprehensive coverage and an open media landscape can transform political engagement among Japanese citizens. For media activist Tsuda Daisuke, this potential defines his interest in interactive technologies; YouTube, Nico-Nico, and similar platforms can introduce a broad selection of events to a diverse national body and inspire them to protest, volunteer, or otherwise mobilize. For example, Japanese mothers—historically not an especially political demographic—began lobbying after 2011 for an end to Japan's reliance on nuclear energy under the banner of "*kodomo mamorō!*" (save the children!), as nuclear energy–related events became the focus of the independent media.[42] Unlike regional/selective broadcast or public meetings, internet coverage of protests and action events (such as those held by Tokyo-based Democracy 2.0 and One Voice) encourage remote participation and, as Tsuda argues, can potentially mobilize political action at the national level.[43] Right-wing groups in Japan have similarly co-opted live streaming technologies as a recruitment tool, using their events mostly as a means of converting internet viewers to supporters of their cause—as anthropologist Tomomi Yamaguchi summarizes, they use "live-streaming . . . as a means of activism."[44] The comparison complicates the work of freelance journalists in the organizations described here. At once overlapping with the publics for whom they seek to create content, they also seek to frame and legitimize their work in terms of conventional media practice. This necessitates consistently distancing their work from a right-wing association with the platforms (e.g., NN) and methods (live streaming) that they use.

The FPAJ sought to introduce hybrid forms of participation to the conventional press conference format, retrofitting an old system rather than attempting to dismantle it through new technology. Its events represented media ritual at its most self-consciously performative, their utterances rehearsed and revised, and the acceptable positions for reporters and equipment mapped out on the floor (often with masking tape). They were also a type of rehearsed and bounded spectacle, typically requiring the framing of the *kisha* club conference room. The FPAJ's use of NicoNico was therefore a significant part of a broader strategy (also seen in chapter 2) to disrupt traditional gatekeeping practices while maintaining allegiance to the integrity of journalistic praxis. However, as in the example of right-wing groups, it was also about performing for the live streaming cameras, attracting an audience to the FPAJ's channel, and soliciting the feedback that NN users typed across the live video feed while watching an event. But the independent media, despite featuring some of the usual newsmakers in settings that visually mimicked a traditional press conference, represented a more direct conduit for the discursive flows of audiences to media producers. This proximity undermined their work even as they pursued legitimization by appropriating some of the rituals of mainstream news production.

On one occasion, during the September 5, 2012, press conference of a visiting American nuclear scientist, I was seated in the same row as NN's news division chief. The NN app was open on his tablet, the press conference room reproduced in miniature on his screen. Although it was early in the presentation, the signature NN image-overlaid comments passed rapidly over the face of the conference's presenter on the video feed (as one television company employee described it, NN comments are *barabara*, like a barrage of gunfire). Two thousand people were already watching online, and after downloading and installing the app on my own tablet, I tried to follow their commentary's rapid progression across my screen. Most of the comments passing across the FPAJ's video stream were typical internet fare: that is, astute commentary shared space with humorous insults, anti-American/Korean sentiment, and no shortage of the right-wing conspiracy theories for which sites like 2chan are known. Kitada Akihiro and Hamano Satoshi have written about the pleasure in participating in spaces like NN or 2chan, and the extent to which the content of a video stream or of individual comments is less important than the energy of participation.[45] In other words, "people are interacting because of the pleasure in the social communication itself," and the content of the comments becomes as much about the pleasure of trolling as about any genuinely held political beliefs.[46] By five minutes and forty seconds into the press conference, the online audience had surpassed five thousand.

Gesturing toward the intention of the FPAJ's experiment, the NN news chief frequently broke through the typical press conference din of frantic typing and camera shutter clicking to solicit the mic and ask questions on behalf of internet audiences. As he spoke, a line of golden text appeared over the internet video feed stating that his question was harvested directly from the online viewers for whom this press conference was primarily staged. On this occasion, the 30,535 users now watching the live stream erupted into messages of appreciation at their inscription into the event: *Oshare!* (Nice!) The context provided by the FPAJ provided intersecting channels within which professional and citizen journalists could respond to the news, and through which journalists in attendance at the event could craft articles in response to concerns raised by publics in real time. Typically, they alternated between live tweeting the event, commenting on NN, and frantically taking notes—the event becoming more about its translation online than the embodied experience.

Uesugi Takashi articulated his vision for the organization in profoundly idealistic terms, underscoring the significance of his ongoing struggle against the system of Japanese journalism: "[Earlier in this statement] I referred to the third 'opening up' of Japan. The first was the Meiji Restoration, and the second was the rise from the destruction of WWII. Together, these constituted revolutions that have fundamentally altered the social composition of the whole country and society. If events on this scale in the past constituted the first and second 'opening up' of Japan, then what's going on now globally with social media surely has the potential to be the third for us."[47] In crafting this mission statement Uesugi referenced what were then major sources of inspiration for those attempting to organize resistance movements online at that time—the Arab Spring and Occupy Wall Street protests, as well as Japan's own antinuclear energy actions and youth movements (such as the *freeters* and later the Students' Emergency Action for Liberal Democracy), which relied extensively on social media as an organization tool.[48]

In seeking to harness the energy of contemporary global social activism, the FPAJ nonetheless had to contend with the unique limitations of Japan's journalistic environment. Despite the FPAJ's attempt to promote its open-access press conferences as politically objective based on their inclusivity, Uesugi's aggressive questioning of politicians challenged this stance and contributed to their general discomfort with the open press conference model. *Kisha* club events provide officials greater control over the way their messages are received and where and disincentivize polemical writing by member journalists.[49] While Anne Cooper-Chen has argued that mainstream journalism in Japan is not about confrontation,[50] the replacement of corporate-embedded journalists with amateur online Others introduces its possibility. Live-streamed broadcasts in Japan are particularly susceptible to trolling and attacks by right-wing internet extremists (the *netto uyoku*)—notably frequent visitors to the anonymous forum 2chan, who gravitate to other anonymous platforms like NN and who are unmoored from the checks and balances of social position by the anonymity that these sites provide. A former advertising executive thus found it amusing when I asked him about the site:

ER: How much do you think 2chan drives internet trends in Japan?
OKADA: (Laughing) 2chan *is* the internet here.

And Okada was right: when we had this conversation 2chan was the world's largest web forum, accessed regularly by an estimated 10 percent of Japan.[51] The flood of extremist (e.g., xenophobic, misogynistic) comments seen on many politically oriented NN live streams complicated the FPAJ's assertion that the online component of these press conferences contributed anything of substantial value, and it seemed to validate mainstream journalism's aggressive use of gatekeeping strategies. (See figure 3.3.) By nevertheless refusing to exclude anyone from commenting or to enforce baseline standards, the independent media effectively marginalized its endeavors and deterred politicians and mainstream journalists from participating in its events. Those who attended virtually often found their contribution lost in the melee, while in-person attendees were subject to online heckling.

3.3 A Free Press Association of Japan press conference with somewhat typical comments overlayed upon the NicoNico Nama Hōsō live stream.

The resultant free-for-all sometimes repelled powerful people who saw no professional benefit to enduring unmoderated trolling. For instance, then–prime minister Noda Yoshihiko was a no-show at his September 18, 2012, FPAJ press conference. After his assistant reportedly warned him about the unruly and often right-wing orientation of the NicoNico users to whom it would broadcast, he deemed the audience undesirable, and the event too risky so close to a general election. What remained for many press conferences was an environment suited to those who enjoy the banter of 2chan, and independent journalists devoted enough to the FPAJ's mission to endure the live stream's chronic misogyny and racism. Thus, while the FPAJ quickly succeeded in functioning as a conduit for (remote) public participation, it remained unclear whether the nature of this participation would eventually discourage attendance by most of the politicians and cultural figures who provided news content, and the journalists necessary to curate it.

Despite some notable successes, the FPAJ press conferences were generally appraised with skepticism by mainstream journalists. Their inconsistent participation in the FPAJ's press conferences underscored the point that some found safety within Japan's inflexible system for news gathering despite its primary function of protecting the reputations and interests of governmental and business elites. The status quo was indeed not disparaged by all; for some members the *kisha* clubs constitute a useful means of enforcing journalistic ethics, in addition to keeping out the trolls.[52] Meanwhile, as Uesugi and fellow media activist Horie Takufumi observed, even when the FPAJ's press conferences generated leads for mainstream journalists, the FPAJ was not acknowledged—though other institutions outside of the *kisha* club system (like the Foreign Correspondents Club of Japan) often received such credit.[53]

The antagonism that attracted online neonationalists to the FPAJ was rooted in the overtly liberal politics of many who called themselves independent journalists and who sought to challenge news outlets they perceived as dangerously conservative and withholding critical safety information from the public after 3/11. Many of these journalists took a stance against the opaque praxis of their mainstream counterparts by using social media to transparently argue their politics rather than performing journalistic neutrality or hinting at personal beliefs around links to their appropriately "fair and balanced" news output. Journalists affiliated with the FPAJ and IWJ were generally consistent in their modes of self-representation, which meant consistently making polemical arguments on Twitter, personal blogs, and organizational newsletters.[54] And although this helped them gain like-minded followers and increase independent media associations' visibility, it also drew unwanted attention from the Far Right. Additionally, activist Uesugi Takashi himself has long been a reliably controversial figure in Japan's public sphere. Although the FPAJ was certainly not a solo venture, as its public face, Uesugi became the individual most prominently associated with the organization and one of its most tireless promoters. By serving as the FPAJ's principal representative he insured that many would have preconceptions about the organization's agenda writ large.[55]

Abandoning Neutrality

Within a year of its founding in 2011, the FPAJ seemed to be gaining momentum. On the heels of a press conference with the Dalai Lama, the major news organizations were attentive to its presence if not actually influenced by it. Occasionally, FPAJ press conferences achieved successful appropriation and framing within a major television news program, and events such as the FPAJ's November 2012 debate between Tokyo's mayoral candidates attracted a sizable mainstream media cohort.[56] But this was insufficient to bridge the divide between the mainstream and independent news media.

Questions of appropriate journalistic conduct and credentialing were raised in response to nearly all the FPAJ's activities.

While the independent media's Twitter use often resembled that of Western journalists, it starkly contrasted with mainstream Japanese practice.[57] Comportment of FPAJ press conference attendees also followed this less formal model in person, leading to occasional confrontations between freelancers and employees of the major media conglomerates that hindered the FPAJ's overall mission and chance of longevity. During the summer of 2012, there was still substantial chatter among members of Tokyo's journalistic set about a 2011 confrontation during an FPAJ press conference between a reporter from the conservative newspaper *Yomiuri Shinbun*, Iwakami Yasumi (of the Independent Web Journal), and Uesugi Takashi. Pursuant to the transparency of the FPAJ's process, the entire *"Jiyū hōdō kyōkai/Yomiuri Shinbun jiken"* (FPAJ/*Yomiuri Shinbun* incident), which took place during a question-and-answer session with prominent politician and former DJP representative Ichirō Ozawa, had been streamed live on NN. Audiences commented on the argument in real time and subsequently edited/compiled it into a twenty-minute clip that they uploaded to YouTube with the title "Uesugi and Iwakami [Yasumi] Flip Out at Stupid Yomiuri Reporter."[58]

During FPAJ press conferences, rules of conduct loosely resembled those of the *kisha* club conferences and were recited each time in a rather pro forma and matter-of-fact way by a volunteer moderator: reporters were to wait to be called on and handed the microphone, state their affiliation, limit themselves to a single question (unless time permitted), and exercise brevity in the asking of their question. In the video, the *Yomiuri* reporter's speech surpassed the format of "question" to become enduring monolog, and the semiotics of this moment were belied by the camera's oscillation between his face and Ozawa's. As Ozawa first interjected and then retreated into impassivity, the reporter quickly entered the territory of social breach. Rather than the prototypical journalistic inquiry, his was a lengthy polemic designed to both challenge and provoke its target. As he recounted this story to me at the Foreign Correspondents' Club, one freelance reporter opined that the conservative *Yomiuri Shinbun* had sent someone to deliberately disrupt an FPAJ press conference; he interpreted the incident as a form of sabotage, with the FPAJ having unwittingly taken the bait.

The impropriety of this breach was underscored by the physical reactions of fellow journalists, who shifted in their chairs and muttered audibly, a perceptible but passive attempt at censoring the wayward individual. After allowing Ozawa the briefest of responses, the *Yomiuri* reporter declined to solicit the microphone before continuing—his speech increasing in speed as he raced the rising tide of collective ire. He held up his hands, still warding off the moderator's attempts to interject, and addressed Ozawa again. The camera cut to Ozawa, who maintained engagement with the reporter as the moderator attempted apologetic intervention, saying, "We need to move on."

Uesugi and Iwakami Yasumi eventually attempted to confront the wayward reporter. Video of the altercation shows a ring of curious onlookers forming around the three men, whose conversation is at first muffled before growing into a din of shouting and effusive display of hand gestures. In proportion to his anger, the speed and volume of Uesugi's speech increases over time until it is diverted into physical obstruction. He stands in front of and close to the reporter and blocks his exit. The incident, as recorded, lasts fifteen minutes.

Months later the FPAJ's office manager, Mariko, and fellow board member Nishizaki winced and sighed, remembering the incident. "It was an embarrassment," Nishizaki explained in a hushed tone.

When organizing a symposium on news start-ups at Tokyo University, I was warned multiple times about covert pushback by faculty against inviting Uesugi Takashi to campus: many read the *Yomiuri* incident as one of inappropriate journalistic intimidation and proof of the need for institutional constraint on individual behavior. Internet chatter about the confrontation (including YouTube comments) tended to favor institutional journalism over the FPAJ, Uesugi Takashi, or Iwakami Yasumi. In particular, the Japanese "alt-right" heavily represented on 2chan and NND relished the opportunity to mock Uesugi and Iwakami's response, which they labeled disproportionate and odd (*iyō*). One commenter made a pun on Uesugi's name by writing *Uesugiru* (*sugiru* being the Japanese verb used to represent an excess of something or "too much").

Backed into a corner, Uesugi eventually apologized on both Twitter and his own website and resigned as FPAJ representative. The usual body of critical internet users followed the incident closely, juxtaposing the triumphant tone of FPAJ members' tweets during the scuffle with their eventual reversal and assumption of a repentant stance. The internet's position was that an external backlash (*kazeatari*) manufactured the FPAJ's change in perspective, but similar social approbation was never applied to the wayward *Yomiuri* reporter.[59] Somewhat more tepidly (amid the usual racial slurs, conspiracy theories, and attacks on FPAJ members), the NN users voiced mild displeasure with the offending reporter and his breaches of etiquette. Nonneutrality, it seemed, was less tolerable for a nonestablishment journalist than it was for an establishment one.

If neutrality, codified as an essential component of journalistic selfhood, and performances of objectivity maintain the boundary separating professional and citizen (or independent journalists), then the FPAJ's in-person attendees often blurred the lines between these two. In the FPAJ press conference room, journalists' questions often revealed the political orientation of those who posed them. Uesugi specifically took every opportunity to press prominent politicians on whether they'd be willing to hold open press conferences, and to reiterate the FPAJ's position on the *kisha* club problem. As he usually asked the first question at events, he set the tone for a discussion that tended to be much more polemical than those at *kisha* club press conferences.

It has been argued in several places that journalism in the absence of orthodox practices potentially occupies a different category of information.[60] In cases like the FPAJ, the efforts of unorthodox journalism neglect to replace or even supplement conventional journalism but rather act as source material for the more disciplined mode of praxis.[61] This is to say, the practice of independent journalism in Japan runs the risk of being more newsworthy than the content it produces if it fails to maintain careful discipline. Ironically for the FPAJ's tricky mix of objectivity-minded production practices and a nonneutral journalistic stance, the *Yomiuri* dispute would likely have not escaped the press conference room had the group not livestreamed it. But by its efforts to make the raw material of newsgathering available to all, the FPAJ inadvertently provided its (and Uesugi's) critics with ammunition to argue that he was not a serious journalist and was incapable of the restraint stipulated by the profession.

If independent Japanese journalists occupy a liminal space between professional and audience comportment, and between mainstream American and Japanese praxis in terms of social media use and habitus, then what is the difference between an independent journalist and a troll? At FPAJ's open-access press conferences, both trolls and independent journalists engaged in polemical debate, and there was occasional overlap in the nature of their advocacy or protest. The primary difference, however, was in the anonymity and crowd energy that governed the *uyo-chu* commentators.[62] Although Uesugi Takashi was branded a troll (*arashi*) and an opportunist by these commentators,[63] his name was prominently attached to his various political and professional endeavors. While he and other independent journalists often worked tirelessly and visibly to promote their causes,[64] trolling, which fed on the crowd energy and safety of anonymous spaces, was more about "social copresence" in most cases than the political issues at hand.

Eventually Uesugi's prominence in the FPAJ and ensuant targeting by right-wing internet users would help drive the organization's dissolution. As donations to the FPAJ waned over the course of 2012, the group perceived the problem as a failure of Japanese society and began to reach outside the country to websites like GlobalGiving. Board members questioned how they could pay for the conference room, and on one brisk day in late January, when the office was particularly cold, I was told they could not afford to turn the heat on.

The budget issues dominating its 2013 meetings, although not uncommon for independent media (or start-ups of any kind), were a problem of both reputation and circumstance for the FPAJ. As time passed after the March 2011 disasters, the capacity of public anger to manifest substantial social change began to seem less inevitable, and a certain amount of fatigue had crept into the discourse. Moreover, the organization's reliance on volunteer labor to solicit contributions subjected it to a tension common to news start-ups, wherein their contributing journalists frequently couldn't maintain a commitment to both the FPAJ and paid work. In a difficult fund-raising landscape, the FPAJ's efforts to stay afloat had suffered from two allegations, seized on by antagonistic 2chan users who tirelessly kept Uesugi's name at the top of the site's list of active topics. These challenges to the FPAJ's reputation involved allegations of financial mismanagement and plagiarism by Uesugi Takashi, and both had become public enough as issues to necessitate a formal response by the FPAJ. The accounting problems stemmed from concerns about funds from the organization's publication of a book about 3/11: *Jiyū Hōdō Kyōkai ga Otta 3.11* (The FPAJ pursues 3/11). According to FPAJ founding member Hatakeyama Michiyoshi, controversy had arisen over the handling of royalties from this book project—specifically, rumors of accounting irregularities and a failure to donate the proceeds to charity as promised in the book.[65] Potentially survivable by a smaller organization, the controversies immediately became the main topic of conversation among members, and a source of glee among those who had hoped to see the organization fail.

The allegations of plagiarism were as follows: In a March 23, 2011, article in *Diamond Online* (*Daiyamondo Onrain*, an online newspaper), Uesugi Takashi had appropriated a data table that had been published by the *Yomiuri*

Shinbun on March 19, 2011, without citing it. However, this was not his first use of the table, as it had appeared in his own newsletter days earlier. And it was not the last, as he later included it in his November 2011 book *Kokka no Haji* (National shame).[66] Uesugi argued that he'd been given the table by a journalistic acquaintance and had been ignorant of its distribution to and use by another reporter. However, the controversy allowed individuals both online and off to reaffirm their position that the formal structure of Japanese journalism acted to weed out the unethical and undisciplined and to further cement Uesugi's identification with the "victim position" relative to mainstream journalism.[67]

The FPAJ was divided about whether to issue a formal response, and Uesugi reported that his lawyer had advised him to refrain from (further) public comment as his libel suit progressed. As individuals affiliated with the organization chose to speak out independently, the FPAJ eventually found itself having to issue a statement.[68] Within two weeks, in March 2013, the FPAJ would effectively be no more, and Uesugi would open an office across town for his online newspaper, *Newslog*.

A More Troubled Definition of an Engaged Citizenry

The social media–dependent independent media landscape in Japan has performed a function consistent with the theorization of anthropologists Paul Manning and Ilana Gershon, by permitting new participants to enter a national conversation and driving national protest movements.[69] That the forums created by open-access and progressive news groups would be seized on by large numbers of alt-right nationalists (*netto uyoku*) who would dominate spaces of engagement and shape the quality of discourse was not anticipated by the media activists spearheading this movement, even though they were undoubtedly familiar with the reach and tenor of 2chan. While social media was heralded by Japanese media activists (and idealistic TV professionals) for its potential to fulfill Manning and Gershon's model, a basic premise of this hopeful rhetoric was that communities that it had made possible would be in support of—and *know* how to support—diversity in virtual spaces. But as the FPAJ's experience showed, audiences can be remarkably conservative even when the status quo they defend would eliminate spaces that made their own unfettered self-expression possible.

Research on Japanese right-wing online communities supports the experience of liberal news groups as targets of their ire. Specifically, *netto uyoku* infiltration of Japan's anonymous platforms was a side effect of a significant increase in xenophobic right-wing internet activity that began in the early 2000s and became particularly inescapable during the FPAJ's tenure.[70] While scholarship in this area points to many Japanese internet users gravitating more to the experience of communicating anonymously, and the enjoyment of belonging through learning the social codes of these forums, than to any profound identification with extreme political beliefs, it has been written of these groups: "They seem to believe in journalistic integrity even more than do journalists themselves."[71] However, in its self-appointed role as media watchdog, 2chan typically finds fault with and considers the mainstream media to be too liberal, so overtly left-wing media are subject to especial derision. And the right-wing information that circulated in these forums during the FPAJ's peak was responsible for a landslide victory for the conservative Liberal Democratic Party (LDP) in 2012, which took the mainstream media—but not the liberal independent media—by surprise.[72]

Despite this negative engagement with their platforms, independent media dream of providing a function consistent with an ideal model of mass media outlined by anthropologist Sara Dickey, by designating (alternative) platforms within which to "create and contest representations of self and other."[73] But sites like NN represent a different and politically significant category of human interaction; as Anne Allison writes of disembodied relationships, "Identification is more ghostly than mimetic—the ghostliness that adheres to images not of 'us', per se, but of interactions in which 'we' appear only as a part."[74] This line of argumentation gestures to a space within which subjectivity can be redefined; if Japanese virtual spaces provide a means to rearticulate selfhood and reestablish belonging in ways that depart from that which is expected and performed in embodied social spaces, then increased participation has the potential to promote more honest expressions of belief or mobilize new communities around alternate forms of expression—however offensive they may be. For instance, Dickey outlines the ways in which online communities can become politicized, particularly in cases where fandom follows the object(s) of its attention in crossing over into advocacy and affective relationships with audiences are appropriated in the service of political change (a model that is becoming increasingly common around the world).[75] By being detached from the infrastructure of mass media, independent journalists are closer to the intersection of producer and consumer than their *kisha* club peers are. Even when allowed access to some of the same press conferences as members of the Japan Newspaper and Magazine Associations, their outsider status shaped the discursive flows they created and the ways they imagined publics. As members of associations that lacked social capital, they were governed by a "people first" approach that was simultaneously bogged down by the triple challenge of mediating news, technology, and users of that technology. Nonetheless, a vision of interactivity as a means to help publics "gather information freely" drove their willingness to endure the downsides of a free exchange of ideas.[76]

Conclusion

Each monthly meeting saw increased momentum for GoHoo. In November 2012, Yanai excitedly announces to the group that *Nihon Hōdō Kenshō Kikō* had officially been registered as a nonprofit entity and proposes that the group begin staking out potential locations for their office space—to move past their appropriation of the Social Entrepreneur School's first-floor meeting area toward something more official.

"*Subarashii*" (excellent), a professor named Koizumi replies, smiling broadly. And then, quietly again to himself again as he flips through the meeting's agenda, "*Subarashii*." A smaller smile.

Members toss around potential Tokyo office locations based on their proximity to other journalistic outposts and news hubs: Akasaka, Kojimachi, or maybe Yotsuya? One of the lawyers proposes recruiting unpaid student interns to drive website output. His argument defers to GoHoo's operating budget, which he argues is best spent pursuing the legitimizing framework of dedicated office space rather than paying employees— particularly when tech-savvy students with free time are readily available.

Despite the forces acting to stymie efforts like those of the FPAJ, GoHoo, and IWJ, the independent media market in Japan should not be considered doomed to fight against the mainstream or right-wing disinformation in futility. The IWJ has been able to maintain its byzantine network of reporters and continues to recruit enthusiastic labor, by contrast with many of its peer organizations. Despite the labor involved in coordinating people and information streams, it has maintained or improved on its infrastructure and process over time. The FPAJ, for its part, was up against some formidable challenges—from a need for nonstop fund-raising to the aggressive opposition of anonymous 2chan and NN communities. And the institutional power behind the *kisha* club system further grants it the power to marginalize smaller news start-ups, which rely on genuine grassroots enthusiasm to make any gains. Yet, despite these impediments and its internal scandals, the FPAJ conspicuously raised substantial questions about what constitutes a journalist in Japan and actively remade press conferences as participatory media events that inscribed both home audiences and all manner of journalists—by providing them with the raw "stuff" of news, to use however they liked. Each of these organizations, and the new start-ups that have arisen since then, participated in a global conversation by complicating the practice and profession of journalism and blurring the line between audience and journalist.

Recalling this point, the July 2013 GoHoo members' forum was an open call for nonvolunteers to hear about the organization's strategy and status. In formal presentation mode, Yanai outlined its progress and activities thus far: the launch of gohoo.org, its press conferences, the magazines and website writeups it's secured, the monthly "GoHoo Report" emails, and the seminars it's organized. The group's dreams included increasing the site's participatory features, allowing journalists and random users to issue rebuttals of and feedback on GoHoo's fact checking. This collaborative system, a fellow board member explained, underscored GoHoo's core mission of reimagining news stories as living, evolving documents.

This dialog between content authors and site visitors, a model of ideal journalistic interactivity, was common to several of GoHoo's peer organizations, including one whose founder was in attendance that day: Hori Jun trained in new media studies at UCLA, but his "8-Bit News" project was inspired by his experiences working in mainstream Japanese broadcast.[77] Like GoHoo, 8-Bit News (8bitnews.org) encourages users to perform the role of journalists by recording and uploading videos to YouTube *"jibun jishin haishin suru"* (to distribute [content] themselves in the service of a better society).[78] In chapter 5, I will take a closer look at the process of binding together audiences and media makers in one citizen journalism start-up. But first, we return to the ways that television is currently using interactivity in the service of pure entertainment and explore what effect this has on the subjectivity of home and in-studio participants and authors.

4

The New Interactive Television

It was multimedia arts and engineering collective teamLab's foray into interactive television that first led me to its office. Although most experimental Japanese television made use of established celebrities to drive viewership, teamLab had solicited the participation of one of Japan's most spectacle-worthy entities: a hugely popular boy band. Tucked into a small building up the street from the University of Tokyo, the collective's six-floor workspace is filled with the castoffs from its experiments in projection mapping and immersive environments. Our meeting is held at what looks like an eight-bit video-game rendering of a table and is built, I am told, of the same military-grade cardboard as a cannon in the corner. A cannon that is also a projector, powered by jumping on a trampoline.

The program in question is called *Ongaku no Chikara/Arashi feat. You*, starring what was then the top Japanese boy band, Arashi. As a high-profile live NTV event, this project was unique among social TV experiments for its prime-time slot (9 p.m. on Saturday, July 6, 2013) and, ultimately, its ratings. The event evolved from a 2011 interactive greeting-card application that allowed users to create and send customized songs featuring

4.1 The interface for the *Arashi feat. You* game, including instructions on how to play.

instrument-wielding eight-bit characters. (See figure 4.1.) In its final realization, the show unfolded with the energy of a massive concert, coupled with the dramatic tension common to all interactive television.

The band appears before its usual crowd, on a stage wrapped in a blue and gray lit-up staircase. As the crowd's cheering slows to allow band member Ohno Satoshi to speak, he announces that he's going to explain how we can participate in the music making. Ohno gestures to a video screen on each side of the stage. When animated, scrolling musical notes pass across a yellow line, we are to push designated buttons on our smart devices, laptops, or TV remote controllers. Following the instructions himself, Ohno tells us in a pseudointimate register that he thinks "we" all need to practice. In time with a syncopated background beat, the band cheers and counts "1-2-3 Hai!" as the crowd presses its buttons in time with the beat. After a minute of these drills, fellow band member Sakurai Sho announces the start of this concert with practiced enthusiasm: "*Nippon zenkoku no minasan: tanoshimimashō!*" (Everyone in Japan, let's have fun!)[1]

Arashi's use of *zenkoku* (the whole country) deploys a salutation commonly used by Japanese television. Combined here with the spectacle of a popular concert and the use of interactive television as a novel form of mass public ritual, it spoke in ways that were alternately familiar and new. In this chapter, I present four examples of early Japanese experiments in interactive television. Developed as part of a strategy to push back against what was then a newly imported American model of on-demand viewing, these gamified programs asserted that live broadcast remained not just relevant, but essential, to televisual storytelling.[2] Specifically, producers hoped to use interactivity to cultivate a sense of national belonging and communitas among participants. Appropriating the pleasures of the playful interaction that drives traffic to places like 2chan and NN,[3] producers designed a form of play that united participants in shared missions and diverged from the individualizing blueprint of social media. Here I argue that strategies of invoking community used by these programs rely on conventional tropes and bypass any meaningful overhaul of the way these communities interact with one another through interactive technologies.

Early interactive TV programs were distributed among four broadcasters—NTV, Fuji TV, NHK, and TV Tokyo—and shared the common ground of each being developed as a one-time special and an application of innovative technology. While NTV's *Arashi* special stood apart in being promoted heavily and aired in a prime-time slot (much like the joint NHK/NTV special, *60 Ban Shōbu*, discussed in chapter 1), other programs, like Bascule's *Bloody Tube* and *The Last Award*, tested their experimental technologies more quietly. These were accompanied by recurring interactive game events like NHK's National Participation Popular Quiz Show QB47 (*Kokumin-sō sanka kuizu shō! QB47*) that were less experimental conceptually. As objects of study, these programs are useful for the ways that they reinforced hegemonic concepts of national identity, regulated the breadth of diversity, and refined certain deeply rooted practices in Japanese mass media. The shows discussed in this chapter differ from previous examples in a significant way: they were designed as games. Nonetheless, they engage in methods of addressing and cultivating a viewing public that are consistent with the central project of interactivity by creating spaces in which communities can feed off composite energy and negotiate shared identity. These shows also appropriated formulae common to Japanese variety shows, known for their use of *tarento* (TV celebrities) to guide audiences through shared consumption of content—whether it be reporters' visit to a new restaurant, video of a zany stunt, or the subjection of the *tarento* themselves to a remarkable situation. As variety and game shows already contained procedural overlap, fusing aspects of both to test social TV technology was the easiest part of developing such programs.

Publics are fostered by TV in multiple ways—through the construction of fandoms or the use of liveness, spectacle, ritual, or event.[4] But while viewing publics have transitioned from public spaces to family viewing to connecting online, the category of interactive television examined in this chapter takes the process a step further by appropriating the energy of simultaneous remote participation and directing it toward a mission that not only affects a specific outcome within the program but constitutes the program itself. Ien Ang once pushed back against the idea that media producers understood the needs of audiences so much as they sought to define them. But more so than the American television about which Ang originally wrote, Japanese TV operates with exceptional conviction about who its audience is, and with confidence in its mandate to direct them. Kitada Akihiro and Fabian Schäfer's discussion of early Japanese media theory unpacks this self-conception and clarifies that "the press has basically two functions: a 'mediatory function' (*baikai kinō*) and a 'leading function' (*yūdō kinō*). Indeed, as a consequence of this leading function, nationalism is performed consistently on television. Even while playing variety show games an assumption of homogeneity permeates the discourse which strives to "evoke a similar consciousness—in the sense of a unitary public opinion (*yoron*)."[5] Specific kinds of people are to be scrutinized (non-Japanese, chiefly),[6] and the idea of bidding the whole country good night feels inscriptive rather than corny.

National Identity and Belonging

NTV's *Arashi feat. You* was a large-scale effort by Japanese television to turn a live concert into a technologically mediated participatory event. While it anticipated the embodied and remote attendance of fans, it also hoped that the novelty of new technology-on-display might be capable of seducing even those who would not typically endure an Arashi song. In its postmortem about the program, teamLab summarized its intentions: "The idea was to turn the scheduled musical performance from boy-band Arashi into a nation-wide interactive rhythm game where fans could use their mobile phones, computers, or even their TV remote controls to keep up with the beat visualized on screen."[7] Thus, while the program was marketed specifically to Arashi fans, it was also ever mindful of the nation as a conceptual category.

I watched the event unfold, live, on July 6, 2013, with a small group of television directors and producers. The band moves from the main stage to a platform in the center of the program's venue, harmonizing gracefully while women cover their mouths in wide-eyed amazement, reach out to touch the men's bodies, and politely sing along. It's hard, even for the at-home participant, to avoid affective engagement with this moment, even as it seems remarkably well behaved. The crowd stops short of excessive emotional display, and while enjoyment is palpable, it is also well managed and homogeneous.

Despite predictable audience fragmentation along age and gender lines represented by boy-band fandom, the *Arashi* set reflects its creators' anticipation of an impressively large-scale event. A large flickering screen just behind the band members tracks the number of game players, which approaches 1 million as the band finishes its first song. The final figure claimed by NTV of 1.3 million participants represents more than 1 percent of Japan's entire population.[8] Of these, the majority (899,658 users) accessed the game via a smartphone/tablet, 333,630 users via *dēta hōsō* (data broadcast), and 139,023 users via computer.

The common use of the term *zenkoku*, as in Sakurai Sho's enthusiastic announcement, functions to dispel the unknowability of audiences as an aggregate and collapses them into a reductive national body redolent of the notion of "audience" itself. Indeed, the members of phenomenally popular fellow idol band AKB48 have been referred to as "national idols" (*kokuminteki aidoru*) or "the performers 'we' Japanese 'all' know and love."[9] The use of the term *zenkoku* is inequivalent to the language used in countries like the United States to inspire feelings of patriotism, or even that of other countries with a single time zone and relatively small geographical footprints. Indeed, concepts like the "national imaginary" or, in particular, "publics" or the Habermasian "public sphere" (*kōkyō-sei*) did not straightforwardly translate to Japanese and took decades to catch on as intellectual concepts.[10] Repeated use by the government had established a monopoly of meaning over the term "public" (*kōkyō*) in contexts meant to foment nationalism and, indeed, define a collective. Therefore, the term and its associated theory were initially unappealing to many intellectuals and gestured toward the manipulation of citizens toward a national consensus as a similar language used in the mass media can do. Yet this aversion to proscriptive consensus existed alongside the construction of publics by a mass media exercising its soft power. While not overtly labeled as such, these publics were molded around an assumption that the richly variegated discourse of unmanaged publics could be channeled into something more uniform. Though the public itself is not a fixed body, but rather a wide form of discourse in and out of media systems, these interactive games tried to fix it to familiar touchpoints, such as blood type, prefecture, and fandom.

The willful collapsing of diversity within Japanese popular culture has been problematized by scholars for many years, with the greatest attention being paid to the genre of literature known as *Nihonjinron* (generally translated or interpreted as "theories of Japanese uniqueness"). Discourse on race in Japan is inevitably linked to historical narratives that promoted the idea of ethnic and cultural homogeneity and worked to erase the diversity that exists within the country. An example of this kind of erasure can be found in the promotion of census outcomes, which claim that Japan is 97.8 percent "Japanese"—using legal status as a stand-in for ethnic diversity.[11] If the cultivation of national identity is an ongoing mission of Japanese broadcasting, the infrastructure of the Japanese television industry contributes to its capacity to think of its viewership in national terms, even as it divides this body up into consumer profiles. There are only five major television companies, and only nine main channels in the Tokyo area. Thus, to borrow Sakurai Sho's wording, "*Nippon zenkoku no minasan*" might have historically been presumed to be tuning in live. This is consistent with the networks' own sense of their role (particularly NHK), based on television's legacy as the curator of a "national time structure" around which people organized their lives to catch popular dramas and other prime-time programming.[12] That television used to be so instrumental in shaping national identity, especially in the 1960s and '70s, is something to which it seeks to return by introducing technologies so compelling they can compete with everything that erases the need for live viewership.

An additional performative strategy that comprises this exclusionary/inclusionary mode of mass address can be located in the ways Japanese TV programs hail audiences by performing the idea of an appropriate or common emotional reaction to particular kinds of surprise or discomfort.[13] The fast-paced and ostensibly anarchic Japanese *waidō shō* (variety program) format creates space within which both home and in-studio observers, as well as participants, may be (within predictable parameters) caught off guard, eliciting seemingly genuine and spontaneous reactions that both teach culture and reinforce sameness.[14] We see this too in the way television makes of "foreigners" objects of fascination, arranging encounters between Japanese and Others that frequently emphasize differences and establish an audience for the "coolness" of Japan.[15] Media strategies that nurture uniformity may complicate Western notions of publics, but they do not represent a departure for mass media in Japan or elsewhere. However, the promotion of consensus through media events raises questions about whether the discursive flows produced by such institutions constitute publics after all.

The experiments in Japanese interactive TV discussed here maintained a program of reifying collective identity and reducing differences to a finite number of taxonomic categories. These categories offer a qualified agency to audiences by becoming the teams with which audiences can affiliate to play games together. In a vivid example, NHK's popular interactive quiz special QB47 appropriated interactivity between 2012 and 2015 to pit the prefectures of Japan against one another in a trivia contest.[16] Teams were represented by *tarento* from each region, and viewers could choose their team independent of embodied location. Serving as a visual reminder of the idea of Japan were maps displaying live national participation. The successes of each prefecture were repeatedly ranked on this national map, with bonus points for the percentage of participants by area population. By classifying participants by region and using this information first to create live maps and to rally teams for a collective mission, participants were encouraged to adopt a local identity even as it was repeatedly linked back to the national and given meaning through this broader context. Through this visualization of national belonging and the hosts' excited banter about the program's reach, the homogenizing impulse of such programming both subsumed and celebrated the diversity of Japan by means of ongoing performance and assignation of Japanese-ness. This containment of diversity toward reifying the national imaginary is performed through a variety of themes that go beyond the regional and are a significant part of interactive game shows' strategy.

While *Arashi feat. You* cultivated belonging through difference by allowing users to select their preferred musical instrument (which is really grouping them by which band member they prefer), Bascule's June 15, 2013, show *Bloody Tube*, one of the most technologically sophisticated early social TV experiments, sorted participants according to their blood type and recruited hosts representing each of the possible blood types.[17] In this show, participants in each blood type category raced through a simulation of a well-known model/idol (*aidoru*)'s blood vessels using controls on their smartphones—metaphorically invading her body, which has been not only conquered by their spacecraft but colonized by billboard-like advertisements featuring the show's sponsors. Objectification of the female body is apparent from the opening sequence of the show: A young woman, Dan Mitsu, enters a room, clad in a bathrobe. Her hair appears damp as if she has recently bathed. Eyelids half-lowered, she pouts for the camera, and slowly

4.2 Dan Mitsu, taking the stage as the *Bloody Tube* girl. This program was a project of Bascule, Inc.

allows her robe to fall away—revealing the sheer white bra and underpants beneath. Her skin glows softly, golden, in the warm lighting of this soundstage. As Dan slowly mugs for the camera in a manner resembling nothing if not soft-core porn, a voice-over tells the audience that we're about to play a game. And the game will take place in her body. The word LIVE shimmers across the screen, top left. To its right appear the words "*ketsuekigata rēsu* [blood-type race] BLOODY TUBE." (See figure 4.2.)

As she lies motionless before us, we enter her body; assigned to teams by our blood type, we will use smartphones, tablets, laptops, and remote controls to navigate our rocketships through a simulation of her veins and earn real-world currency in the form of Ponta Points (a currency redeemable in stores).

Problematic as the presumptive heterosexual male gaze is in *Bloody Tube*, it does not stop producers from marketing the show to a general family audience. As Bascule's postbroadcast ad on YouTube announces alongside images of multigenerational families, families with young children, and mixed groups of young adults in rapt and excited engagement with the game, "The game is easy but very fun for old and young, men and women."[18] Collective enjoyment is therefore a significant part of interactive TV's strategy to domesticate the individualizing tendencies of mobile devices and internet use patterns and render them a productive tool for broadcast TV to cultivate national identity and belonging. More than that is necessary, however, to elicit feelings of identification from the audience, and another key element of this nascent genre of interactive TV is the use of *tarento*, or TV celebrities, as stand-ins for the reactions and participation of audiences.

On-Screen Surrogacy, from *Tarento* and Staged Intimacy to Guest Experts

In *Bloody Tube*, with the opening sequence over, Dan Mitsu moves on the screen into her position for gameplay, and we hear the voices of the male *tarento* issue unabashed utterances of appreciation as she settles onto the platform to become object. Not simply a recipient of the gaze in a conventional sense, she is the platform within which this program's game will occur. Even as we are reminded of her physicality by the immersive simulation of her body's internal structure, Dan is stripped of even the appearance of consciousness. The *tarento* watch her, we watch her, and we watch them watching her as we access *Bloody Tube*'s mobile-responsive game interface. With her eyes closed, her body frozen in place, Dan is the machine without the ghost.

A common feature of Japanese variety shows, in general, is their recruitment of familiar celebrity TV guests to act on behalf of audiences—to experience a new consumer product, react to prerecorded content, or participate in a stunt. Applied to interactive television, productions assign *tarento* the task of learning about and testing program user interfaces and synchronically with home audiences, to demonstrate what "we" should all be doing. Such *tarento* are accessible in the sense that they are not necessarily famous as actors or musicians. Instead, their purpose is to appear on television, exhibit a "relatable" persona, and increase audiences' emotional satisfaction with variety shows.[19] To this end, *tarento* in Japan are both friendly and famous, objects of fantasy and simultaneously approachable. Most *tarento*, but especially women, tend not to be particularly talented, but rather "friendly looking."[20] For interactive game shows, (e.g., *Bloody Tube*, QB47) *tarento* are recruited as team members based on a characteristic they possess (i.e., blood type, a specific hometown), and expected to embody ideal engagement, react to their team's progress, and serve as its de facto mascot. While celebrities famous for other things can be used in this role—such as the members of Arashi—this effect differs and is generally deployed when a program's goal is widespread audience recruitment. In other words, while the fandom surrounding actors and pop music stars innately produces large audiences, *tarento* restore intimacy to the interactive experience.

Fandom is always an asymmetrical relationship between one (or five, in Arashi's case) and many; to feel a connection with the star, fans must do substantial work to transcend that star's inaccessibility, privilege, and prestige.[21] The capacity of *tarento* to help make this connection less strenuous is underscored by the ability of the Japanese language to convey social distance or proximity; as Japanese studies researcher Andrew Painter notes, television show fans have historically addressed *tarento* informally in letters, while their correspondence with film stars reflected an elevated grammar.[22] Further emphasizing this, a television producer named Takashi, who was active in the local interactive TV "think tanks," commented to me, "Of course, we are using the tradition of showing well-liked *tarento* introducing the interactive technology. What is a better way to get people to use it than if they can picture themselves playing a game with their favorite celebrities?"[23] The use of *tarento* in social TV facilitates audience identification, but in doing so, it also helps address a central anxiety pervading interactive TV: the question of what interaction or participation should look like.

Experiments in social TV often fall prey to the dilemma outlined by Henry Jenkins within which [television] producers and consumers alike acknowledge a progression toward such technologies without consensus on what participation should or does mean.[24] In Japan, however, a potential solution already existed within the television industry. Japanese studies researchers Caroline Stevens and Shuhei Hosokawa note that Japanese TV is, in general, dedicated to a project of staged intimacy; much of the medium comprises stars bantering with one another, discussing each other's art, performing each other's songs, and conversing with the program's MCs.[25] Rather than genuine intimacy, they note, these interactions are performances of appropriate social behavior; older stars are treated with respect, and everyone is politely careful with one another.[26] This practice of behavior modeling in Japanese TV is widespread; while television in many countries guides viewers toward the recognition of a predetermined narrative, it ultimately leaves room for subjective decoding. But Japanese television frequently cuts between documentary-style content and the reactions and discussion of celebrity panelists, replacing implicit direction through narrative with dictation of meaning. This enactment of behavioral norms is part of a comprehensive effort to instruct audiences. Going beyond simply choosing subject matter, camera shots, and so forth, it transfers suggestions regarding how to interpret such content from the realm of the implicit to a mimetic performance.[27] Through the established use of *tarento* by the TV industry, the human uncertainties associated with television are partly managed, and audiences need not be trusted to orient themselves to new technologies without an explicit model for how to do so.

Demonstration of how audiences should be positioned relative to a user interface and/or broadcast narrative extends to the role of guest experts, who have similarly made the transition from traditional TV programming to interactive TV. The connection that the "talking heads" of television create with audiences diverges from that of *tarento*, being less about emotive performance and more about rational judgment. Corresponding to an ideal of democratic participation, the relationship between TV expert and interactive public becomes a site of significant knowledge production and rehearsal of mainstream values. This is not by accident: as Koichi Iwabuchi observes of Japanese TV commentators, "We need to interrogate how supposedly spontaneous voices on the show are actually shaped under the production format of the talk show genre and whether a highly commodified and exaggerated debate on TV can be seen as a public forum."[28] Rather than leaving audiences to assemble interpretations of its content, television guides their opinions by invoking expertise as a mediator between audiences, newsmakers, and current events. This entrenched structure is part of what made the FPAJ a radical departure from traditional models of information dissemination, as it formed channels that directly connected publics and the news (see chapter 3).[29] For entertainment-oriented interactive television, this careful management of the audiences' capacity to form judgment does not so much aspire to the ideals of journalism as constitute a cynical version of Kantian aesthetic judgment,[30] as in the interactive video contest show *The Last Award*.

The Last Award

On September 29, 2013, at five minutes to midnight, Bascule—one of the primary agencies driving interactive television—debuted another experimental program on Fuji Television.[31] Cohosted by Bascule's president, Boku Masayoshi, its concept was again pioneering. Audience members were invited to submit a video of no more than sixty seconds, representing the idea of "a one-minute image to send off the day." Submitted videos were then aired on the program and evaluated simultaneously by a panel of experts and the home audience, with results displayed on-screen in real time. The framing of the on-screen panel experts as distinct from but parallel to home audience members occurs immediately. *The Last Award* opens by credentialing these experts as judges and representatives of the home audience—a step necessary to establish their credibility as the show's primary evaluators considering their obscurity relative to the usual TV *tarento*. Boku's profile is brief but champions his role as judge by running through a "best of" showcase featuring Bascule's recent experiments with image mapping and interactivity and credential signaling by highlighting an impressive collection of awards in its office lobby. The role of participating audiences is subsequently defined: if they want to vote on a series of audience-submitted animated short videos, viewer/users must first create an account on the program's mobile-responsive website. This allows them to rate each video as it is played on TV and comment within the program's webspace. As with most televised talent shows, the agency of users is regulated, their contributions filtered through media checkpoints. Videos for which viewers can cast a vote have been selected by producers as part of the same collaborative and compromise-filled process as other media content.[32] Unlike in any other talent competition, however, the format here presents as collaborative, like that of a classroom art critique.

One at a time, the expert and home audiences view the user-submitted videos, and as each one ends in a swirl of animated leaves, sleepy eyes, or families watching TV together, voting begins on the application. Tapping upward on a cartoon eye opens its lid wider, and a corresponding numerical rating ascends from one to ten (see figure 4.3). As viewers vote, ten columns of animated eyes stream on-screen behind the five judges. (The more eyes passing through a numerical column, the greater the number of users who have assigned a video that score.) The experts reserve judgment, and in a model that contradicts that of most global television contests, refrain from commentary that might guide or instruct audiences. In this program, expertise is contrasted with democratic perception, and home audiences have greater power than usual, if not an equivalent platform, to assign merit to participants.

As animated eyeballs scroll vertically in rapid succession, the experts point and laugh—noting the number of fives, in one case, and ones in another. With exaggerated theatricality, their faces contort in response to the strictness of home audiences, who seem at first to assign lower scores than do the judges themselves. Expert judgment follows the announcement of an aggregate audience score, as the judges award three eights and two fours to the first submission. Ultimately, audience voices are represented only by numerical figures and comments entered in a web field, while experts sit before the broadcast camera and pronounce audible judgment on

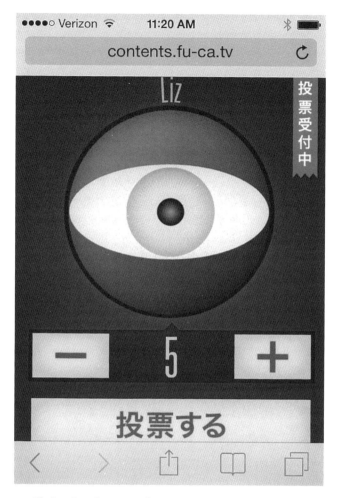

4.3 *The Last Award*'s user interface in action. Here, I am voting a "5" on the video submission that we just screened.

the short films. The difference in the reach and likelihood of exposure between viewers' comments on the television-hosted social media accounts and those of the program's in-studio judges calls attention to the lingering differences between mass and social media (the multichannel din of social media always belonging to the realm of potential massification, and television nervously scanning for signs that it is losing its historic privilege). Whether or not one body identifies as "commensurably elite" within Bourdieusian taxonomies of capital, the other inevitably possesses greater access to socioeconomic and cultural resources. Moreover, there remains a conventional orientation to the direction in which identification occurs, with TV audiences more likely to self-identify as media experts themselves than the show's expert panel is to take the imaginative leap of identifying with an unknown body of contributor/users. Though this program does work to blur categories and complicate notions of media and power by turning users and audiences into content producers and involving panelists in the show's production, it remains grounded in the status quo—manifesting a typical awareness of professional success and privilege and underscoring the access to media platforms that power facilitates. In *The Last Award*, the agency of users is varied and overlapping—not all are participants, and not all are contributors. But they share the need to bid for a voice in the program. Conversely, members of the expert panel need not solicit media inscription but are worthy of its attention by virtue of their professional network and recognition by peer experts.

Through its social TV component, *The Last Award* unifies expertise and (somewhat) democratic participation to a greater extent than most vote-at-home television specials. By allowing audience feedback to guide expert judgment rather than follow it, the usual orientation of expert relative to home audience member is granted a nuance it usually lacks. Like Fuji TV's interactive news discussion show *The Compass*, where participants gathered in virtual spaces to debate news alongside TV panelists (see chapter 2), *The Last Award*'s limited overture to an unknown body of users tries to go a step further than conventional television toward unifying expertise and democratic participation in pursuit of a common goal. While the renegotiation of representation is a consistent motif in all of Bascule's TV experiments, *The Last Award* foregrounds the performance of expertise in a few provocative ways—most notable being the capacity to evaluate and label media according to learned standards for what constitutes "good" and "successful." Second is the way that this expertise shares space with the audience's perceptions and means of interacting with the program's structure and content. And third is the program's appropriation of user-submitted media, its use of the mass media platform to broadcast videos that one might otherwise watch on YouTube. For the interactive television viewers, this means adapting the framing of their usual evaluation of small-scale media production. This has been done before—in the United States, for example, *America's Funniest Home Videos* experimented with positioning audience-crafted content as televisual in the late 1980s and 1990s. But while earlier programs were limited by a need to define participation as a benefit of studio presence or introduce delays between voting and the announcement of results, *The Last Award* (and the *60 Ban Shōbu*) take audience feedback and introduce it to the tension of live broadcast, allowing audience comments to collide with those of the judges. Despite the novelty of this program's user interface, it was not widely advertised, and Bascule declines to even mention it on its list of past interactive TV projects.[33]

A New Imaginary

In Japan (and elsewhere), the nostalgic idea of members of a three-generation family wrestling over the remote control, staking out their preferred programs, and viewing together regardless of preference, is one that is commonly invoked in contrast with today's viewing habits. In a 2013 public service video and Twitter discussion arranged by Japan's Association for the Promotion of Digital Broadcasting to demonstrate the features of contemporary digital broadcast,[34] one of the featured *tarento*, Tetsu, explains precisely this: "Three generations of us were living together, so when I wanted to watch TV I always had a fight with Grandpa over which channel to watch."[35] Television content was consumed simply as an element of family routine, its communal viewing a means of reifying ties by acquiescing to the interests of others and enjoying television as a shared experience.[36] One might interpret Tetsu's musings as a kind of Fordist nostalgia filtered through the lens of Gramscian philosophy; here the home is the quintessential romantic space of perceived historical innocence, its cozy multigenerational TV viewing a foil against rapid national industrialization. Fordism, it has been said, made the family the core and normative social unit, as Henry Ford himself balanced the compromises demanded by his industrial policies with a nostalgia for a perceived simpler personal life of times past.[37]

Prominent social television promoter and founder of the Sōsharu Terebi Suishin Kaigi (Social TV Promotion Collective) Sakai Osamu also writes with sensuous detail about this bygone era of television consumption in such a way that recalls American viewing habits of the past: the family would gather around a twenty-inch set, eating dinner together while watching TV in the *(o)cha no ma*.[38] By contrast, contemporary viewing means a disorganized procession of family members gazing at the LCD screen from sofas or a Western-style dining table, eating separately. This transformation has been lexicographically indexed by the vanishing of the phrase "*cha no ma*" in favor of the loanwords "living room" (*ribingurūmu*)."[39] Sakai's sentimental portrait of familial utopia and a bygone era of television culture is reinforced by the language he uses to describe it; television once delivered "dreams" to the *cha no ma*. Fathers watched the news, children sat wide-eyed, hearts racing (*dokidoki*) to see their favorite heroes, wives excitedly consumed the dramas and content from the United States, and everyone watched commercials to learn about consumer fashions.[40]

Social television has, in a sense, tried to restore this era by focusing on rebuilding the collective experience around television. Dividing audiences into teams (by blood type, region, etc.) further reinforces the audience's sense of belonging to a group and locates the individual within a managed whole—a national imaginary. Among the production goals of each of these projects was an attempt to cultivate and manipulate identification and identity and to better discipline audiences by dividing them according to categories considered immutable and commensurate. Relevantly, when I asked about community-building in interactive television programs, an assistant director contracting at Fuji TV observed, "People are easily manipulated. It doesn't matter what *we* want—we just have to get people excited using the formulas we know. That is what the [TV] executives want."[41]

In determining what will appeal to the spectator, television professionals are self-aware about their use of the most pessimistic notions of the audience as uninformed, manipulable, sentimental, and tolerant (if not enthusiastic) about television's relentless implementation of the same old formulas. The effects of this approach can be seen in the way that the interfaces and barriers used by these programs govern the energy of participants and massage the unruly energy of the crowd into that of a managed public. Despite enthusiasm for and idealism of the internet's capacity to introduce interactivity to broadcast, the "*nama koe*" (raw voices) of users are kept segregated from official TV messaging and isolated within the comment section of each program's web interface. The energy instantiated by a program's "liveness" is simultaneously repressed and incorporated—similar to how anthropologist William Mazzarella describes cinema's capacity to appropriate both the physical energy of embodied crowds and that of virtual publics watching the film elsewhere.[42] Japanese social TV producers' appropriation of community as a core value of social TV is therefore a strategic pivot; it selectively expends the energy of a crowd to bridge the traditional sentiment of the *cha no ma* heyday of Japanese communal television viewing to a newly reconstituted sense of national identity. Certainly, the need for this unbroken knowability of the audience remains rooted in the economic imperative driving the television industry, as a managed public is one to whom advertising might be optimally delivered.

After eyeballs are tapped in *The Last Award*'s user interface, and the scores of the audience and judging panel are relayed, the judges spend time invoking professional credentials and experience in defense of their decision. Meanwhile, users of *The Last Award*'s app complain about the frequency of the show's advertising breaks—both the program's constant disruption by short bursts of commercial video and the jarring juxtaposition of slick sponsor advertising with DIY user content. These complaints are naturally unsuitable for appropriation by the program itself, and Fuji TV filters out the majority of what they say; audience critiques of commercial sponsorship have little place on the television screen.

Although audience members are encouraged to interact with the show and imagine themselves as a collective body based on their shared experience, the engagement for remote participants is bidirectional only where user and technology meet. Direct communication with other audience members is permitted but sidelined by the show itself: although *Arashi feat. You* establishes a direct link between home audience members and the screen, the lateral connection between users is more tenuous. As the embodied crowd seen on the TV screen, and the connections made between individual audience members, become part of the program's energy, the virtual interactivity of the musical game diverges by excluding direct connection within or directed at the broadcast space. Thus, television's drive to discover individual audience members is enacted through technologies built not for the benefit of audiences, but for that of television as a business from which everything proceeds from a capacity to sell detailed profiles of the audiences to advertisers.

That the knowability of individual audience members serves a dual purpose of marketing and reifying a sense of national belonging is indeed part of its appeal to television networks. Such programs frequently appropriate common demographic categories to suggest to users that they are part of a mass collective event—Nick Couldry's media ritual on a (now) reduced scale.[43] In addition to benefiting advertisers and therefore the networks themselves, the integration of live user data into programmatic content reinforces a sense of connected nationhood. A genuine desire to facilitate community and belonging, along with an interest in how new technologies might evolve their audience's relationship with television, was (and is) a critical driver of social TV projects.

Nonetheless, attempting to harness the passive energy of the observer into the kinetic energy of collective action—while maintaining control over the volatility of crowds—requires a delicate touch and resolutely uncontroversial content. Social TV is consistently mindful of the dangers of editing television's traditional barriers, and of social media's potential to become unmanageable (as it did for the independent media). We've seen poignant examples of this during recent political protests in the United States, Hong Kong, and Iran, but it was the Arab Spring that was on the minds of mass media producers during the early days of interactive TV experimentation—in particular, the power of Twitter (multiple voices) when connected with mass broadcast (privileged platform). The visceral energy of mass participation, even at the virtual level, could therefore be said to justify television's policy of containment. In other words, a combination of its latency and the brevity of such programs stymies the accumulation of tension and enforces a cooling distance that turns users into a managed public.

Conclusion

Social connection is one of the most central themes promoted by social TV developers and continues to drive more recent experiments. Bascule's 2016 program *Ryūsei Hōsō Kyoku* (Meteor broadcast network) was described as a tool to allow Japan to experience the Geminid meteor shower "together at the same time" (*dōjikoku ni issho ni*).[44] Like many social TV programs, this one harnessed data to reinforce a sense of togetherness, prominently displaying at the top of the app and television screen the number of people holding their smartphones over the sky and experiencing the meteors together.

However, a major problem remains interactive TV's (in)capacity to foster meaningful intimacy. The recent/current generation of social TV entertainment programming permits a degree of participation from viewers that exceeds both the much more circumscribed participation of early 2010s interactive news discussion shows and the attempts by the independent news media to increase political engagement through direct internet participation. And the feelings of community these make possible are largely expressed in terms of national belonging and maintenance of an intangible or imagined national ethos. Publics being constituted by this technology are asked to conform to join in, and even antagonistic participation requires considering one's identity relative to others. Abandoning nuance, users acquiesce to the group dynamic knowing their contribution is mostly measured quantitatively in the form of a binary signal rather than as meaningful discourse. Missing is the intimacy or jostling of the crowd as a body that knows one another too well, yet not well enough, and extracting these energies to feed media content while sidelining generative critique risks frustrating the publics these programs need to recruit.

Currently, user contributions and concerns are reflected at them coyly, and with nowhere to go, this crowd energy threatens to spill out elsewhere online, or into the real world. As a fixture of modern life, virtual crowd energy often erupts into virtual effervescence: hysteria, "flame wars," cyberbullying, political action, and so on. With an awareness of the risk that such crowds can have to the manicured space of television, it is no great surprise that each of these programs' apps constrains the interaction that users can have in a way that NicoNico and the independent media could not, while still letting them play along. Fortunately, in Lauren Berlant's theorization of an intimate public, intimacy and virtual synchronicity can be decoupled.[45] And that is what chapter 5 of this book turns to, the intimate relationship between "audience" and "media maker" in citizen journalism.

5

Teaching Citizen Journalism

MEDIA ACTIVISM AND OUR PLANET-TV

In early May 2013 fourteen of us are assembled for one of Our Planet-TV's three-month video production workshops.[1] We find seats around a series of conference tables arranged amid the cozy clutter of bookshelves overflowing with carefully labeled videotapes and awards. Participants ranging in age from their twenties through their fifties flip through workshop packets and thumb through the required reading: Our Planet-TV founder Shiraishi Hajime's book *Bideokamera de Ikō* (Let's go with a video camera).[2]

We are in the brainstorming stage now, our packets composed of thirteen proposals for a documentary. The task on this Thursday night will be to pitch them to the group, to narrow the potential projects down to six, among which the workshop participants can choose to join one team. Therefore, one by one each participant tries to sell their idea while Shiraishi asks questions intended to flush out the practicality of the project, the extent to which its author has thought through issues of access, the difference between narrative versus topic, and so on.

The proposed topics mostly fall under the heading of what could be called ethnographic film and are inspired by people and places that their authors have found compelling around Tokyo. One young woman hopes to make a film about the many reasons for delayed marriage in Japan. She cites a page of statistics that she's brought with her and then, placing this paper back on the table before her, looks around at the group to gauge its response. But in the end, hers is not one of the pitches chosen for further development—exercising its own form of gatekeeping,[3] the class's final list includes projects profiling a neighborhood experimental film group, street musicians, a dance troupe, an oncologist, and an innovative Japanese-language instructor.

Our Planet-TV is a venture founded in 2001 by Shiraishi Hajime, who began her career at one of the major commercial broadcasters, TV Asahi. By her explanation, she eventually quit TV Asahi with the intention of trying to force diversification in Japanese media by training citizens to craft counternarratives and take ownership of the media representation of their experiences.[4] While maintaining a commitment to producing her own award-winning documentaries,[5] Shiraishi also dedicates time to her role as an educator by running workshops, cultivating Our Planet as a pedagogical resource for media production, and authoring books on filming techniques and the structural problems with contemporary Japanese mass media. Like Uesugi Takashi, Shiraishi has identified the nation's *kisha* club system as especially problematic and defined her work as sustaining an alternative space for news production.

In her exposition on Our Planet-TV's mission, Shiraishi cites Habermasian theory of the public sphere and emphasizes her desire to increase the representation of "small voices" (*chīsa na koe*) and diverse news materials in that space. However, Our Planet-TV is hoping to go one step further than even the Independent Web Journal (IWJ) or Free Press Association of Japan (FPAJ) (see chapter 3), by producing a cadre of citizen journalists who will challenge traditional divisions between producers and consumers of news—the journalistic interlopers of recent academic attention (and frequent critique on matters of quality control).[6] Its workshops introduce a new relationship between individual participants and the media, providing citizens with the conceptual and material tools with which to engage mass media content more critically and to approach it as the outcome of a series of decisions made by individual actors.[7]

In this chapter, I will pick up my discussion of the approaches taken by the independent media to create a participatory alternative to the mass media and to allow viewers to participate in media in a way that allows them to retain direct control over their representation even as it gives them control over the representation of others by inscribing the subjects of its production in ways that are conceptually like that of mainstream television. My analysis here represents the experiences and efforts of my Our Planet-TV workshop group, which included one middle-aged Japanese-language instructor (Seiji) who drove our filming and narrative choices, a college student (Kaori) who focused mostly on editing and composition, and a middle-aged woman (Mitsuko) interested in video production work who storyboarded and scripted much of our project. As the author of our group's film concept, Seiji served as the de facto producer/director, and the rest of us functioned as his assistant directors while also, of necessity, being involved in production, interviewing, and editorial decision-making. Beyond the physical construction of a documentary, one of the additional tasks of our group was negotiating between discrepancies in our perception of audiences and our relationship with media content while identifying a voice for our narrative that appropriately hailed audiences.

On the second day of documentary project planning in May 2013, those authors whose pitches were chosen by the group for further development present their outlines for a June filming schedule—including locations and lists of interviewees. Of these individuals, four have brought printouts for the group, one has prepared a PowerPoint presentation, and the last elects to narrate their concept without supporting materials. From these six potential projects, our task will be to select four finalists; therefore, the presentation of schedules and defense of feasibility are as much an exercise in persuasiveness as they are a means to encourage organization. A lack of tangible documentation seems to drive negative reception of a cancer-treatment project idea, while a Suginami-ku neighborhood-cinema proposal wins in a landslide after its author presents a detailed catalog of potential filming sites and interview contacts. Seiji's project, about an exceptionally effective Japanese-language teacher, is one of the projects chosen. To force a more equal distribution of volunteers across the documentary topics, we revote twice, and everyone cooperatively shuffles between groups until these are balanced.

As Shiraishi's rhetoric makes Our Planet-TV's objective a challenge to dominant public discourse, the task of any single group was not massively metonymic, but symbolic. In building a narrative for our group's project, its members did not speak in terms of public sphere(s) as did Shiraishi but defined the documentary as having a goal of conscientious representation and a mandate to remain faithful to a subject in a way that routinely eludes mainstream media (for whom intimacy is not innate but engineered). Our group's decoupling from the commercial pressures of television shifted the project's focus from that of entertaining the audience to authentically capturing a subject in the context of their routine. The process became about representing those with whom a Japanese public may not necessarily identify but with whom they might find connection through our portrayal.

Our Planet-TV was not the only independent media organization that engaged in training non–media professionals to perform the work of media producers and film crews. The IWJ, which sought to provide supplementary (unedited) coverage to the mainstream news, routinely hired individuals with no media production experience to be on its staff and relied on short periods of apprenticeship to prepare them to cover news events. Compared to Our Planet-TV, however, the urgency of the IWJ's need for reporters meant its training was relatively brief and foregrounded the technical rather than the ideological or aesthetic conditions of media production. I learned this firsthand: during my second visit in September 2012, I was trained alongside two new part-time staff members in how to cover events and upload video to the appropriate IWJ UStream channels. This entailed specific procedural instructions:

> Hardware = connect camera to laptop, launch correct software, select a standby image.
>
> Don't forget: name the files using the "date-iwj" formula. Connect to the proper channel. The Bluetooth mic, mobile Wi-Fi, and UStream connection devices must also be connected correctly. (See figure 5.1.)

To test our capacity to carry out these instructions, the three of us are sent out to roam the Azabu neighborhood and build a coherent tour, largely for the amusement of colleagues watching our progress from the office. It's a muggy summer day, and we are sweating as we attempt to maintain the steadiness of the camera while recording each other's walking tours and isolating the sounds of our speech from the sounds of street traffic. Ultimately there is no real evaluation process or critical feedback on our efforts. Back inside the offices, where an older woman sits fanning herself while other staff members devour cup ramen and cigarettes, the youngest in our group is immediately assigned to a press conference, and I am invited to help film the protests outside of the National Diet. Training over.[8]

As I acknowledged earlier, there is much overlap between categories of knowledge production as well as between the kinds of Gramscian organic intellectuals who are its authors.[9] But there continues to be slippage between the categories of journalist and audience under the current

5.1 The Independent Web Journal broadcast setup (properly connected). Photo by author.

conditions of media production, a destabilizing of concrete roles despite the continued emphasis on training. Accordingly, claims like "Citizen journalism may borrow the *craftsmanship* developed through a century of journalistic work, but citizen journalists will never be professionals until they have the skills, knowledge, and sources of the professional journalist" disqualify the documentary efforts of many IWJ employees from belonging to this category.[10] TV professional Inai Eiichirou underscores this point by arguing that media produced by amateurs are categorically different from professional output; the training inherent in television production refines and elevates the craft of its authors, contrary to the naive formulations of a public armed with consumer-grade tools.[11] But for the activists involved in Japan's independent media scene, expertise can be not just elevating, but also innately compromising. Their answer to the objections, offered largely by those with a stake in calcifying taxonomic differences, is to train citizens to make their own media. Indeed, this is the primary work of Our Planet-TV, whose training focuses on the slower process of storytelling (and the accompanying leisure to address aesthetic and ideological concerns) rather than the urgency of daily news production.

If journalism was once conceived of as a means to establish and maintain publics and, perhaps most aspirationally, to further national unity by promoting a common body of information (as Japanese television still seeks to do), the nature of media dissemination in the twenty-first century has both engaged with and necessitated a different approach.[12] Historically speaking, institutional journalism regrouped under the banner of objectivity and neutrality to address a politically diverse readership and "unite [readers] under the sign of the factual."[13] But ultimate reception of an appropriately balanced news article was considered essentially unknowable and beyond the scope of journalistic practice. Citizen journalism often represents a departure from this prevailing journalistic model of disciplined neutrality and performance of objectivity; instead, it legitimates its pursuit by arguing for the need to represent a particular perspective that is presumed to be overlooked by extant media. As such, it falls well within the mission of the independent media, who argue that the conservatism of the mainstream Japanese press has put the safety of its people at risk and belied a tendency for corporate journalism to protect its interests (i.e., those of its advertisers) over all else.[14]

Back in May 2013, the Our Planet Japanese-language teacher documentary group settles in to begin planning, Seiji, a Japanese-language teacher himself, places his notes on top of his copy of Shiraishi's book and outlines his vision: We will meet early on Wednesday to observe two different levels of Japanese-language class taught by the documentary's protagonist, Koshino Sensei. Seiji outlines his desired shot list, which includes filming the Sensei working at his desk, engaging in class prep, and interacting with his family at home, and he notes that we will need to seek out the students themselves for interviews to create a balanced portrait of the Sensei and Japanese-language learning. As our group rejoins the others in Our Planet's media workshop, the conversation turns to the equipment we should all bring to our production sites this week; at the minimum, a boom mic and a digicam are recommended by Our Planet's staff, while we can use our own headphones to monitor sound. This was remarkably like the production trips I'd been on with the major TV networks, apart from our lesser equipment resources and the absence of amusingly jaded camera-operating contractors. The more leisurely timeline alone was evocative of citizen journalism's more self-governing mode of praxis.

Preproduction

Seiji's Our Planet group meets at Tokyo's Higashi Nakano Station as planned the following Wednesday in May to scout the language school building and determine how to capture Koshino Sensei's routine. Sitting at a large wooden table in the reception area, we observe students arriving and collecting their name tags from bins near the front door. This school is overwhelmingly attended by students from other East Asian countries, Seiji informs us, with South Koreans representing the largest subgroup. In his estimation, this is reflective of the audience this school has chosen to target to differentiate itself from other Japanese-language schools. Mitsuko and I write this down.

Our group spends the afternoon in an advanced-level (*jōkyū*) class taking notes on the room, the way the Sensei and his students interact, and the parts of his workday that might metonymically indicate his commitment to teaching. Later we dissect these at a nearby coffee shop; Kaori suggests that Koshino Sensei speaks sufficiently loudly in his classroom that a boom mic is unnecessary. Moreover, the narrowness of the space and the potentially disruptive repercussions for our video of accidentally catching the mics on camera make it desirable to use only handicams. Placing her hand to her mouth thoughtfully, Mitsuko adds that it's hard to tell what the students are thinking based purely on observation, and Kaori affirms Seiji's initial opinion that we'll need to interview them rather than assigning them perspectives ourselves.

That the public sphere is a fiction authored by the mass media is a common suspicion in the twenty-first century—in Japan, allegations that most television news is *yarase* (scripted) are commonplace. Further, conspiracy-minded online audiences claim that networks use actors for *gaitō intabyū* ("person on the street"–type interviews) and have circulated screen captures online to show the same individuals being interviewed multiple times for different stories.[15] This practice—taking the form of both *gaitō intabyū* interviews and those I labeled "impacted person" interviews—is often deployed to reinforce producers' chosen narrative. Although they are intended as means to invoke bidirectionality, representation remains the privilege of producers and editors. People are therefore sensitive to the camera as risky, as potentially appropriating one's image in a way that one cannot manage.

My group's discussion turns to one of production technique: Seiji wants the group to film with two cameras simultaneously in the classroom. He asks if we've ever noticed the way a video can cut from one perspective to another in the same filmic space,[16] and he proposes that we replicate this effect to represent the classroom as though the camera were looking through the eyes of the professor, and then the students. The audience gaze remains a dominant theme in subsequent production meetings; as the group sits around a table in Our Planet's "Media Cafe" space, we discuss the potential impact of the documentary. Do we want viewers to come away from it saying to themselves, "I want to be a Japanese-language teacher?" (Everyone considers this possibility.) What kind of image do we want to present of the school?

Seiji's group, although composed of amateur content creators, places their documentary in the context of their own media exposure as they make decisions about who to interview and how to construct a story from a combination of these interviews and live footage. Noting that what we choose to film can dramatically impact the form that Japanese-language education takes in the minds of viewers, Seiji asserts that we must focus on recording the school space in a way that conveys what is unique about it. But also, he posits, most natives of Japan don't have a sense of the climate (*funiki*) of a Japanese-language classroom. In other words, we have a chance to be ambassadors for a context this documentary's audience is unlikely to experience firsthand.

Our group's evolving media practice throughout the workshop extends to how we interact with the technical and physical aspects of our work. The creation of any kind of video-based media involves the transportation of heavy equipment and, unlike print journalism, still necessitates embodied attendance; that is, it remains an intrinsically physical practice. During my time at the IWJ, the interaction between bodies and physical equipment was also the dominant theme of media production, unmistakable during the ebb and flow of staff to press conferences. One staff member would enter the room, sweating and dragging bags of equipment behind him, while another two would sort through and pick batteries, a mic, and a UStream box from the plastic storage units behind a broad kitchen table. It seemed inevitable that all the members of my Our Planet-TV production group were (or hoped to be) educators and were, therefore, taxonomically speaking, intellectual laborers. But in the world of television and independent media production, there is no easy Marxian divide between intellectual and physical labor.

Typically, in major production outlets the more junior the employee, the more equipment they are tasked with, while contracted cameramen are perpetually lugging oversized and unnecessarily bulky cameras and define their labor very much as a series of demands on the body. On one occasion during fieldwork with a major network in 2011, while we waited for a network producer named Shinji to obtain filming clearance, a *kamera-san* explained to me why heavy Betacams were still so ubiquitous in broadcast journalism when smaller cameras can garner the same quality footage: "I prefer using the smaller SD card-driven cameras, or at least the ones that take mini tapes, but when people see this [big] camera they think, 'Oh, they are making television!' Otherwise, they think I am just some *ojisan* (old guy) with a video camera." I ask him about the weight of the massive camera, and he lets me hold it. When I exclaim at its heaviness, he retorts in a way that recalls John Caldwell's interpretation of television's physical labor as highly gendered:[17] "That's why they need strong (*ganjō*) young men like me to carry them." Shinji climbs back in the van just in time to overhear this and rolls his eyes.

The production of video on a smaller scale, such as the IWJ's nonstop coverage of national events and press conferences, or my Our Planet group's trips to the language school to shadow Koshino Sensei, are also dominated by experimentation with our tools and invocation of physicality. During one day of the workshop in June 2013, we break away from our documentary groups, where everyone has been examining scripts and playing with the settings on handicams, for an audio lesson. We cluster around Hiro, the Our Planet staff member who, apart from Shiraishi-san, spends the most time training us on equipment and methods. Hiro frequently emphasizes that competent video can be made on cameras costing as little as US$500 (he recommends Sony) and still be shown in any theater. An older male student asks, "Why are TV cameramen often seen on the streets wearing headphones and lugging large boom microphones that hang over the heads of interviewees like umbrellas?" Hiro, smiling and nodding, says, "Everyone, plug a simple set of earbuds into your cameras. Have a member of your group speak in a normal voice near the camera." Seiji taps Mitsuko to try this exercise with him, and after a beat, he ventures a guess: "You can hear the sound quality in real time (*jitsujikan*)." Hiro points emphatically into the air, exclaiming, "*Sō desu yo!*" (Right!)

He moves on to the rationale behind external mic use, composing a diagram redolent of those used in music classrooms to explain basic acoustics. "Directional range," he says, is why those television directors use external mics. (See figure 5.2.) In other words, they pick up sound very well from

5.2 Hiro explains acoustics to the Our Planet project team. Photo by author.

directly in front of them and soften the sound from around the edges. We all try this as an exercise—plugging one of the big external mics into our cameras and listening to the audio on headphones. Kaori, who wears the headphones while I speak into the mic, notes enthusiastically that the resultant sound is lovely and clear—she can hear "really well." Seiji listens with an expression of deep concentration as Mitsuko speaks near the camera, switching between its built-in mic and one he's brought from home. Watching over his shoulder, Kaori remarks in surprise that the video seems so high quality for a handheld, consumer-level camera.

Hiro resumes his lecture: if we want to capture environmental noise, forgoing an external mic is best. For interviews, pin mics (*pin maiku*) are the current convention among documentarians, but television stations employ expensive lapel mics (aka *taipin-gata*, or "tie-pin mics"—because they clip onto one's necktie) when conducting interviews. "The IWJ," he notes, and several people look up, "employ wireless microphones most of the time."[18] Next to me, Seiji jots this information down in his notebook, below his reproduction of Hiro's microphone sound diagram.

Fostering insight into the mechanics of mass media production is one of the main goals of these workshops, and students bring to this experience

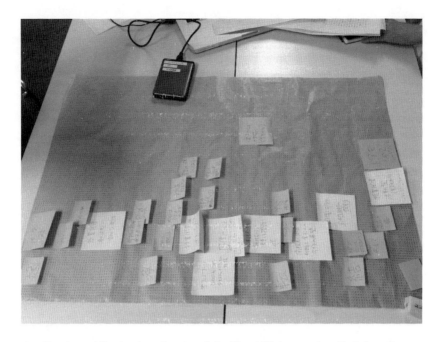

5.3 Mapping out the structure of our team's Our Planet-TV documentary. Photo by author.

incisive observations on the technicalities of its creation. Mitsuko has brought to this meeting an outline of potential interview questions for Ko-shino Sensei and his students as well as another outline of how they might weave themes from these interviews into their shot choices. For his part, Seiji has followed Shiraishi's textbook example and storyboarded his own minute-by-minute filming timeline—including camera positioning, shot type, and the goal of each "scene change" (see figure 5.3). As Kaori and Seiji read through the pile of documents and rearticulate the documentary's themes, Hiro approaches to ask us if we understand how best to position the camera during an interview. "Tripod," he announces, reminding us that we can't risk having our hands shake while we focus on a face that is likely to remain relatively steady. "Don't tilt the camera, pan only. Slowly." He asks us what else we have noticed about broadcast interviews, and Seiji comments that their subject is generally seated. "Right!" Hiro confirms. "And what else?" After a pause during which nobody ventures a guess, he suggests that the interviewer is generally neither seen nor heard on camera. Raising his voice so the rest of the class can hear, he encourages us to think of an "imaginary line" (said in English), behind which the camera must film. One of the older members of the other group pipes up in consternation to insist that he sees television staff appear on camera all the time. Hiro nods, conceding that when done, the practice is part of a Japanese strategy to invoke intimacy by breaking the fourth wall.

There are other differences between the treatment of interviews by mainstream television and Our Planet-TV–style citizen journalism. Earlier, I mentioned the widespread use of person-on-the-street interviews, and although these are common on Japanese TV, their ubiquity does not seem to have engendered widespread comfort with participation. Perhaps this is due to an accurate sense that to take part in such projects is to lose control over one's image, to permit it to be edited, reconstructed, and appropriated in a manner that represents its authors' best hopes for what one might have said. During my time with a major broadcast network, I observed one of my network TV interlocutors, Shinji, hail potential subjects with a self-introduction that moved from the general to the specific: "[Network name] *no* [Program Name] *no* [His Name]." His vinyl armband, comparable to those worn by most affiliated with the news media (including IWJ staff), offered credentialing and legitimization. And though he called out with friendly familiarity "*Onēsan!*" (lit. "older sister") or "*Onīsan!*" ("older brother") as he approached people, the sight of the camera was enough to elicit defensive gestures and uncomfortable murmuring before his subjects were even sufficiently close to read Shinji's identifying band or hear his affiliation.

Although hesitation and self-consciousness of interviewees also impact independent news creation, the process of building media from these encounters diverges according to the handling of recorded footage back in the studios. When we have returned to his network's building after collecting interviews about consumer fears of radiation-contaminated rice, I sit next to Shinji at his desk on the twelfth floor while he assembles a narrative for the segment and sends an assistant director down to the eleventh floor to search for a transcriber. I join the AD in her search, and when we eventually locate the bespectacled, buzz-cut Toshio, the AD hands over a piece of paper on which she has scrawled the names of interviewees; Toshio will input their speech into a central database to become another signature element of Japanese television—the colorful and animated selective *komentoforō* (subtitling).[19] Within the fluorescent-lit cubicle maze of transcribers, several young men and women sit with headphones on, moving backward and forward through footage of person-on-the-street interviews from festivals, concerts, and as always, the streets of Tokyo.

Ultimately, the shape of any professional news segment is born of the intentions and actions of many individuals, who pass tapes and notes between one another in a process resembling a relay race.[20] As I screen Shinji's interviews over and over again during the transcription process, I am struck by the extent to which the narrative is most self-consciously manipulated at the level of embodied interaction, hewn by producers who coax desired reactions from interviewees.[21] With one exception, the individuals Shinji approaches are unaware that officials suspect radioactive contamination of local rice crops, and he must explain this to them before asking once again if they are concerned.

In the case of the independent media, the presence of a camera and the explanation of an unknown project or recitation of an obscure affiliation before the surname of the producer prompts less of a palpable retreat on the part of bystanders, although the nature of a particular project and the risk of associating with anything unsavory/politically immoderate induce some visible hesitation.

Filming in Progress

On a muggy Sunday in June, we interview Koshino Sensei in his three-story home near Shinkoiwa Station. While his wife accepts the flowers and sweets brought by Mitsuko and arranges both on the table, Koshino Sensei asks us questions about the documentary and workshop. Seiji's group eventually becomes distracted by practical concerns: the second-floor lighting is unsuitable for filming, and the scene is too informal and domestic. After we move to Koshino Sensei's third-floor office, Seiji must reassure him that we intend to frame him tightly; filmic images are always bounded, and this one can erase a messy, toy-covered bed in the corner. Mitsuko and Kaori want to painstakingly record the room's personal artifacts and film the Sensei flipping through his notes for our B-roll, pretending to work so that this too might be combined nondiegetically with a voice-over. And Kaori, mimicking teachers of interview technique, recommends that they begin by asking him simple questions to relax him, such as "How long has he been a Japanese teacher?" and "Where did he first start teaching?"

Despite the use of an external mic, sound is our main complication, as we need to close the office door against the excited shrieks of the Sensei's son playing downstairs, then repeat a question about common language-learning mistakes after his cat begins meowing loudly. Further, Kaori cannot help but make noises of affirmation as Koshino Sensei speaks, despite her self-flagellation. Nobody crosses the invisible line until, jokingly, we talk about wanting to include behind-the-scenes bonus footage with DVDs of the documentary, and Seiji points the camera at each of us in turn.

In theorizing the potential reception of their product, Seiji and the rest of the group lack the taxonomic and quantitative tools that mass media rely on to bring audiences into relative focus. But Seiji's group is nearly always anticipating and debating the goals of its audience, even though the Our Planet workshop has been mostly concerned with the technical aspects of filming. Newly learned camera techniques are always interpreted by the group through an imagined and largely self-referential audience gaze. For example, the use of a hand mic instead of the one built into our cameras is articulated as indicative of certain savvy professionalism, or the skill to maintain viewers' attention and lend merit to their chosen subject matter while performing technical competence. A lengthy discussion about the format of Koshino Sensei's interview becomes a matter of balancing the amount of exposition they can introduce into the storyline without losing audience interest. Certainly, they want to hear an in-depth explanation of Koshino's journey to becoming a language teacher, but they also want the documentary to have *flow*—to use many voices to tell his story and move between them at an appropriate pace.

If Seiji's Our Planet group is less cynical than many major network producers about their capacity to translate concepts to their audience (see chapter 2), this is grounded in a sense of proximity to the audience, of borrowing techniques from the mainstream media but still being outsiders to its social and professional worlds. Yet, we do not entirely depart from this discrimination, and our self-perception as authors seems born of the convergence of our own experience as audience members, our training, and similar unflattering impressions about the philistinism of the Japanese public. There is therefore a sometimes-conflicting sense in how we discuss this project that our editing and narrating decision-making reflect how we would want to consume the topic, but also that our audience may be more unrefined than us or even antagonistic toward our material. That we are here, that we have studied media production to the extent that we have, already casts us into the liminal space of citizen journalists—somewhere between the professionals and the audience.

Filming unfolded in Koshino Sensei's classroom as a dance between the preplanned and highly organized system decided on by the group, and improvised movement around and behind the class to capture students writing in their workbooks, helping each other, and reacting to the lesson. During a break in filming, the group huddles and turns its attention again to matters of representation—particularly which shots of the Sensei to use so that the documentary conveys a balanced sense of him as *ningen* and *kyōshi* (human being/teacher). Kaori emphasizes to the group that it is essential we correct the stereotype that anyone can teach Japanese. "Who thinks that?" I ask, interrupting. She replies quickly, *"Minna mo sō omotte iru."* (Everyone thinks that.) Mitsuko corrects her, *"Nihonjin wa."* (Japanese people.)

Seiji picks up this train of thought to raise the question of how we might best correct the impression of unskilled labor and convey a Japanese teacher's societal role. By only featuring Koshino Sensei in this documentary, he worries that we risk representing the most esteemed teacher in the school as conventional. A pause. He decides that juxtaposing interviews with the other teachers would functionally prove Koshino's exceptionality. At the most basic level, the difference will be semiotically apparent; the tie-wearing Koshino will, by contrast to his more casual colleagues, appear even more diligent and the audience can be trusted at this moment to infer rather than being told.

Even in this brief biographical film, the group returns consistently to two themes: (1) an obligation to correct a mistaken impression at the societal level and (2) telling a story that will sustain attention and improve the likelihood that they may succeed at #1. To balance these priorities, the group spoke in terms of a mandate to adhere as closely as possible to mainstream filmic convention and to succeed in this workshop by mastering the formula of a successful documentary.

Editing and Final Screening

By July, Mitsuko is lamenting, "We've recorded too much." Without the round-the-clock and/or expansive staff of a major production group, editing is a task impossible to finish in the remaining four workshop days and must be distributed as homework. Leaning over our shoulders, Hiro exclaims *"sugoi kirei"* (very lovely) about our interview with Koshino. Unfortunately, the group decides that in the service of creating a decent story we need to sacrifice some of the content that best represents him as *ningen* and prioritize those that frame him as *kyōshi*. With headphones on, we are watching as a group; the dialog is intermittent and generally coincides with a shuffling of the Post-it notes that the group has finally arranged on our poster board.

S: We don't need this.

K: (*Where Koshino is explaining important reasons to teach Japanese to foreigners*) I think this is important.

M: (*Watching interview footage where Koshino describes an incident in which he became angry at a student*) I'd like to hear that.

K: *snickering*

M: I want to cut this.

S: But before this dark bit is the part where Koshino is explaining about those photos.

K: (*About one of the student interviews*) It's too quiet here.

M: Yeah, too hard to hear. But if we just use subtitles here . . .

S: (*Cutting a chunk of slow class-time footage*) Is it okay if I cut it like this?

K: We can't put all of the discussion with [Koshino's] coworkers in.

S: Koshino's smiling face. . . . We'll finish with his smiling face because that feels really documentary-ish. Before that, the "how was today's class" segment.

K, M, S: (*Voices overlapping as they practice fading out audio*) Subtly fade? This is weird here. I think we can do it a little. . . . This is hard to understand. Is this yellow line the volume?

Again here, my groupmates' vision for our documentary unfolds relative to those for which they have functioned as audience members/consumers. The group's process of seeking a balance between our mission to educate and one to entertain is one that is common to many forms of television and film "infotainment," as well as journalism in general.[22] Material conditions of labor have a substantial impact on the outcomes of video production, however, and although the gap between professional- and citizen-generated footage is narrowing, it remains discernible even without considering the habitus of professional videographers.[23] Observing both the painstaking editing of footage intended for TV broadcast, and that of citizen journalists intended for web distribution, I am struck by the palpable *televisuality* of the professional version, the gulf introduced by its access to more expensive equipment, as well as the well-rehearsed framing, reproduction of its subjects, and aggressive elimination of imperfect material.[24] Herein, it seems clear that the context within which knowledge is produced constitutes aesthetic decision-making. Just as lengthy training/apprenticeship is a prerequisite for television director roles, video camera operators who wish to pass from the category of amateur to that

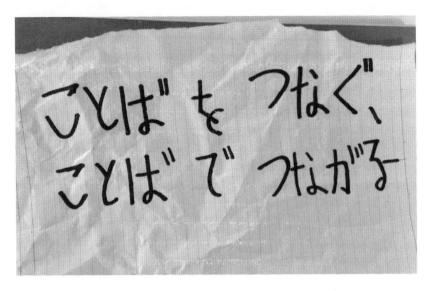

5.4 This drawing became the title image for our group's documentary. Photo by author.

of professional log many hours observing and imitating the credentialed outcomes of their seniors' labor.[25]

Despite an exhaustive editing process, my Our Planet-TV groupmates are less than confident in the coherence of their footage and the balance they've sought between cut content and compensatory voice-over narration. But finally, it is July 18, 2013, the night of the documentary screenings. The documentary authors fidget anxiously in their chairs, their finalized films burned to DVD and stacked in a queue, waiting for their turn. Shiraishi rises from her seat, introducing the event by stating that she is always impressed by how quickly workshop participants transition from their role as consumers of documentary content to producers capable of manipulating its visual conventions. "There is truly a lot of well-done work," she says.[26] Koshino Sensei arrives just as Shiraishi concludes her opening remarks, unable to bring his family because of the late hour. We accordingly screen our documentary, "Connecting Words, Connecting with Words," first (see figure 5.4).[27] As Koshino looks up at the screen, his face begins to flush a deep red, and his eyes fill with tears. He gazes at his own likeness, appearing overwhelmed and holding his hand to his mouth as his colleagues and students praise him. As the credits appear, Shiraishi probes him for his reaction.

"How can I comment on such material?" Konshino asks.

The Interactive Dialectic of Public, Audience,
and Media Maker in Citizen Journalism

In creating "public interest" media, there seems to be endless debate about how to gauge what actually interests publics—but even more so, whether publics are qualified to steer broadcast decision-making, or whether decisions are best made paternalistically.[28] While there often seemed to be a consensus among media professionals that entertainment and pedagogy are incompatible, Seiji's group nonetheless sought to balance the two even without any meaningful expectation of attracting an audience, or concerns about commercial viability. They were steered primarily by the blueprints in Shiraishi's book, formal instruction from Our Planet-TV staff, and their integration of common representational techniques. As my team moved around the language school, the objects, people, and events at which they chose to point a camera reflected their interests, but also their new training. The documentary *had* to tell a story. Absent a need to make production contingent on marketability and potential advertising revenue, the group still defaulted to a way of articulating narrative decisions that mirrored those I heard in broadcast television conference rooms. Facilitating this process, Shiraishi's books about media production, and the contents of Our Planet's workshops, are informed by her tenure as a TV Asahi employee—indeed many of those I encountered in the world of "interloper media" had learned their craft through prior employment at one of the mass media conglomerates.[29]

Recalling Susan Sontag's foundational work on the degree to which our perception of everyday experiences is colored by our internalization of filmic techniques, this overlap was also due to the aesthetic language of both professionals and amateurs having been constituted by their media exposure, and filmic technique being more a matter of tradition than born of individual ingenuity.[30] Just as media scholar Barry Dornfeld gleaned from his participant observation in public broadcast that producers take on the role of media consumers in their consideration of audience needs and future decoding of texts, the participants in the Our Planet workshop oscillate between assuming the technical gaze of a media producer and the interpretive position of their imagined audience.[31] In both cases, media consumed outside of a production context inform ultimate artistic output and encourage producers to call on their own experience of viewership within professional praxis.

I experience this firsthand almost a year earlier during fieldwork with IWJ when on a Friday I am invited to attend and help film the weekly anti–nuclear energy demonstrations outside of the National Diet. It is my first time piling into an IWJ van, my first time operating an IWJ camera, and my first time watching the viewer count on the UStream transmitter climb as we continue filming. The experience feels every bit like guerrilla journalism, as we seek to represent the ebullient energy of the protesters without permit or parameter.[32] Operating the cameras under such conditions—with no mounts or ladders, and only one's hands to hold the camera over the crowd and convey the scope of the protest—dramatically foregrounds the process of editing and filtering and makes it as much a physical as a technological performance. Ours is a process of mimetically reproducing the ways I have seen protest captured before, including what is attended to and what is excluded. I zoom in on what makes the most noise: a Guy Fawkes mask in the crowd, an elderly couple dressed as cockroaches.[33] The process of creating documentary coverage is less one of deterritorialization, and more an exercise in the collection of "echo objects."[34]

In media scholar Anna Everett's formulation of activism and its appropriation of "the logic of network news gathering," the capacity of Black American women to successfully appropriate the language of mainstream broadcast indicates the capacity of new technology to take back television's power to represent, by self-representing and "recod[ing]" with consumer-level tools.[35] At the same time, this self-representation—of the viewer/consumer's desires through a producer's lens—establishes an intimate and liminal space between aspects of the self. There is an enduring tug-of-war among what an author desires to show, what audiences wish to see, and the author's compromise where they perceive these positions to overlap. This close relationship and resultant dialectic between the selves of the media maker and audience creates new and unexpected interactivity within the process of citizen journalism. Further, it contributes another dimension to the concept of interactive/social TV: a dialectic between the media maker as creator and the audience as receiver, both conceived as parts of a unified whole.

Conclusion

Although the needs of audiences are unpacked in a theoretical and potential way during media construction, producers' capacities to anticipate the needs of audiences are informed by their experience in that role. At the major networks, demographic viewer data allow producers to transcend (if not escape) the metonymic use of themselves as audience surrogates by gesturing to the perceived neutrality of these numbers. However, at small independent media organizations like Our Planet-TV and IWJ, media makers rely on their instincts about how they might best communicate to audiences by interpolating their own experiences as media consumers. Although the IWJ can often see in real time whether their assumptions manifest in viewership as the number of live stream viewers fluctuates, this feedback resembles the crude "yes/no" (watching/not watching) of traditional television and is incomplete feedback.

Recalling Seiji's group's discussions about the balance between exposition and flow, citizen media makers realize first that they must consistently manage expectations about what they can expect of their audiences, and second, that the closest point of reference they have for audiences is their perceptions of how the Japanese mass media engages publics and pushes narratives. During our group's editing sessions (in between shoptalk), the conversation in the room oscillated between microscale comparisons of favorite authors and their specific publics, and the invocation of a "we" that was of national scale. As was the case within the mainstream variety shows I discussed in chapter 4 the audience for most content was repeatedly identified as "Japanese people" by my group members. Yet it was unclear where my group members' self-conception as part of this group alternated with possession of a journalistic identity and fledgling habitus that cast them in the role of observer of this national body.

Interactivity, when enacted within the production structure of citizen journalism, draws equally on the seeing and producing self, the self that desires, and the self that reaches out. It captures a desire for media to engender authentic connection, where the connection appears to begin within oneself. Could there be anything new about how my group invokes nationhood compared with the history of such monolithic forms of national address by the mainstream media and informed by group members' sense of their relationship to nationalism?

Throughout our project, my groupmates operated on the assumption that our documentary had an obligation to both Koshino Sensei and a misinformed national audience to redeem the oft-disparaged profession of language instruction. Shiraishi's mission for Our Planet-TV recalled an attitude toward media born of 1960s American and Japanese counterculture and "founded on a belief in liberation via the democratic pluralism of television—[ideally] anyone could control the means of production, anyone could and should be an artist."[36] As such, my groupmates, inspired by Shiraishi's vision of Our Planet's workshops as helping to facilitate the transfer of power over media representation from entrenched corporate entities to any member of Japanese democratic society, described our project as driven by a mandate to improve public discourse by capturing our subject authentically. But the twentieth-century notion that technological development would birth a more democratic and utopian version of the public sphere than was allowed under the management of media conglomerates has been largely relegated to the bin of dated rhetoric. Nonetheless, within the pockets of optimism represented by independent media, the goal of liberation remains an emancipatory process in which my groupmates could partake. In the dialectic between media maker and audience embodied by the practices of citizen journalism, liberator and liberated are not separate, but one.

Interactivity, as it turns out, is not a cure for media monopolies under late capitalism. Rather than functioning as a cudgel against the structure of mainstream journalism, it represents the industry's acknowledgment of an evolving relationship between media makers and audiences. Meanwhile, audiences have witnessed internet movements become the content and concerns of the mass media, and in this era of media "bricolage,"[37] the public's sense of its capacity for resistance has grown. But the inconvenient side effect represented by audiences generating their own flows of discourse is perhaps the main point of interactivity rather than a disturbance that must be managed. This also suggests that the future of television might be more effectively realized by bringing media makers and audiences together in new configurations rather than trying to replicate traditional alignments using new technology. Interactivity has taken steps to solicit audience input on the future direction of mass media but has so far self-limited by looking solely through the capitalistic lens of potential profit and advertiser benefit. The most idealistic media professionals have worked within this infrastructure to renegotiate their relationship with audiences, and these first overtures toward interactivity will not be the last strategy they try in pursuit of a new relationship with nationalism and national publics.

Conclusion

In the introduction, I wrote about the open and closed systems of knowledge production as one of the core binaries operating in this book. This
insider/outsider divergence remains a significant theme of my research,
owing to the contrast between well-promoted and well-funded projects on
the scale of *Arashi feat. You* and the *60 Ban Shōbu* versus the lower-budget
press conferences of the Free Press Association of Japan (FPAJ) and the
documentaries of Our Planet-TV. But there are other binaries. One can
be found in the way interactivity is applied to news versus entertainment
content, regardless of budget, as significant overlap exists between the vision of independent and mainstream broadcast journalists. While projects
like those of the FPAJ and Independent Web Journal (IWJ) discussed in
chapter 3 are unambiguously news oriented, game shows like *Bloody Tube*
self-describe as entertainment. But other programs are positioned more
equivocally: news discussion shows like *The Compass* (chapter 2) are as
much entertainment as they are news, while the human-interest documentaries authored by Our Planet-TV represent news insofar as they report
on contemporary social phenomena but depart from this classification by

focusing on ongoing societal challenges instead of breaking stories. Finally, contrasts appear within the degree of control exercised by a system/project, and the range of potential cocreation possible within each programmatic space. The FPAJ, for example, represents the extreme of allowing audiences to comment freely on press conferences online while eliminating embodied gatekeeping and granting open access to its press conference broadcast facilities. The IWJ offers another example of reimagined boundaries by replicating traditional news gathering (to an extent) but removing the mediating process of editing and interpreting for audiences. Further, audience participation ranges even within the projects of major TV networks— some allow audiences to directly act on their content (*Bloody Tube, Arashi*) while others limit the audience role to voting yes or no (*The Last Award, 60 Ban Shōbu*) and relegate communications between audience members to a dedicated chat space sequestered from the broadcast screen.

As this discussion suggests, however, the continuum of interactive media cocreation is not much of a continuum. Rather, it constitutes a set of discursive opportunities, moments of flow between authors and audiences within the framework of various systems. An experiment that breaks ground for how it allows participants to control programmatic outcomes may co-opt the most bounded and inflexible tools to maintain conventional boundaries between producers, TV talent, and audiences (as in most of Bascule's projects). Meanwhile, projects that initially appear to be thoroughly regulated, like *The Compass*, might offer audiences greater latitude to converse with one another and access TV staff by funneling crowd energy into more open-ended participation rather than engaging it in game playing. Nonetheless, interactivity appears within the desire for and intention of producers to facilitate cocreative opportunities as much as the actualization of any specific approach to interactivity. Those opportunities can largely be condensed into three categories: anonymous live commenting, preference indicating (voting, "liking," clicking on), and team-based game playing. Yet as I maintain throughout this book, each technique for interaction, while innovative in its own way, remained beholden to the infrastructure and long-standing practices of conventional mass media. Such practices—ranging from a contingent workforce inside and outside the media conglomerates, to preoccupation with commercial appeal, to insufficient resources—represent the human and structural elements that are inextricably tied to the technological project of interactivity.

In 1969 Konno Tsutomu of TV Man Union wrote about power's relationship with, or control over, our experience of time, describing power as "that which has the right to restructure time politically as a matter of course and then present it as 'history,'" and television as a threat to that power when it tries to present time as it is. He wrote that "only by *creating/developing the present* can television determine its own future."[1] Indeed, this is the position that the FPAJ, IWJ, and others took relative to Japan's media conglomerates, as they considered their decision to broadcast unedited live streams a contestation of television's self-protective and deceptive editing practices. Their strategy is/was one of taking back power over the narratives that become history—even when, for the FPAJ, transparency meant transmitting moments harmful to its own reputation. This strategy also epitomizes the challenge that the industry insiders (which the TV Man Union founders also were) posed to their own networks. Rather than simply presenting conventionally edited material, they chose to challenge the dominant system by allowing people to comment live on events unfolding in real time. This model worked for journalistic fare and for interactive games by introducing audiences to the temporal sphere of television even as they remained cloistered in spaces that maintained TV's power.

Throughout the twenty-first century, one of the biggest barriers to a more ambitious and radical implementation of interactivity as a benchmark for mass media has indeed been television itself. While some of the most ambitious and idealistic practitioners in the industry tried to define what was possible and desirable for a more inclusive future, the potential for interactive technology collided with the self-protective interests of a medium that was constantly moving the guideposts of possibility and impeding advancement. Advances in technology always accompanied concerns about unacceptable rhetoric making its way into a broadcast or bleeding excessively into the spaces where politicians humored journalists with their presence. Thus, television could feel simultaneously "slippery" and obstinate to both insiders and outsiders, a shape-shifter uncertain of its evolving role but bounded by entrenched conditions.[2] After decades of debate among scholars and media producers, the medium is no closer to settling into a specific relationship with representation or narrative. Even the news functions in the service of collective imaginaries, and when it neglects to tell stories, ratings suffer.[3]

Insight into the professional practices of television producers reinforced my sense that despite the above ambiguity, the medium is dominated by an exasperating intractability. Unlike journalism, which was regularly described by those inside and outside of the major Japanese news corporations as having reached a breaking point, the status of television was rarely spoken of as a "crisis" (*kuraishisu*, or any other synonym) by industry insiders. Rather, the situation was conceived of in terms of potential—as a puzzle to be solved, and an opportunity to engage and experiment with new technology despite a series of worrying circumstances surrounding the aging of its most loyal demographics and ever-evolving modes of viewership among younger audiences.

As a former executive for Dentsu (one of the world's largest advertising firms) explained as we stood outside the Tokyo offices of a prominent television production company that now employed him, "Japan is like the Galapagos Islands. There, creatures have been able to exist that do not exist elsewhere and could not exist elsewhere. And some have died out that should have lived. Japan is also an island, and our TV is like those creatures that could not live anywhere else and ought to have died out."[4] These TV "creatures" he gestures toward, along with the daily negotiations and practices of the television and media producers who create them, have been among the subjects of this book.

While there are certainly voices clamoring for changes to TV content, these are muffled in comparison to those of the press releases and ongoing fanfare surrounding technological development. Recently, government-sponsored research collaboration involving rival Japanese television manufacturers (such as the government-backed NexTV-F) resulted in NHK being the first in the world to broadcast in 8K in 2019—a goal it chiefly sought to achieve before South Korea and in preparation for the 2020 Olympics.[5] In launching the world's first Ultra HD broadcast channel (NHK BS8K), the network self-consciously maintained its legacy of firsts, as NHK had earlier been responsible for Asia's first color broadcast in 1960 and the first national HDTV broadcast in 1994.[6] Meanwhile, Japanese commercial networks continue to struggle with the technical quality of their 4K broadcasts, and the benefit to consumers or even their interest in 8K+ broadcast remains unclear.[7] The divide between technology and the social worlds it conceives seemed manifest in Japan's 2022 law vaguely making "online insults" punishable by a year in prison or a fine equivalent to US$2,200, and though its stated goal was to curb cyberbullying, it remains to be seen if the law will impact journalism.[8]

Referring to audience studies, Ien Ang has argued, "More often than not, research is a tool for symbolic politics rather than for rational decision-making."[9] Much like the television professionals and journalists whom I met during fieldwork, media scholars and anthropologists have focused on understanding audiences because of the massive symbolic weight this body has for those who strive to construct meaning through media and theorize the work they do.[10] In many cases, media producers are seeking to reproduce their own identity in the narratives they produce and hope to create a connection with audiences using tools that could result in the validation of these narratives. In cases where the audience is or feels unknowable, the self as media and meaning maker is called into question—the resultant unknowability of what it means to do media work and to hold expertise in this area reflects one's own sense of internal ambiguity.

My study of mass media expertise and professional praxis focused on both interactive TV and journalism to examine two kinds of heightened tension involved in this category of media making. First is the role production anxiety plays in shaping producers' interpretations of audiences. Second is how the logics of interactivity position audiences in a liminal space between content and the physical technologies themselves, where the content will always receive greater protection from the users than users from the content. Although television programming is always designed to target audiences as consumer-viewers, much of the creative work in interactive TV/journalism hails audiences in ways that are intended to facilitate especially precise and thorough data gathering—a natural outcome of how most global TV is funded. Nonetheless, interactive media's interpolation of audiences is still accompanied by overlapping anxieties about allowing audiences greater proximity to a live broadcast. But strategies to safeguard television's business model also cannot be separated from its authors' hopeful (and oft-expressed) consideration of audiences as capable of and deserving of a role in the production of television narratives. A genuinely idealistic perspective drives these experiments, which allow viewer/users to shape narratives and explore virtual spaces with one another alongside novel forms of advertising.

The real-time audience feedback afforded by mobile-responsive/live streaming websites and social media surpasses what is offered by traditional ratings or pilot episode testing and offers producers a more direct connection to viewers through interfaces that encourage open and immediate referendums on programming. Producers can experience the signified meaning they have created and contrast it with the signifiers of their internal (broadcast studio) conversations and their imagination, to gauge whether a signifier provokes any kind of response at all. And although the business and creative sides of media production seek audiences for different reasons–whether for the desire to connect through their creation or merely fill an economic imperative—the capacity to talk to those audiences in real time during a broadcast partially disambiguates them and may facilitate future mass media production that is more responsive to their desires. Although commercial thought processes represent unideal baggage when combined with fantasies of building productive connections with audiences, media producers are largely resigned to these conditions.

Further, both mainstream and independent media producers address audiences simultaneously as a free democratic body and a unified national body—an often-conflicting impulse that mirrors a similar schism in media production: the drive to offer variety while also being generic enough to appeal to mass audiences under the rubric of general interest news and entertainment programming. While Japan calls attention to this tendency frequently through forms of address to "everyone in Japan" and unselfconsciously promotes an image of a country with a very limited range of subjectivity, this general dynamic is also reflected in mass media around the world. That Japan would seek to reproduce conventional modes of address within social TV experiments becomes interesting given that interactivity (at least in the global West) has traditionally been conceived of as a gateway to an unregulated, wild diversity with all its concurrent downsides.

A question I have frequently posed to myself and my interlocutors in mainstream television and the independent media is whether the massive 2011 earthquake and subsequent nuclear accident signified a turning point, a moment of meaningful historical change in the way that their professional communities conduct business. Most of the television professionals with whom I worked replied in the negative or demurred and argued, in essence, that history is still unfolding. But independent journalists often cited these events as ongoing inspiration for their work or as the origin story of their respective ventures. Their organizations and labor have, at minimum, introduced the possibility of alternative narratives to Japanese society by stimulating a movement to blog, tweet, information-share, and consult a variety of sources for news content, which prompted activist May Shigenobu to compare the aftermath of Fukushima to the Arab Spring.[11] By making media a site of contestation, even if on a small scale, their efforts represent an intense and passionate struggle that continues to generate small changes in the way Japan "conducts media."

For television writ large, balancing the economic, political, and cultural imperatives of national broadcast remains trickier. Internet content thrives because of the comparatively low barrier to entry required to join the conversation. But as unpacked in my discussion of citizen journalism, this means great inconsistency in the quality of the content (and commentary)—which television attempts to eliminate as much as possible under the banner of appropriateness. That television broadcast operates under a mandate to which internet broadcast is not subject is discernible in moments when its seemingly innate authority breaks down as it stumbles in its appearance of neutrality, for example. While the freedom granted online viewers in Japan can be attributed to a lack of accountability to institutional power sources, media executives circulate in proximity to politicians and are largely responsible for enforcing an institutional "trickle-down" effect.[12] The system grants politicians a wide berth to manipulate broadcasters through boycotts, public censure, and so on, as each station depends on government approval for the renewal of its broadcast licenses.[13]

The oligarchical nature of the broadcast industry also demands of TV a certain dance between the necessary fragmentation of targeted marketing and these forms of address suited to national bodies.[14] Simply put, with only six television stations, the burden of responsibility is distributed among relatively few entities. Interactive television is particularly intriguing for how it processes diversity: rather than pacifying the viewer, isolating one in the particularity of one's experience, "social television" takes a step back from the fragmented marketing of mass entertainment in Japan and gestures toward reconstituting the national imaginary. Once again, however, the extent to which social TV has consented to lessen its authoritative hold over media programming—to allow the actions of unseen masses to directly act on content—remains limited, the gatekeeper role intact. And the question of democracy, or whether interactivity will eventually allow greater democratic speech and participation in the political and cultural processes of Japanese society, remains to be seen.

Television in Japan also continues to face fears of what an aging population means for advertising revenue. Data from NHK from 2010 showed that 11 percent of the country consumed no television, and after 2015 the percentage declined drastically among individuals under forty years old—a phenomenon media consultant Ujiie Natsuhiko has called "the beginning of the end of television."[15] This is what concerns TV staff the most and drives their decision-making: specifically, since 2018, audiences have spent even more time using the internet than watching on-demand television.[16] And despite the impact of the COVID-19 pandemic on individual mobility in the early 2020s, home television viewership did not rebound.[17] Yet the logics of television in Japan, which are anchored in an entrenched system of national broadcast, widespread viewership, and predictable advertising revenue, allow networks to maintain assurance that scale will protect them from the effects of evolving consumption patterns.

Though affected by the same neoliberal economic forces that have pushed so many other large companies and institutions to outsource and rely on contingent labor, to require workers to diversify skill sets, and to perform the jobs previously assigned to multiple individuals, television has adapted to contemporary economic conditions and is still producing hits. The massively popular 2013/2020 TV drama *Hanzawa Naoki*, for example, remains loyal to the formulas and styles of dramas from decades past, apart from improvements in technical quality. If anything, television retains its basic profile as a content factory because it has spent the past two decades manipulating puzzle pieces in attempts to fit interactivity to television without changing television overmuch.[18]

With television producers and independent journalists sharing many of the same ideals as media scholars about the potential sociopolitical ramifications of a more bidirectional mass media (and much the same skepticism/cynicism),[19] it can be tempting to interpret with excessive optimism the ways that viewer contributions have been integrated into programming and the effects of these on broadcasts' central narratives. But has the integration of Twitter comments into news broadcasts been experienced as fundamentally different from the earlier practices of reading audience letters on-screen or taking calls from viewers? Other, comparable efforts have included appropriating videos uploaded to social media, particularly when they represent organic evidence of an event that unfolded beyond the reach of TV cameras. But these inscriptions hardly suggest a repositioning of television relative to citizen-produced media—they rarely include the video's author and retain the division between journalist/guest expert and citizen found on shows like *The Compass* and *The Last Award*. Where most television remains wed to conventional relationships with audiences, the experiments described in this book appear even more exceptional.

Therefore, if television remains largely a medium characterized as "to be watched," its cachet among theoreticians concerned by its passivity will remain consistently low. Media researcher John Hartley argues that TV will never be considered alongside other "literate" forms of art until audiences can both read *and* write in response to it.[20] This is what interactive television, in its ideal form, offers global audiences. Hartley suggests that media experiments wherein programs are composed of audience-submitted footage (such as Fuji TV's "Japan in a Day" special) start to dissolve the boundaries between producers and consumers, and to an extent, I think this is true.[21] These differ from other means of engaging television through writing (even the kind of "decoding as writing" famously articulated by

Stuart Hall[22]) that have relied on disengagement from the medium itself, as in the case of fan fiction. But could this fan/slash fiction, as discussed by Henry Jenkins, properly be considered audience integration and a step toward dissolving the distinction between producers and audiences?[23] Such projects make a gesture toward connecting people within and through art in a way that exceeds the consideration of many philosophers[24]—but they leave television's borders intact.

While interactive television in its current Japanese incarnation tends to strip audiences of readerly liberty, it simultaneously makes space for a new kind of "writing with TV." If technologies like the VCR, and later the TiVo and other DVRs, introduced Umberto Eco's "aberrant decoding," wherein audiences can move programs forward and backward and skip and rewatch portions in a manner resembling that of "literary" reading, interactive TV aims to thwart nonlinear consumption by attempting to render such practices irrelevant or obsolete.[25] That the experience of these programs is contingent on live participation returns audience-users to the paradigm of an earlier era in TV history. It allows them to choose between effervescent crowd energy or the convenience of "time-shifted" viewing and promotes the opportunity to join a project (or a pretense) of collective programmatic authorship.

As Jacques Rancière argues, the purpose of a work of art is to create community, and yet "an aesthetic community is a community structured by disconnection."[26] Nonetheless, the Japanese media remains dedicated to the project of promoting a collective ethos and repairing the connection that technological progress has severed. By mapping the country through culinary tourism, engaging in live coverage of rituals surrounding the emperor, or reminding us that one can view and participate in an interactive NHK quiz show (or Arashi concert) simultaneously from the northernmost to the southernmost parts of the archipelago, Japanese television gestures toward a collective way of being (or at least a capacity for collective enjoyment).[27] National culture is reified through ongoing performances and assignations of Japanese-ness, and while interactive television rarely dabbles in overt performances of tradition or activities deemed culturally specific, it is motivated by the same energy "[that seeks to bind] the Japanese people tightly together in time and space, from one tip of the archipelago to the other."[28] Like cinema, however, social television can address its audiences on more than one level—to allow them to exploit the freedom of anonymity alongside intimate, familiar modes of address. Even in *The Last Award*, where viewer/users don't just play along but supply the program with nearly all of its content, participants using the mobile website remain anonymous. The audience as an unknowable aggregate, however, is moving toward extinction.

The "we" that is claimed by interactive television represents a natural progression from the ways that television producers hail national audiences and seek a relationship with them that may be bidirectional (for the producer) but remains abstract on both sides. Classical philosophy was interested in accounting for this abstract space, naming emotional/affective encounters between people and art and creating the language to account for the relationships formed between the creator, art object, and consumer. But as discussed in chapter 2, interactive media seeks to orient its audiences away from conventional modes of detached consumption, and although this practice may hinder the kinds of aesthetic contemplation considered ideal by a canonical philosophy of aesthetics,[29] it induces a different kind of ecstasy and sublimation of the self. Rather than encouraging rational contemplation, interactive TV plays with affect by manipulating distance. Distance between audience members paradoxically both increases and decreases within virtual spaces, while the space between audiences and a program's creators is complicated by interactive TV, maintaining existing power imbalances at the same time it brings the two bodies closer. Audiences as collaborators and cocreators are still encouraged to act within groups (often teams), to behave as a crowd, and to retain their individuality only as data that can be bought and sold. As TV commercials become increasingly integrated into on-demand viewing, and if Gracenote's work in the past decade is any indication, they will soon be able to target their marketing more precisely than before.

The idea (and sometimes the hope) that the mass media was in trouble with advertisers and needed to rapidly adapt its content and its practices was a specter that haunted industry events around Tokyo, and the nature of the threat was always changing. Initially, it came from the time-shifted viewing made possible by DVRs or DVD subscription services like Tsutaya's DISCAS,[30] which were considered disruptive insofar as their users passed in and out of visibility while actively consuming content—conventionally uncountable, unsaleable, but always tantalizing insofar as they were assumed to be viewing. When NHK and NTV teamed up to create the *60 Ban Shōbu* (and in the process satirized the tensions between these networks that existed during the early years of broadcast), they broke with convention by asking viewers to voluntarily step into the light to be counted and to convey to sponsors when they were watching and how by pressing buttons at regular intervals. During postmortems on *60 Ban Shōbu*, producers made a practice of scrutinizing these precise moments in time when audiences experienced peak enjoyment. This wealth of data could be processed alongside detailed graphs reporting the locations, ages, and genders of individual viewers now known to be actively and synchronously reaching toward on-screen *tarento* and program staff. Savvy marketers quickly conscripted this model for advertising using Japan's unique *dēta hōsō* technology; a program or ad might indicate that a viewer could take a quiz after a commercial for Mister Donut; they press the D button on their remote control to access the questions and to earn a coupon. Smartphone applications that can listen for and respond to targeted television content are being developed for similar purposes.

Observing emerging forms of TV advertising, a former marketing executive named Okada complained about the ways that Japanese brands interact with audiences: "[Bidirectionality as a strength] is what we've found with Facebook. . . . So, if you're following a company and leave a comment, you expect the company to comment back. But . . . for so many Japanese companies, their idea of how to build a website is to put up some pretty pictures of the brand, and you just mention the [company's] contact details and that's it. That's something we've found, that there's just one-way communication."[31] Okada's frustration with the ways that advertisers (and mass media) pretend to embrace interactivity and its supposed capacity to formulate intimacy between producers and consumers mirrors the skepticism of academic communications studies, within which some scholars have polemically pushed back on the notion that the nature of television (and journalism) will meaningfully change with the introduction of much-heralded participatory technologies.[32] Instead, according to Mark Andrejevic's Marxian critique of interactive television, participation is another way for capitalism to exploit the labor of consumers who are now engaged in generating content on behalf of media conglomerates.[33] Audiences, by agreeing to join the virtual spaces and teams defined for them, are also agreeing to be exploited insofar as agency is possible relative to modern systems. But audiences are mostly aware of and resigned to the trade-offs. During a July 2013 focus group I held with thirty-five convenience-sampled TV viewers in Tokyo, this was what they told me. In essence, "It has become so difficult to track the paths our data takes. We accept it as a condition of technology use."[34]

Critiques of television as excessively paternalistic and audiences as unfailingly passive have progressed from the culture industry to more complicated assessments of audiences and the eventual deployment of ethnographic fieldwork as a further corrective.[35] Indeed, a problem with a cynical view of interactive media is not that it misrepresents the material conditions of its production, but that it *oversimplifies the motivations of those who create it* and substitutes the idealism of earlier scholars of interactivity for the lingering idealism of contemporary media makers. It is true, though, that the mass media producers whom I met during fieldwork do not see themselves as equivalent to their audiences and especially not to citizen journalists. Combining social media with the news has thus amounted to less than was promised by communications scholars, while alternative news channels have arguably amounted to more, especially since 2016.[36]

Globally, social media has become a significant challenge to the authority and workflow of professional journalists.[37] According to communications scholar Elizabeth Bird's interviews, by 2009 journalists were already defending a sense of themselves as trained experts, distanced from the work of those without credentials or conventional forms of affiliation.[38] Reinforcing this point, chapter 3 shows that while the professional practices of Japanese independent journalists might more closely represent an ideal model of Western journalism—thus reflecting the fulfillment of their aspirations to emulate this model—the incumbent journalists belonging to the *kisha* clubs emphatically resist acknowledging work done outside of the major newspapers and their parent TV companies. My interlocutors also argued that the reason for low newspaper and TV news consumption among younger demographics is that they are always in contact with information. This is because a lack of interest in consuming news in conventional forms does not indicate a lack of interest in news, and generally, social media–using tech-savvy young adults will instead encounter significant current events information through their networks. If stories emerge through interpersonal communication, then, the interest of television and journalism must be in presenting the right information in the right format and appropriating the urge to share stories with one's network (more cocreation as free labor). Some of the technologies discussed in this book were intended to facilitate this kind of transaction but have faded from relevance in the past five to seven years.

Despite the aspirations of independent media, citizen journalism, and social TV, their success in constituting publics seems to eventually rely on mass media as a framing device (fringe websites use social media to self-promote and drive traffic, the mainstream news covers them, etc.). Michael Warner has argued, in his canonical work on the subject, that a public cannot be created from discourse operating in the model of sender-receiver, even insofar as such pared-down performances can be considered to exist: "Texts themselves," he writes, cannot create publics, but demand the "concatenation of texts through time."[39] Warner's definition does not require the active participation of all subjects within earshot, but it does require a dialog that operates within the range of their hearing. The space of Nico-Nico constitutes that possibility, as does that of interactive television, but not everyone using the system will do more than observe the comments of others. Our Planet-TV too exists as part of this paradigm, by encouraging media consumers to produce original works to supplement perceived journalistic oversight or failure—to engage with sensitive topics and, by engaging, formulate a rebuttal in the language of mass media itself. This is the "regular flow of discourse in and out" that defines publics, and while television edits incoming/outgoing discourse, so does print media.[40] I would argue it is the intent to create such a dialog and its manifestation, even in truncated form, that makes of it a public.

Meanwhile, interactive television and independent journalism dabble in publics in a cyclical process wherein its hosts notice the input of audiences, comment on it, and encourage further commentary from audiences. Pushing the button, in other words, can describe a conversation involving media maker and audience both acting as transmitter and receiver, with the push of one button triggering a reciprocal pushback.[41] This happened at Free Press Association press conferences when journalists read comments from the NicoNico live stream and posed questions aloud to guest speakers. Likewise, interactive television has tried to transcend the "fake reciprocity" it was accused of and by which its twentieth-century experiments (such as those of NHK) were largely implicated. And although mass media will never be democratic, the authors of the media described in this book fought to create a greater interchange between makers and users and to push experiments in interactivity outside of the realm of aficionados and specialists.

As anthropologist Tom Boellstorff observes in writing about rapidly evolving technologies, "I see it as a strength that this text will be dated by the time it appears in print."[42] For me, this must also be true. That many of the technologies depicted herein have largely maintained a holding pattern since the early 2010s is one thing about them. Another is the paradoxical feeling shared with me by TV producers and journalists that last year's project is already a hundred thousand projects ago. As in Boellstorff's work, distance has allowed me to focus less on the sensationalism of individual programs, and more on the ripples they created or the ways that they did (or did not) change Japanese broadcast.

Independent media still has its strengths, despite its marginalization in Japan: According to activist Michiko Ishizu, there will always be a place for citizen journalists in the country as long as they conduct themselves ethically, stand behind their work, and do something to differentiate themselves from the mass media.[43] If my fieldwork within the left-wing alternative media suggests anything, it is that the comparative agility with which independent media can experiment with new technology will permit it to stand apart from mainstream television and journalism and maintain its efforts to decenter news production and information flows.[44] Although some of these news start-ups have ceased to exist, so have many of the technologies and projects of the mass media. Technology is impatient, whomever its driver.

NOTES

Introduction

1   Information about Bascule, Inc. can be found at "Play with Future," Bascule, https://bascule.co.jp.

2   TVMANUNION, "Kigyō Rinen." Also, see chapter 2, where I discuss this subcontracting relationship from the perspective of the subcontractors.

3   Hagimoto, Muraki, and Konno, *Tada no Genzai ni Suginai*. This manifesto's title is also translated in English as "You Are Nothing but the Present"; Gerow, "Film to Television."

4   Sas, "Culture Industries" 237.

5   Konno, "Kanōsei no Teiji ni Mukatte," 91.

6   Chun, *Hundred Million*, 6.

7   Uesugi, *Kokka no Haji*. The full title is *Kokka no haji: Ichioku sō Sen'nō-ka no Shinjitsu Tankō* (National shame: The truth about the brainwashing of 100 million people). Uesugi-san was a big part of my fieldwork, as seen especially in chapter 3.

8   I am referring here to the 2003 Sofia Coppola film, which portrays fading celebrity Bob Harris (played by Bill Murray) visiting Tokyo to appear in Suntory whisky commercials and make appearances on Japanese television. One of the themes of this movie is essentially that Japanese television is incomprehensible to non-Japanese.

9   *Los Angeles Times*, "Japanese Journalist."

10   Clammer, "Consuming Bodies," 197.

11   Carpentier, "Concept of Participation."

12   McKenna, *Real People*, xxxiv.

13   Nishida, "Terebi to Sōsharumedia."

14   Hartley, "Republic of Letters."

15 NHK Hōsō Bunka Kenkyūjo, "2013-Nen Kenkyū."

16 Hakuhodo-DYMedia-Partners, *Sumātofon no Fukyū*. Also, this has continued to be true according to more recent studies like the one cited in the next endnote. Korean parent company Naver's messaging software Line exploded in popularity during my fieldwork (2012–13), largely because it was ahead of other communication tools in allowing users to send "sticker" reaction images to one another and to easily send messages internationally.

17 Video Research Co. Ltd., "Media Teiten Chōsa."

18 Morofuji and Watanabe, *Changes and Trends*.

19 This remains true despite mobile viewing ventures like TVer, which was launched in 2015.

20 Hakuhodo-Co. Ltd., *Seikatsu-Sha*.

21 Hakuhodo-Co. Ltd., *Seikatsu-Sha*, 5.

22 *Dēta hōsō* (data broadcast) provides a separate "layer" to Japanese broadcast which, without requiring an internet connection, allows viewers to access specific information on demand, such as the weather, natural disaster information, or one's horoscope. Individual programs, like QB47, also use *dēta hōsō* for quizzes and other bonus program-related content, and such content may be engaged via remote control. For more information on the technology, see NHK's What Is *Dēta hōsō*? website, https://www.nhk.or.jp/data/about/.

23 Horkheimer and Adorno, *Dialectic of Enlightenment*, 97. A useful summary of the relationship between the Frankfurt School and television can be found in Kellner, "Critical Perspectives."

24 Postman, *Amusing Ourselves to Death*.

25 For a thorough discussion of these positions, see Schultz, "Concept of Interactivity," 206.

26 Rodwell, "Machine without the Ghost."

27 Ujiie, "Terebi no Mirai."

28 McCurry, "Japan."

29 Tsuda, *Dōin no Kakumei*, 168.

30 For comprehensive histories of the Japanese television industry see Chun, *Hundred Million*; Ivy, "Formations of Mass Culture"; Moeran, *Advertising*.

31 Cooper-Chen, *Mass Communication*, 5.

32 Shigenobu, *Arabu no Haru*.

33 Freeman, "Mobilizing and Demobilizing," 236.

34 Borowiec, "Writers of Wrongs"; Freeman, "Mobilizing and Demobilizing"; Kingston, "Watchdog Journalism"; Krauss, "Portraying the State"; Snow, "NHK, Abe and the World."

35 Kingston, "Watchdog Journalism"; Mulgan, "Media Muzzling."

36 Sekiguchi, "Japanese Politicians," paras. 5, 6.

37 Mulgan, "Media Muzzling"; Nakano, "Right-Wing Media."

38 Kingston, *Press Freedom*; Mulgan, "Media Muzzling." During the editing process for this chapter in 2022, Abe Shinzo was assassinated by a man named Tetsuya Yamagami using a homemade gun. That this could happen during a media event is of little surprise to those who have participated in them. The security at outdoor events especially was generally minimal.

39 Borowiec, "Writers of Wrongs," 49; Fackler, "Silencing."

40 Sieg, "Japanese Media Self-Censorship," para. 7.

41 Tsuda, *Dōin no Kakumei.*

42 eMarketer, "Strongest Markets."

43 This process foreshadowed the media climate in the contemporary United States.

44 Ōta, "Producing."

45 Ōta, "Producing," 79.

46 Ujiie, "Terebi o Minai."

47 NTV began broadcasting on August 28, 1953, months after public broadcaster NTV went on air on February 1, 1953. At the time only 866 television sets existed in Tokyo. Thus, as I describe in chapter 1, the two networks banded together to celebrate their sixtieth anniversary on February 1, 2013. Yoshimi, "Japanese Television," 540; Chun, *Hundred Million*, 109.

48 Stronach, "Japanese Television."

49 In the 1970s Kanai Nobutaka, the chairman of Fuji TV, criticized Japan's newspapers for the ramifications of this setup and claimed that the newspapers had prevented Japanese television from modernizing by protecting their own interests (see Westney, "Mass Media.") In solidarity with Kanai's assessment, industry insiders overwhelmingly gestured to the example of TBS (Tokyo Broadcasting System), whose capacity to aggressively engage new media trends was seen to be a result of comparatively weak ties to its parent company's newspaper, *Mainichi Shinbun*—which suffered from systemic financial problems that made it undesirable for its parent company to privilege it to the detriment of TBS. Indeed, by 1990 TBS's news department, TNS (Tokyo News Service), was the largest among the commercial broadcasters, able to pay the equivalent of US$12 million to send one of its TV news reporters, Akiyama Toyohiro, aboard a Russian spacecraft as Japan's first citizen in space. The resultant broadcast netted ratings of around 36 percent (Times Wire Service).

50 At the same time, Japanese television was reliably risk averse even when it came to areas less concerned with nationalistic pride. It endures what anthropologists Dominic Boyer and Cymene Howe have referred to, quoting Alexi Yurchak, as "hypernormalization" ("Portable Analytics," 12), preferring to recirculate texts that have at one point proven themselves effective and to engage in experimentation only within designated zones (such as the predictably unpredictable stunts seen on variety shows). Professionalization of TV content creators demands integration of the status quo and competent performance of representational habitus and rewards

those who best perform relative originality within accepted framing by elevating them in a rigid system of institutional rank. In other words, something of the autopoietic nature of television can be found in the production process itself. In John Caldwell's assessment, television is engaged in a constant self-referential process of metacritique, with each new product in conversation with those of the past. The insularity of Japanese television made this especially true (*Production Culture*, 1).

51 These are the national stations. In Tokyo there is also TV Tokyo, for example. An enduring impression that Fuji TV is anti-Japanese, driven by online disinformation campaigns about its relationship with Korean content, has affected perceptions of the network and resulted in it being ranked least favorably in public opinion polls (Yoshino, "Fuji wa Naze," para. 5). If this was Fuji TV's reputation despite its ownership of the conversative newspaper *Sankei Shinbun*, the other networks responsible for what has been sardonically labeled "*masugomi*"—a play on the words for mass communication (*masukomi*) and trash (*gomi*)—haven't fared much better. Although characterization of each network naturally depends on who you ask, public broadcaster NHK typically performs the best in public sentiment for its ambitious documentaries, despite recognition of its institutional conservatism (Yahoo.jp, "Geneki Terebi"; Onecareer.jp, "Gyōkai Kenkyū"). Of the others, NTV is identified in audience surveys for wide-ranging programming and for its investment in new technologies (e.g., it bought Hulu Japan). TV Asahi in turn is identified with sports and a tendency to follow rather than lead, and TBS is known for its drama series.

52 Interview, November 1, 2012.

53 Yoshino, *Fujiterebi wa Naze*.

54 Ujiie, "Terebi no Mirai."

55 Jenkins, *Convergence Culture*, 243.

56 In the interest of protecting my hosts at each of these networks, who have asked me not to identify their workplaces by name, I am obscuring locations in this text as much as possible when referring to conversations with individuals.

57 Condry, *Hip-Hop*, 6.

58 I discuss NicoNico in depth in chapter 2, and 2chan in chapter 3.

59 Gusterson, "Studying Up Revisited," 116.

60 Deuze, "Media Life," 137.

61 For more on some of the theory that informed this approach, see Postill, "Introduction."

62 Stocker, "Yoshimoto Kogyo and Manzai," 247.

63 Pharr, "Media," 37; Postill, "Introduction."

64 Hannerz, "Transnationals."

65 Mahon, "Cultural Producers."

66 For a comprehensive look at market segmentation in Japan, see Lukács, *Scripted Affects*.

67 Behar and Gordon, *Women Writing Culture*; Clifford and Marcus, *Writing Culture*.

68 User experience professionals talk about buttons a lot, including reflections on best practices for default states, appearance, placement, and so forth.

1. The Interactive Consumer-Viewer

1 Chun, *Hundred Million*; Stronach, "Japanese Television."

2 Sakai Osamu explains why this button is not the "*ii ne*" (いいね) of Facebook, but a katana "*ii*" (イイ), using the syllabary that is traditionally reserved for foreign loan words in Japanese. He writes: "It's not '*ii ne*' [in hiragana], it's '*ii*' in katakana, because Japan's Kenjiro Takayanagi, the developer of the cathode-ray tube television system, first used it to transmit a katakana '*i*'" (Sakai, Terebi wa Terebi, para. 9).

3 Nippon Hōsō Kyōkai, "Sōsharumedia."

4 Buschow, Schneider, and Ueberheide, "Tweeting Television"; Giglietto and Selva, "Second Screen and Participation"; Harrington, Highfield, and Bruns, "Backchannel."

5 Chun, *Hundred Million*, 44.

6 The STSK has since changed its name. I am declining to mention the new name here, as the group is private on social media. The ways that the STSK talked about television's potential and its future echoed the ideas of the pioneering collective TV (*Terebi*) Man Union in the 1970s. This group of former TBS network producers also authored an influential 1969 book of broadcast theory: *Omae wa tada no Genzai ni Suginai: Terebi ni Nani ga Kanō ka?* (You Are Just the Present: What Is Possible for Television?). The book was reissued in 2008 for its fortieth anniversary. Current TV Man Union members are still active in television thought leadership and attend STSK meetings.

7 These were the figures circulating around Tokyo in 2013. Also see Citation Japan Co., Ltd., "Terebi to Sōsharumedia."

8 "*Terebi shichouritsu to sosharu media (SNS to ka) o tsukainagara, terebi o miru koto no percento wa kankei ga arimasen ka?*"

9 Yamamoto, "Shibaitai."

10 NHK, "Terebi Hōsō."

11 See Allison, *Precarious Japan*.

12 Gaia Co. Ltd., "2020-Nen 5 Tsuki Kōshin."

13 Sakai, *Ikinokoreru*.

14 Sakai, *Ikinokoreru*.

15 The Gyao website can still be found at https://gyao.yahoo.co.jp/, but the page that announces the service has been terminated as of March 2023.

16 Sakai, *Ikinokoreru*.

17 Chun, *Hundred Million*; Yoshimi, "Japanese Television."

18 "*Terebi wa media no ōsama*," as he puts it.

19 The means of accounting for these kinds of viewing are different, and generally diary/survey based.

20 Yamamoto, "Shibaitai."

21 Author's field notes, March 21, 2023.

22 Moeran, *Advertising*.

23 Honma, *Dentsū to Genpatsu*.

24 Fackler was nominated for a Pulitzer Prize based on his post-Fukushima coverage. During 2013, he became a figurehead for the body of individuals critical of the press by publishing a book in Japanese—*Hontō no Koto o Tsutaenai Nihon no Shinbun* (Japanese newspapers do not tell the truth)—and giving public lectures on his post–March 11 experiences. He presents a scathing account of the *kisha* club system.

25 Cooper-Chen, *Mass Communication*; Honma, *Dentsū to Genpatsu*.

26 Honma, *Dentsū to Genpatsu*, 31.

27 Horie and Uesugi, *Terebi ni Kirawareru*.

28 Mazzarella, *Censorium*.

29 Mazzarella, *Censorium*.

30 Moeran, *Advertising*.

31 Moeran, *Advertising*, 248.

32 Moeran, *Advertising*.

33 Wolferen, *Japanese Power*, 176.

34 Bourdon and Méadel, "Inside Television," 794.

35 "*Nihon no baai, shichō-ritsu no bijinesu moderu ga ōkibona tame, tōmen wa kono ōrudo bijinesu moderu o dō kīpu suru ka ga; terebikyoku no saidai no kadai desu . . . terebi juzō-ki no shichō-ritsu ga ayashiku natte iru genzai, 'shichō-ritsu' no kangaekata o, terebi juzō-ki kara sumātofon ya pasokon made hirogete ikitai no ga*" (interview, April 2013). Shin'ichiro is a pseudonym, as are all names that are not those of named book authors or media personalities.

36 Ang, *Desperately*, 75; Video Research Ltd., "Taimushifuto."

37 Lukács, *Scripted Affects*; Moeran, *Advertising*.

38 Also see chapter 4 for a discussion of Ponta Points as used for rewards in the interactive TV program "*Bloody Tube*."

39 Chun, *Hundred Million*, 219.

40 Cubitt, "Virilio," 132.

41 South Korean programming has especially been a scapegoat for this issue in Japan. See the introduction for my mention of the protests at Fuji Television's headquarters over imported programming.

42 Mankekar, *Screening Culture*.

43 For a comprehensive examination of the segmentation into market demographics, see Lukács, *Scripted Affects*. YouTube and NicoVideo (NicoNico) are among the most popular online video sites in Japan. On-demand viewing was accepted relatively late, and it is still substantially less popular in Japan than in the United States.

44 Chun, *Hundred Million*.

45 Chun, *Hundred Million*.

46 Gracenote's parent company is the American ratings stalwart Nielsen.

47 Since 2018 Gracenote has since implemented this project in the United States and integrated it with its other Nielsen offerings. (See, for example, Nielsen, "Nielsen Expands.") Also, this is a point that was raised earlier in the chapter by Yamamoto.

48 "*Jikayōsha wa otōsan no meigi ni natteite mo kazoku zennin o noseru kagiri setai-zaidesu. Sentakuki wa kazoku zennin no ifuku o arau kagiri wa setai-zaidesu.... Kodomo-tachi ga ima ni itte kazoku minna de terebi o miru jikan ga aru kagiri, terebi wa setai-zaidesu.... Tada, sono jikan ga zuibun hette kiteiru node areba, terebi no setai-zai toshite no tokuchō wa ushinawa retsutsu aru to iubekida to omou no desu*" (Yamamoto, para. 12–13).

49 Bourdon and Méadel, "Inside Television."

50 For example, during my fieldwork I found that the industry had neglected to formulate a response to the rising ubiquity of DVRs, which allowed users to skip commercials and whose viewing metrics eluded the ratings system until 2012. After 2012, Video Research Ltd. began to solve this problem. (See "Taimushifuto shichōritsu" [Time shifted viewership], Video Research Ltd., https://www.videor.co.jp/tvrating/timeshift/backnumber/.) Even in 2013 much commentary was devoted to the implications of an estimated one-third to one-half of TV being consumed as "time shifted"—the metric varies heavily depending on the genre (Nakaoka, "Taimushifuto"). Besides the ability to view programs at one's convenience, the ability to skip commercials was cited by 2chan users as the most common reason to record television: "You can watch a one-hour program in thirty minutes!" (*Haya mawashi de miru to 1-jikan bangumi ga 30-bun gurai de mirarerushi*!, nao, "Terebi Kyoku," para. 5.) This problem will probably remain relevant with the introduction of technologies like Toshiba's Blu-Ray recorder with automatic commercial skipping, a feature likely to become normalized in DVRs and impact station revenue long-term.

51 Video Research Ltd., "Sabisu."

52 It should be noted that VR Ltd. is a subsidiary of the advertising behemoth Dentsu.

53 Video Research Ltd. describes es XMP (*īesu kurosumedia paneru*) as a tool to help advertisers understand smartphone use, engagement with brands, and the relationship between smartphone usage and television content. You can read more about the system on the company's website: "es XMP," Video Research Ltd., https://www.videor.co.jp/service/media-data/esxmp.html.

54 *Sankei News*, "20% Dai."

55 Caldwell, "Cultural Studies," 110.

56 Furuhata, *Cinema of Actuality*, 5.

57 Kitada and Schäfer, "Media/Communication Studies," 429.

58 A Frankfurt School joke that makes itself.

59 Sakai, "Terebi wa Terebi," para. 17, 24.

60 "*Ima masa ni terebi to iu media no furēmu o mojidōri kowasou to shite iru.*" Sakai, "Terebi wa Terebi," para. 25.

61 Boyer and Howe, "Portable Analytics," 30.

62 This is a pseudonym. Because the membership of this group is not public facing (apart from Sakai Osamu), I am deliberately not identifying this presenter.

63 "*Kaiketsusaku wa AR desu.*"

64 This Asahi Broadcasting app was based on an anime series of the same name and was released in 2013 (for iPhone, and later for Android). It has gone through a few iterations since and is now called *Mahōtsukai Purikyua*.

65 For example, the essays in Carpentier, Schrøder, and Hallett, *Audience Transformations*; Evans, "Engaging Screens"; Hill, "Push–Pull Dynamics"; Livingstone, "Active Audiences?"

66 For a useful summary of research as it pertains to the United States, see Parigi and Henson, "Social Isolation in America." And for a counterpoint in Japan, see Tateno et al., "Internet Addiction."

67 Lukács, *Scripted Affects*.

68 Ang, *Desperately*.

69 Ratings for this program exceeded 30 percent, a figure that was generally described as belonging to the television of yesteryear.

70 Email interview, March 2014.

71 Seaver, "Captivating Algorithms."

2. Interactivity and Gatekeeping

1   NicoNico (nicovideo.jp), which contains the NicoNico Douga and NicoNico Namahōsō sections, was generally referred to affectionately as "*nicodō*" by both mainstream and independent journalists during my fieldwork. I have historically used the acronym NND to refer to the site in English, in a nod to the *nicodō* nickname, but I have updated it here to NN to refer to the service (app/website) in general. I have also capitalized the name for the sake of readability though the romanized logo is in all lowercase letters (niconico), or sometimes Niconico.

2   When it first launched, NicoNico relied on YouTube to host its videos, but it sent so much traffic to YouTube that it was eventually blocked and forced to relaunch with its own video streaming capabilities.

3 Lore holds that those who listened to this debate on the radio thought Nixon to have won, while those who watched on TV thought Kennedy to have won. This theory has been refuted by media scholars (see Schudson, *Power of News*), but the idea persists and was mentioned on *The Compass*.

4 Koh, "Twitter CEO."

5 A user poll featured at the end showed that 78.9 percent of NN users thought the program was "very good" (*totemo yokatta*) and 17.6 percent indicated that it was "pretty good" (*ma ma yokatta*).

6 The assembled personnel included the general manager of Fuji TV's Information Production Center (*Jōhō Seisaku Sentā*) and some of his staff.

7 Auslander, "Digital Liveness," 3.

8 Taylor, "Television 2.0," 1.

9 Parks, "Flexible Microcasting," 133.

10 Fuwa, "Yūchūbu"; Dwango, *Introducing Niconico*; Dwango, "Nikoniko."

11 Work-Data, "Nikoniko Dōga"; Dwango, *Introducing Niconico*.

12 NicoNico, "2019 Dēta." When I wrote to NicoNico's parent company Dwango asking for more updated data, they replied that this was still the most recent they had.

13 "*Sōhōkō-sei ni nareta sedai wa, terebi wa oshitsukegamashī to kanjirun janai deshou ka.*" (*Asahi Shimbun*, "Netto ni Makenai.")

14 Tsuda, *Dōin no Kakumei*.

15 Kitada, "Cynical," 79. I return to this again in the next chapter.

16 Parks, "Flexible Microcasting," 138.

17 Parks, "Flexible Microcasting."

18 Quoted in Auslander, "Digital Liveness," 6.

19 Gripsrud, "Broadcast Television," 213.

20 Auslander, "Digital Liveness," 6, 8.

21 Fieldnotes, July 7, 2013.

22 Lubarsky, "Ten O'Clock," 313.

23 Perreault and Ferrucci, "What Is Digital Journalism?"

24 Kitada and Zahlten discuss the distinction between *baitai* and *media* in depth when analyzing the Kantian media theory of Nakai Masakazu (see Kitada and Zahlten, "Meaning").

25 Hagimoto, Muraki, and Konno, *Tada no Genzai ni Suginai*, 194.

26 Kitada and Zahlten, "Meaning," 89–90.

27 To this end, the topic was raised more than fifty years ago in the above-mentioned book by the founders of TV Man Union (Hagimoto, Muraki, and Konno). The authors initiated and informed the discussion about what is possible through

television and what is limited by the nature of the medium and the nature of the media makers themselves.

28 Boudana, "A Definition of Journalistic Objectivity."

29 Boudana, "A Definition of Journalistic Objectivity," 386.

30 Oi and Sako, *Journalists*, 2. A special thank-you to Tanjev Schultz for calling my attention to this survey.

31 Eki, personal email, November 24, 2014.

32 Uricchio, "Television's Next Generation."

33 *"Tekunorojī wa kakujitsu ni shinpo shimasu."*

34 *"Terebi no mirai wa akumade kontentsu no seisaku nōryoku ni sayū sareru to omoimasu."*

35 *"Terebi ga shichō-sha ni taishite geigō shiteiru to omoimasu."*

36 Author's field notes, November 27, 2012.

37 Mazzarella, *Shoveling Smoke*.

38 Anstead and O'Loughlin, "Emerging Viewertariat"; Carpentier and De Cleen, "Bringing Discourse"; Doughty, Rowland, and Lawson, "Sofa"; van Dijck, "Users Like You?"

39 Gripsrud, "Broadcast Television."

40 Caldwell, *Production Culture*.

41 This worst-case scenario happened in England, where the mobile app associated with *The Singer Takes It All* failed during the program's first episode.

42 Galloway, "Unworkable," 946.

43 Luhmann, *Art as a Social System*, 57.

44 Ihlebæk and Krumsvik, "Editorial Power," 472.

45 Hill, "Media Audiences"; Evans, *Transmedia*; Ang, *Desperately*; Carpentier, "Concept of Participation"; Carpentier, Schrøder, and Hallett, *Audience Transformations*; Livingstone, "Active Audiences?"; Morley, "Unanswered Questions"; Ytre-Arne and Das, "Agenda."

46 Ang, *Desperately*; Carpentier, "Concept of Participation"; Carpentier, Schrøder, and Hallett, *Audience Transformations*; Evans, *Transmedia*; Hill, "Media Audiences"; Livingstone, "Active Audiences?"; Morley, "Unanswered Questions"; Ytre-Arne and Das, "Agenda."

3. Cultures of Independent Journalism

1 I specifically chose to refer to them as "cameramen" rather than "camera operators" or another gender-neutral term, because in Japan I never met anyone other than male-identified individuals in this role, and I want to draw attention to the ways that heteronormative masculinity was a core component of their professional discourse.

2 Since then, Dwango has been acquired by Japanese media conglomerate Kadokawa Corporation and is now a subsidiary of that company.

3   The American web-streaming company UStream was acquired in 2016 by IBM, and became IBM Cloud Video, then IBM Watson Media.

4   Although the word for misinformation would typically be Romanized as *"gohō,"* the group wrote its name as "GoHoo" on the website and promotional materials.

5   *"Masukomi no hōdō o chekku suru."* Employing fact-checkers is one of the main strategies proposed in a policy brief by the European Research Council (2021–2022) to fight extreme speech and disinformation online. See Udupa et al., *Extreme Speech* (LMU Munich 2021), 17.

6   Russell, *Journalism as Activism*, 7.

7   The FPAJ operated through donations and a partnership with Dwango, NicoNico's parent company. One of my jobs as an intern for the Free Press Association was to translate its financial records into English to send them to fund-raising site globalgiving.org, which reviews this information and vets organizations before accepting them as partners. Thus, I can confirm that its funding came from individuals, though donations ranged in size. (For more on the FPAJ and its solicitation of donations, one of its founders wrote a useful explanation on his blog: Hatakeyama, "Jiyū Hōdō Kyōkai o Yameta.") The FPAJ's infrastructure was therefore relatively pared down: a one-room Kojimachi office in the heart of many reporters' beats, and a rented press conference room open to TV cameras and internet live streaming. Its camera setup closely resembled that of other Tokyo media start-ups in using lightweight consumer-grade video cameras rather than the bulky equipment favored by the television industry.

8   Here Uesugi is referring to Yasumi's Independent Web Journal (IWJ), discussed in this chapter, and Shiraishi Hajime's Our Planet-TV, discussed in chapter 5.

9   *"Shuzai katsudo wa dekinai to iu funiki."*

10   Uesugi, "Free Press Association."

11   Yamaguchi, "Xenophobia."

12   *"Amerika no bai wa, korekushon shite iu pēji ga mainichi aru desu ne,"* interview, April 2013.

13   For example, a Japanese-language version of the *Huffington Post*, run by major Japanese national newspaper *Asahi Shinbun*, launched during my fieldwork.

14   Whether one considers the press to be offensively conservative or offensively liberal depends on the corners of the internet one frequents. Participants in the anonymous 2chan forum (discussed in this chapter) claimed that the mainstream media is too left-wing (Yamaguchi, "Xenophobia," 105).

15   *"Kifu bunka ga nai"* (There is no donation culture), I was often told. Anthropologist Anne Allison learned the same thing during a pre-2011 group interview she conducted with college students in Japan. One student stated, "We Japanese don't volunteer; it's not part of the tradition," and the others agreed. Moreover, they elaborated that giving money to a homeless person on the street (for example) would feel shameful to both parties (Allison, *Precarious Japan*, 146). In Allison's understanding, this way of thinking was informed in part by the Reaganesque

neoliberal policies of former Japanese prime minister Koizumi Junichiro, whose notion of *jiko sekinin* (self-responsibility) meant that citizens should not expect help from others and ought to likewise refuse support to them.

16 Peterson, "Getting to the Story," 201.

17 Perreault and Ferrucci, "What Is Digital Journalism?," 1301; Eldridge, "Where Do We Draw the Line?," 10.

18 Dickinson and Memon, "Press Clubs," 617.

19 Kingston, "Watchdog Journalism."

20 Reporters without Borders, "Japan: Tradition and Business Interests"; Reporters without Borders, "Japan | RSF."

21 Reporters without Borders, "2014: Asia-Pacific," paras. 10–11.

22 Borowiec, "Writers of Wrongs," 50; Kingston, "Watchdog Journalism."

23 Borowiec, "Writers of Wrongs"; Freeman, *Closing the Shop*; Kingston, "Watchdog Journalism"; Krauss, "Changing Television News in Japan"; Snow, "NHK, Abe and the World."

24 Borowiec, "Writers of Wrongs"; Freeman, *Closing the Shop*; Krauss, "Portraying the State"; Yamakawa, "Kisha Kurabu."

25 Borowiec, "Writers of Wrongs," 49.

26 Under the formerly conventional model of lifetime employment in Japan, where seniority determined promotion and employees spent their entire professional lives among the same individuals, antagonism led to guaranteed misery.

27 Farley, "Japan's Press"; Freeman, *Closing the Shop*.

28 Krauss, "Changing Television News in Japan."

29 Tsuda, *Dōin no Kakumei*, 129.

30 Freeman, *Closing the Shop*, 238.

31 Freeman, *Closing the Shop*, 241.

32 Nippon.com, "Shinbun Yomanai."

33 This was before the recent increase in research and journalistic attention to the ways that social media facilitates the circulation of misinformation, and its effects on politics and the COVID-19 pandemic.

34 OurPlanet-TV, "Kokkai Kisha Kaikan."

35 OurPlanet-TV, "Kokkai Kisha Kaikan."

36 Field notes, September 12, 2012.

37 Boyer, *Life Informatic*.

38 Although Yanai tells me GoHoo does have a VCR for recording television, the effort required to review content each day was daunting.

39 Freeman, *Closing the Shop*, 238.

40 Iwakami et al., "Media Akutibizumu."

41 Referred to in Japanese as *indipendento* or *furī* (free) *jānarisumu*. For more about the definition of independent journalism, refer to this book's introduction.

42 Allison, *Millennial Monsters.*

43 Tsuda, *Dōin no Kakumei*, 41–42. For more on youth activism in Japan see, for example, O'Day, "Differentiating SEALDS."

44 Yamaguchi, "Xenophobia," 104, 109.

45 Hamano, *Ākitekucha*, 195–240; Kitada, "Cynical." The site 2channeru (2Channel) was originally located on 2ch.net, and now is located on 2ch.sc and 5ch.net after an international tug-of-war over the domain. The forum was launched in 1999 and allowed users to post anonymously about a wide range of topics. The forum 2chan is known as the home of the right-wing internet trolls in Japan, the *netto uyoku*, and spawned a similar American (English-language) counterpart, 4chan. (For more information see Sakamoto, "Koreans, Go Home!"; Yamaguchi, "Xenophobia"; Kaigo, "Aggregators.")

46 Kitada, "Cynical," 79.

47 Uesugi, "Free Press Association," para. 6.

48 O'Day, "Differentiating SEALDS," 111; Yamaguchi, "Xenophobia," 111. In brief, the *freeters* are a youth movement of part-time, irregular, and temporary workers in Japan. The Students' Emergency Action for Liberal Democracy (SEALDs) were a student activist group organized in protest of then–prime minister Abe Shinzo's government and its policies.

49 Motoki, "Naze Kisha Kurabu."

50 Cooper-Chen, *Mass Communication.*

51 Kitada, "Cynical," 72.

52 Nihon Shinbun Kyōkai Henshū Iinkai, "Kisha Kurabu Ni Kansuru."

53 This was true in my experience of seeing footage from the FCCJ and FPAJ incorporated into mainstream television broadcast. Even when you could see the FPAJ's logo screen in the background, it was never acknowledged.

54 Aşık, "Politics, Power, and Performativity," 589.

55 Since the immediate post-Fukushima years, Uesugi has run for governor of Tokyo (2016) and now serves as secretary-general for the Party to Protect the People from NHK (NHK kara Kokumin o Mamoru Tō).

56 Standing in the back of the room for lack of available seating, one TV network reporter commented, "This event is utterly unique to the FPAJ. Nobody else is having an event where all of the candidates are in one place and debating one another, so all of us [journalists] are here." Network logo–branded and bulky news cameras filled the back of the room, and the telltale din of numerous clicking keyboards and camera shutters created a semiotic indication of newsworthiness by their presence. The interns and FPAJ representatives dressed in suits underscored the gravity of the conference as event.

57 See Ahmad, "Twitter"; Metag and Rauchfleisch, "Political Tweets"; Molyneux, "What Journalists Retweet"; Vis, "Twitter."

58 "Yomiuri," nicovideo.jp.

59 "Uesugi Takashi, Iwakami Yasumi."

60 Eldridge, "Where Do We Draw the Line?"

61 Blaagaard, "Shifting Boundaries."

62 As Kitada explains, "The term is derived from *uyoku* (right-wingers) and *chuubou* (middle-school kids), and refers to those who indulge themselves in immature, extremely reactionary postings" ("Cynical," 80–81).

63 Participants in the online forums, which consistently discussed Uesugi, criticized him as neither genuinely right nor left wing, but an opportunist. (See "Uesugi Takashi 122.")

64 Auslander, "Digital Liveness," 6.

65 Hatakeyama, "Jiyū Hōdō Kyōkai o Yameta."

66 Uesugi, *Kokka no Haji*, 188–89.

67 Figenschou and Ihlebæk, "Challenging," 1231.

68 This statement was issued in a February 20, 2013, email to supporters.

69 Manning and Gershon, "Animating Interaction." Also see Tucker et al., "From Liberation to Turmoil."

70 Yamaguchi, "Xenophobia"; Kaigo, "Aggregators"; Kurahashi, "Netto Uyoku."

71 Yamaguchi, "Xenophobia"; Kurahashi, "Netto Uyoku"; quote in Kitada, "Cynical," 81.

72 Yamaguchi, "Xenophobia," 111.

73 Dickey, "Anthropology and Its Contributions," 418.

74 Allison, *Millennial Monsters*, 187.

75 Boyer, "Digital Expertise"; Boyer, *Life Informatic*; Dickey, "Anthropology and Its Contributions."

76 Hatakeyama, "Jiyū Hōdō Kyōkai o Yameta," para. 32.

77 He later also founded Garden Journalism (https://gardenjournalism.com/) with a similar goal of expanding the range of journalistic content available in Japan and providing freelance journalists a space to contribute.

78 Hori, "Ima Koso Motomerareru Ōpun Jānarizumu."

4. The New Interactive Television

1 If you search on "Arashi feat. You" and/or "The Music Day Ongaku No Chikara" on YouTube, you can find a video of the show.

2 Hulu moved into Japan in 2011, and Netflix followed in 2015. Currently Amazon is the lead in streaming services, followed by Netflix and Hulu.

3   Kitada, *Nihon no "Nashonarizumu."*

4   Fujitani, "Electronic Pageantry." Concerning fandom in Japanese media, see the essays in Kelly, *Fanning the Flames*, which thoroughly and effectively unpack this topic.

5   Kitada and Schäfer, "Media/Communication Studies," 412.

6   Hambleton, "Reinforcing."

7   Martin, "Japanese Television Network," para. 1.

8   The figure published on the NTV website is 1,372,311 participants with 171,733,624 button pushes (Martin, "Japanese Television Network").

9   Galbraith and Karlin, "Introduction," 1.

10 Kitada and Schäfer, "Media/Communication Studies," 429. As you will see in chapter 5 though, they did catch on; Our Planet-TV founder Shiraishi Hajime invokes the public sphere in her writing about media.

11 "Kokuseki chikibetsu"; Burgess, "Multicultural Japan?"; Narzary, "The Myths of Japanese Homogeneity."

12 Yoshimi, "Television and Nationalism."

13 Painter, "Japanese Daytime Television," 300.

14 Koichi Iwabuchi emphasizes the scripted and controlled nature of talk shows: "Talk shows are highly stage-managed and controlled by the production side" (Iwabuchi, "Ordinary Foreigners," 41).

15 Furukawa, "Stupidest." I will also add that I sat in on many production meetings for the NHK show *Cool Japan* and observed tapings in the studio. The premise of the show is essentially to introduce non-Japanese visitors to the country to something interesting about Japan and film their reactions. Topics during my observation ranged from Japanese beef (*wagyū*) to calligraphy (*shodō*). The non-Japanese guests for each episode essentially had the job of performing amazement at the cultural product chosen for that episode. A truly entertaining show that launched on TV Tokyo around the same time was called *You wa Nani Shi ni Nippon e?* (Why did you come to Japan?) and followed foreigners arriving at Narita International Airport (usually) on their journey around the country.

16 During its research symposium in 2013, NHK mentioned that QB47 had exceeded the ratings of even the massive annual TV event *Kohaku Uta Gassen*. The program therefore became a series (NHK Hōsō Bunka Kenkyūjo, "2013-Nen Kenkyū").

17 You can read more about the program on Bascule's archive page for the show, "Bloody Tube," at https://bascule.co.jp/work/bloody-tube/; or visit the site the company made to commemorate it, Bloody Tube, at http://pieces.newers.net/2013/bloodytube/en/.

18 As of late 2022, a copy of this advertisement could still be found at "Bascule Inc.—Bloody Tube," YouTube video, 2:00, https://www.youtube.com/watch?v=Nsn_gfomSKw.

19 When an individual *tarento* is at their peak, as determined by NHK surveys, they are on TV more often than not, moving between multiple programs and, occasionally, inadvertently appearing on more than one network at the same time. As many *owarai tarento* are known for one "shtick" in particular, to fail to recognize the signified meaning to which they gesture is to be naive in the face of humor that expects and rewards regular television viewing. For example, being able to identify the costumes, scandals, and events of the massively popular Japanese idol band AKB48 was essential to understanding comedian Kintarō's entire routine when she became a fixture on variety shows in 2012 (Cooper-Chen, *Mass Communication*, 122). This "insider literacy" that TV demands arises from the medium's self-referentiality, and this rewarded viewers who were able to access programmatic "subtext" and "access information external to the media at hand" (Kitada, "Cynical," 74). Frequently, this best described the participants in Japan's anonymous online forums, who used this literacy to approach both independent and mainstream media with cynical humor.

20 Galbraith and Karlin, "Introduction," 2–3, 8.

21 Galbraith and Karlin, "Introduction," 47.

22 Painter, "Japanese Daytime Television," 297.

23 Field notes, July 7, 2013.

24 Jenkins, *Convergence Culture*, 177.

25 Stevens and Hosokawa, "So Close," 236–37.

26 Stevens and Hosokawa, "So Close."

27 Galbraith and Karlin, "Introduction," 16.

28 Iwabuchi, "Ordinary Foreigners," 41.

29 This tension recalls the classic debate between John Dewey and Walter Lippmann in the 1920s, when the duo debated the rationality of humankind and whether democracy would function better if managed by elites (Lippmann) or reimagined as a more participatory form of democracy (Dewey). This captures well the stance of the mainstream Japanese media companies (Lippmann) vs. the independent media (Dewey).

30 Kitada and Zahlten talk about how influential Japanese media theorists like Nakai Masakazu rooted their discussions of the difference between medium and media (*baitai/media*) in Kantian philosophy, and indeed Kant has had a major influence on Japanese theory. Hence my nod to it here (Kitada and Zahlten, "Meaning," 89).

31 An encore aired on April 3, 2014, also shortly before midnight.

32 Postill, "Introduction."

33 "Work," Bascule, March 8, 2023, https://bascule.co.jp/work/. As of late 2022, you could still find it on Fuji TV's website: The Last Award, https://www.fujitv.co.jp/b_hp/thelastaward/.

34 The Association for the Promotion of Digital Broadcasting is known as DPA, or Ippan Shadanhōjin Dejitaru Hōsō Suishin Kyōkai.

35 "*Boku wa ojīchan, obāchan to 3 sedai de kurashite ita node terebi o miru toki ojīchan to itsumo channeru arasoi o shite imashita*" (Ippan Shadanhōjin Dejitaru Hōsō Suishin Kyōkai, digital broadcast, 2013).

36 This is an interesting counterpoint to arguments about the domestication of entertainment breaking down social connection as in Putnam, *Bowling Alone*, 216.

37 Muehlebach and Shoshan, "Introduction."

38 Sakai, *Ikinokoreru*, 10, 49–50. In chapter 1 I engage in a lengthier discussion of these points and elaborate more on Sakai's role.

39 "*Kotoba toshite wa "ribingurūmu" no hō ga fusawashī darou*" (Sakai, *Ikinokoreru*, 49).

40 Sakai, *Ikinokoreru*, 10.

41 Field notes, January 20, 2013.

42 Mazzarella, *Censorium*, 48.

43 Couldry, *Media Rituals*.

44 For the full description of this program, see "Meteor Station," Bascule, https://bascule.co.jp/work/ryusei-tv/.

45 Berlant, *Cruel Optimism*, 226.

5. Teaching Citizen Journalism

1 In Japanese these were called "*Eizō seisaku wākushoppu*." The organization can be found at Our Planet-TV, http://www.ourplanet-tv.org/.

2 Shiraishi, *Bideokamera*.

3 See, for example, Lindner, "Editorial Gatekeeping."

4 Shiraishi writes about this throughout her book *Media o Tsukuru*.

5 In 2014, Our Planet-TV received the Japanese Association of Science and Technology Journalists' "JASTJ Prize," for its film about TEPCO (Tokyo Electric Power Company), beating out national broadcaster NHK for this award.

6 Eldridge, "Where Do We Draw the Line?"; Holt and Karlsson, "Random Acts"; Karlsson and Holt, "Is Anyone out There?"

7 Postill, "Introduction."

8 In November 2012, the IWJ relocated to a spacious new set of offices in the Roppongi neighborhood of Tokyo, with rows of new computers and news tables, and a separate suite for Iwakami to conduct live-streamed interviews. A box of common-use slippers sat by the door to the main office. While I once memorably knocked a cup of coffee into one of the IWJ laptops in the tight quarters of the old office, here I was able to conduct eight more months of fieldwork without knocking over a single thing. And I almost always had my own desk.

9 I am thinking here of the (Gramscian) intellectuals as knowledge producers, discussed by Dominic Boyer in *Spirit and System*, 44.

10 Blaagaard, "Shifting Boundaries," 1088 (emphasis in original).

11 Inai, "Terebi wa Nan."

12 Anderson, *Imagined Communities*; Warner, "Publics."

13 Blaagaard, "Shifting Boundaries," 1078.

14 Honma, *Dentsū to Genpatsu*.

15 Ashcroft, "Television Conspiracy"; Raibudoa Nyūsu, "Terebibangu."

16 He was describing a simple shot/reverse-shot process.

17 Caldwell alludes to this in his work ("Para-Industry," 160), when addressing the relentless physical demands of television production.

18 "*IWJ wa hotondo waiyaresu maiku o tsukaimasu*."

19 This differs from a process like closed-captioning because it is used only to highlight key information, including words emphasized for comedic effect.

20 Again, this is addressed significantly in the "media as practice" literature of anthropology: see Postill, "Introduction."

21 I have seen this done most self-consciously by American reality TV, whose producers aggressively sculpt interviews.

22 Boyer, *Life Informatic*; Dornfeld, *Producing Public Television*.

23 Boyer, "Digital Expertise"; Ihlebæk and Krumsvik, "Editorial Power"; Perreault and Ferrucci, "What Is Digital Journalism?"; Lewis, Kaufhold, and Lasorsa, "Thinking about Citizen Journalism."

24 The Our Planet group's finished documentary incorporates an interview conducted with Koshino Sensei's colleagues even though the telephone rings incessantly in the background. By contrast, a series of motorcycles roaring behind an interviewee for a television news segment are only faintly picked up by the high-quality boom mic, and had this not been the case, the footage would have likely been discarded before broadcast.

25 Here I use "camera operator" rather than "cameraman" to refer to the practice of recording video beyond the (male) gendered labor of the television networks.

26 "*Hontō ni yoku dekita mono ga ōkute*."

27 The title was actually "*Kotoba o Tsunagu, Kotoba de Tsunagaru*" in Japanese.

28 Ang, *Desperately*; Dornfeld, *Producing Public Television*.

29 "Interloper media" is a term used by Scott Eldridge in his article "Where Do We Draw the Line?"

30 Sontag, *Pain of Others*.

31 Dornfeld, *Producing Public Television*.

32 The feeling of the scene and the process of filming reminded me of Luke Goode's 2009 article "Social News."

33 Inspired by its use in the film *V for Vendetta*, the Guy Fawkes mask was appropriated by the hacker/activist group Anonymous and has in many ways come to

be associated with protest in general. For a thorough description of this trope see Coleman, *Hacker, Hoaxer*.

34 "Echo objects" is the title of a book by Barbara Stafford. She uses this term to capture how complex images, patterns, and symbols become mental objects through our prior associations with their context. Hers is an argument that seeks to bring the humanities together with neuroscientific research—a project that is very close to my heart (see Stafford, *Echo Objects*).

35 Everett, "Double Click," 233.

36 Patricia Mellencamp, quoted in Everett, "Double Click," 232; Shiraishi, *Media o Tsukuru*.

37 This is a term I borrowed from Mark Deuze's article "Participation, Remediation, Bricolage."

Conclusion

1 Konno, "Kanōsei no Teiji," 91.

2 Uricchio, "Television's Next Generation," 165.

3 It is not as though live streams in the model of the FPAJ and IWJ haven't been tried on television. In the United States C-SPAN comes to mind. But this is generally not a lucrative practice.

4 *Interview*, July 7, 2011.

5 The 2020 Olympics in Tokyo was rescheduled to 2021 because of the COVID-19 pandemic. Even with the delay, it was still controversial to hold an event with such a high volume of international traffic amid a surge in COVID cases in Japan.

6 Neikirk, "For Japan."

7 Brasor, "No Clear Picture."

8 *Kyodo News*, "Bujoku-zai."

9 Ang, *Desperately*, 18.

10 Ganti, "Ethnography"; e.g., Englehart, "Media Activism"; Kazi, "Religious Television"; Matza, "Moscow's Echo"; Avilés, "Audience Participation."

11 Shigenobu, *Arabu no Haru*.

12 Rodwell, "Open Access, Closed Systems."

13 Cooper-Chen, *Mass Communication*, 208.

14 Lukács, "Dreamwork"; Ujiie, "Terebi no Mirai."

15 Ujiie, "Terebi o Minai."

16 Ministry of Internal Affairs and Communications, *Omona Media*.

17 Senden Kaigi, "Jikeiretsu."

18 Avilés, "Audience Participation."

19 Müller, "Formatted Spaces."

20 Hartley, "Republic of Letters," 402.

21 Hartley, "Republic of Letters," 403.

22 Hall, *Encoding*.

23 Jenkins, *Poachers*.

24 Rancière, *Emancipated Spectator*.

25 Eco, "Semiotic Inquiry," 4.

26 Rancière, *Emancipated Spectator*, 59.

27 Hill, "Media Audiences."

28 Fujitani, "Electronic Pageantry," 832.

29 That is, Kant, Hegel, and Schiller. Kantian aesthetics in particular was taken up by Nakai, *Zenshū* (e.g., vol. 3), and through Kitada Akihiro and Alex Zahlten, e.g., "Meaning."

30 Tsutaya is a massive media retail chain in Japan, which still distributes physical DVDs in addition to hosting streaming content, following Netflix's original model.

31 Interview, November 14, 2012.

32 Müller, "Formatted Spaces."

33 Andrejevic, "Webcam Subculture."

34 Focus group, July 31, 2013, Tokyo, Japan.

35 For audience assessments, see Hill, "Push–Pull Dynamics"; Hill, "Media Audiences and Reception Studies"; Hall, *Encoding*. For ethnographic fieldwork, see for example Dornfeld, *Producing Public Television*; Abu-Lughod, *Dramas of Nationhood*; Moll, "Television Is Not Radio."

36 Figenschou and Ihlebæk, "Challenging"; Figenschou and Ihlebæk, "Media Criticism"; Holt, Ustad Figenschou, and Frischlich, "Dimensions."

37 Boyer, *Life Informatic*; Barnard, "Tweet."

38 Bird, "Future."

39 Warner, "Publics" 62.

40 Warner, "Publics," 66.

41 Ideally this relationship, mediated by buttons, should avoid the "uncanny valley of unbalanced interactivity" described of a 2017 smartphone app experiment called HQ Trivia, where audiences could ask trivia questions and chat in real time (Sauter, "HG Trivia"). HQ Trivia is still around, though in a pared-down form.

42 Boellstorff, *Coming of Age*, 31.

43 Rausch, *Local Newspapers*, 119.

44 An example of how activist-journalists are doing so can be found in Russell, *Activism*.

BIBLIOGRAPHY

Abu-Lughod, Lila. *Dramas of Nationhood: The Politics of Television in Egypt*. Chicago: University of Chicago Press, 2008.

Ahmad, Ali Nobil. "Is Twitter a Useful Tool for Journalists?" *Journal of Media Practice* 11, no. 2 (January 1, 2010): 145–55.

Allison, Anne. *Millennial Monsters: Japanese Toys and the Global Imagination*. Berkeley: University of California Press, 2006.

Allison, Anne. *Precarious Japan*. Durham, NC: Duke University Press, 2013.

Anderson, Benedict. *Imagined Communities: Reflections on the Origin and Spread of Nationalism*. New York: Verso, 2006.

Andrejevic, Mark. "The Webcam Subculture and the Digital Enclosure." In *MediaSpace: Place, Scale and Culture in a Media Age*, edited by Nick Couldry and Anna McCarthy, 193–208. London: Routledge, 2003.

Ang, Ien. *Desperately Seeking the Audience*. New York: Routledge, 1991.

Anstead, Nick, and Ben O'Loughlin. "The Emerging Viewertariat and BBC Question Time: Television Debate and Real-Time Commenting Online." *International Journal of Press/Politics* 16, no. 4 (July 25, 2011): 440–62.

Asahi Shimbun. "Netto ni Makenai 'Daradara Chikara' Mo Ikasu Terebi no Dai Fukkatsu" [A revival of TV that makes the most of its 'dull power' to compete with the internet]. *Asahi Shimbun* (Tokyo), February 15, 2013. Accessed May 5, 2023. https://web.archive.org/web/20130510153522/http://astand.asahi.com/webshinsho/asahipub/aera/product/2013021200006.html.

Ashcroft, Brian. "This Japanese Television Conspiracy Has Familiar Faces." *Kotaku*. July 9, 2014. http://kotaku.com/the-japanese-television-conspiracy-1602285870.

Aşık, Ozan. "Politics, Power, and Performativity in the Newsroom: An Ethnography of Television Journalism in Turkey." *Media, Culture and Society* 41, no. 5 (2019): 587–603.

Auslander, Philip. "Digital Liveness: A Historico-Philosophical Perspective." *PAJ: A Journal of Performance and Art* 34, no. 3 (September 2012): 3–11.

Avilés, Jose Alberto Garcia. "Roles of Audience Participation in Multiplatform Television: From Fans and Consumers, to Collaborators and Activists." *Participations: Journal of Audience and Reception Studies* 9, no. 12 (2012): 429–47.

Barnard, Stephen R. "'Tweet or Be Sacked': Twitter and the New Elements of Journalistic Practice." *Journalism* 17, no. 2 (October 9, 2014): 190–207. http://journals.sagepub.com/doi/10.1177/1464884914553079.

Behar, Ruth, and Deborah A. Gordon. *Women Writing Culture.* Berkeley: University of California Press, 1995.

Berlant, Lauren. *Cruel Optimism.* Durham, NC: Duke University Press, 2011.

Bird, Elizabeth. "The Future of Journalism in the Digital Environment." *Journalism* 10, no. 3 (2009): 293–95.

Blaagaard, Bolette B. "Shifting Boundaries: Objectivity, Citizen Journalism and Tomorrow's Journalists." *Journalism: Theory, Practice and Criticism* 14, no. 8 (2013): 1076–90.

Boellstorff, Tom. *Coming of Age in Second Life: An Anthropologist Explores the Virtually Human.* Princeton, NJ: Princeton University Press, 2008.

Borowiec, Steven. "Writers of Wrongs." *Index on Censorship* 45, no. 2 (June 29, 2016): 48–50.

Boudana, Sandrine. "A Definition of Journalistic Objectivity as a Performance." *Media, Culture and Society* 33, no. 3 (April 19, 2011): 385–98. https://dx.doi.org/10.1177/0163443710394899.

Bourdon, Jérôme, and Cécile Méadel. "Inside Television Audience Measurement: Deconstructing the Ratings Machine." *Media, Culture and Society* 33, no. 5 (2011): 791–800.

Boyer, Dominic. "Digital Expertise in Online Journalism (and Anthropology)." *Anthropological Quarterly* 83, no. 1 (2010): 73–96.

Boyer, Dominic. *The Life Informatic: Newsmaking in the Digital Era.* Ithaca, NY: Cornell University Press, 2013.

Boyer, Dominic. *Spirit and System: Media, Intellectuals, and the Dialectic in Modern German Culture.* Chicago: University of Chicago Press, 2005.

Boyer, Dominic, and Cymene Howe. "Portable Analytics and Lateral Theory." In *Theory Can Be More Than It Used to Be: Learning Anthropology's Method in a Time of Transition,* edited by Dominic Boyer, James D. Faubion, and George E. Marcus. Ithaca, NY: Cornell University Press, 2015.

Brasor, Philip. "No Clear Picture on 4K and 8K Display Differences." *Japan Times,* October 12, 2019. https://www.japantimes.co.jp/news/2019/10/12/national/media-national/no-clear-picture-4k-8k-display-differences/.

Burgess, Chris. "Multicultural Japan? Discourse and the Myth of Homogeneity." *Asia-Pacific Journal: Japan Focus* 5, no. 3 (2007): 1–25.

Buschow, Christopher, Beate Schneider, and Simon Ueberheide. "Tweeting Television: Exploring Communication Activities on Twitter While Watching TV." *Communications* 39, no. 2 (2014): 129–49.

Caldwell, John. "Cultural Studies of Media Production: Critical Industrial Practices." In *Questions of Method in Cultural Studies,* edited by Mimi White and James Schwoch, 109–53. Malden, MA: Blackwell Publishing, 2006.

Caldwell, John. "Para-Industry: Researching Hollywood's Blackwaters." *Cinema Journal* 52, no. 3 (2013): 157–65.

Caldwell, John. *Production Culture: Industrial Reflexivity and Critical Practice in Film and Television*. Durham, NC: Duke University Press, 2008.

Carpentier, Nico. "The Concept of Participation. If They Have Access and Interact, Do They Really Participate?" *Fronteiras—Estudos Midiáticos* 14, no. 2 (August 31, 2012): 1–14.

Carpentier, Nico, and Benjamin De Cleen. "Bringing Discourse Theory into Media Studies: The Applicability of Discourse Theoretical Analysis (DTA) for the Study of Media Practises and Discourses." *Journal of Language and Politics* 6, no. 2 (January 1, 2007): 265–93.

Carpentier, Nico, Kim Christian Schrøder, and Lawrie Hallett, eds. *Audience Transformations: Shifting Audience Positions in Late Modernity*. New York: Routledge, 2014.

Chun, Jayson Makoto. *"A Nation of a Hundred Million Idiots?": A Social History of Japanese Television, 1953–1973*. New York: Routledge, 2006.

Citation Japan Co., Ltd. "Terebi to Sōsharumedia no Kankei-Sei: Jishu Chōsa Kekka" [Relationship between TV and social media: Voluntary survey results]. Citation Japan Co., Ltd., 2020. https://tinyurl.com/75z228b8.

Clammer, John. "Consuming Bodies: Constructing and Representing the Female Body in Contemporary Japanese Print Media." In *Women and Media Consumption in Japan*, edited by Lisa Skov and Brian Moeran, 197–219. New York: Routledge, 1995.

Clifford, James, and George E. Marcus, eds. *Writing Culture: The Poetics and Politics of Ethnography*. Berkeley: University of California Press, 1986.

Coleman, Gabriella. *Hacker, Hoaxer, Whistleblower, Spy: The Many Faces of Anonymous*. New York: Verso, 2014.

Condry, Ian. *Hip-Hop Japan: Rap and the Paths of Cultural Globalization*. Durham, NC: Duke University Press, 2006.

Cooper-Chen, Anne. *Mass Communication in Japan*. New York: Wiley-Blackwell, 1991.

Couldry, Nick. *Media Rituals: A Critical Approach*. New York: Routledge, 2003.

Cubitt, Sean. "Virilio and New Media." In *Paul Virilio: From Modernism to Hypermodernism and Beyond*, edited by John Armitage, 127–42. London: Sage Publications, 2000.

Deuze, Mark. "Media Life." *Media, Culture and Society* 33, no. 1 (2011): 137–48.

Deuze, Mark. "Participation, Remediation, Bricolage: Considering Principal Components of a Digital Culture." *Information Society* 22, no. 2 (April 2006): 63–75.

Dickey, Sara. "Anthropology and Its Contributions to Studies of Mass Media." *International Social Science Journal* 49 (1997): 413–27.

Dickinson, Roger, and Bashir Memon. "Press Clubs, the Journalistic Field and the Practice of Journalism in Pakistan." *Journalism Studies* 13, no. 4 (2012): 616–32.

Dornfeld, Barry. *Producing Public Television, Producing Public Culture*. Princeton, NJ: Princeton University Press, 1998.

Doughty, Mark, Duncan Rowland, and Shaun Lawson. "Who Is on Your Sofa? TV Audience Communities and Second Screening Social Networks." Paper presented at the Tenth European Conference on Interactive TV and Video, New York, July 2012.

Dwango Co., Ltd. *Introducing Niconico*. Report. September 30, 2019. https://site.nico-video.jp/sales_ads/data/ura/niconico_introduction_en_20200124.pdf.

Dwango Co., Ltd. "Nikoniko (Niko Dō Niko-Sei) Kōkoku Sērusushīto | Kabushiki-gaisha Dowango" [Nico Nico (Nico Douga / Nico Live) advertising sales sheet | Dwango Co., Ltd.]. https://site.nicovideo.jp/sales_ads/.

Eco, Umberto. "Towards a Semiotic Inquiry into the Television Message." In *Television: Critical Concepts in Media and Cultural Studies*, edited by Toby Miller, 3–19. London: Routledge, 2003.

Eldridge, Scott A., II. "Where Do We Draw the Line? Interlopers, (Ant)Agonists, and an Unbounded Journalistic Field." *Media and Communication* 7, no. 4 (2019): 8–18.

eMarketer. "Japan Is One of the World's Strongest Markets for Twitter: eMarketer Increases User Estimates for the Country as People Flock to the Platform." eMarketer. July 31, 2018. https://www.emarketer.com/content/japan-is-one-of-the-strongest-markets-in-the-world-for-twitter.

Englehart, Lucinda. "Media Activism in the Screening Room: The Significance of Viewing Locations, Facilitation and Audience Dynamics in the Reception of HIV/AIDS Films in South Africa." *Visual Anthropology Review* 19, no. 1–2 (2003): 73–85.

Evans, Elizabeth. "Engaging Screens: Negotiating 'Engagement' within Transmedia Culture." Paper presented at Television and Platforms in the Digital Age: Narratives, Audiences, Technologies, University of Montreal, March 17–18, 2017.

Evans, Elizabeth. *Transmedia Television: Audiences, New Media, and Daily Life*. London: Taylor and Francis, 2011.

Everett, Anna. "Double Click: The Million Woman March on Television and the Internet." In *Television after TV: Essays on a Medium in Transition*, edited by Lynn Spigel and Jan Olsson, 224–48. Durham, NC: Duke University Press, 2004.

Fackler, Martin. "The Silencing of Japan's Free Press." *Foreign Policy*, May 27, 2016. https://foreignpolicy.com/2016/05/27/the-silencing-of-japans-free-press-shinzo-abe-media/.

Farley, Maggie. "Japan's Press and the Politics of Scandal." In *Media and Politics in Japan*, edited by Ellis S. Krauss and Susan J. Pharr, 133–64. Honolulu: University of Hawai'i Press, 1996.

Figenschou, Tine Ustad, and Karoline Andrea Ihlebæk. "Challenging Journalistic Authority." *Journalism Studies* 20, no. 9 (2019): 1221–37.

Figenschou, Tine Ustad, and Karoline Andrea Ihlebæk. "Media Criticism from the Far-Right: Attacking from Many Angles." *Journalism Practice* 13, no. 8 (2019): 901–5.

Freeman, Laurie. "Mobilizing and Demobilizing the Japanese Public Sphere: Mass Media and the Internet in Japan." In *The State of Civil Society in Japan*, edited by Frank J. Schwartz and Susan J. Pharr, 235–56. Cambridge: Cambridge University Press, 2003.

Freeman, Laurie Anne. *Closing the Shop: Information Cartels and Japan's Mass Media*. Princeton, NJ: Princeton University Press, 2010.

Fujitani, Takashi. "Electronic Pageantry and Japan's 'Symbolic Emperor.'" *Journal of Asian Studies* 51, no. 4 (November 1, 1992): 824–50.

Furuhata, Yuriko. *Cinema of Actuality: Japanese Avant-Garde Filmmaking in the Season of Image Politics.* Durham, NC: Duke University Press, 2013.

Furukawa, Gavin. "'Stupidest of All the Primates': The Role of English in Japanese Television." *Journal of Asian Pacific Communication* 24, no. 2 (2014): 196–220.

Fuwa, Raizo. "Yūchūbu to Niko Dō no Riyō-Ritsu, Dochiraga-Jō ka … Dōga Ya Gazō Kyōyū Sābisu no Riyō Jōkyō" [YouTube vs. Nico Douga, which one is top? Usage of video and image sharing services]. Yahoo.jp. Updated October 17, 2022. Accessed June 6, 2023. https://news.yahoo.co.jp/byline/fuwaraizo/20221017-00319392.

Gaia Co. Ltd. "2020-Nen 5 Tsuki Kōshin! 12 no Sōsharumedia Saishin Dōkō Dēta Matome" [Updated May 2020! 12 social media services latest trend data summary]. Gaia Co. Ltd. Updated May 2020. Accessed July 16, 2020. https://gaiax-socialmedialab.jp/post-30833/.

Galbraith, Patrick W., and Jason G. Karlin. "Introduction: The Mirror of Idols and Celebrity." In *Idols and Celebrity in Japanese Media Culture*, 1–32. New York: Palgrave Macmillan, 2012.

Galloway, Alexander R. "The Unworkable Interface." *New Literary History* 39, no. 4 (2008): 931–55.

Ganti, Tejaswini. "The Value of Ethnography." *Media Industries* 1, no. 1 (2014): 16–20. https://quod.lib.umich.edu/m/mij/15031809.0001.104?view=text;rgn=main.

Gerow, Aaron. "From Film to Television: Early Theories of Television in Japan." In *Media Theory in Japan*, edited by Marc Steinberg and Alexander Zahlten, 56–80. Durham, NC: Duke University Press, 2017.

Giglietto, Fabio, and Donatella Selva. "Second Screen and Participation: A Content Analysis on a Full Season Dataset of Tweets." *Journal of Communication* 64, no. 2 (March 19, 2014): 260–77. https://academic.oup.com/joc/article/64/2/260-277/4085976.

Goode, Luke. "Social News, Citizen Journalism and Democracy." *New Media and Society* 11, no. 8 (2009): 1287–305.

Gripsrud, Jostein. "Broadcast Television: The Chances of Its Survival in a Digital Age." In *Television after TV: Essays on a Medium in Transition*, edited by Lynn Spigel and Jan Olsson, 210–23. Durham, NC: Duke University Press, 2004.

Gusterson, Hugh. "Studying Up Revisited." *PoLAR: Political and Legal Anthropology Review* 20, no. 1 (1997): 114–19.

Hagimoto, Haruhiko, Yoshihiko Muraki, and Tsutomu Konno. *Omae wa Tada no Genzai ni Suginai: Terebi ni Nani ga Kanō ka?* [You are just the present: What is possible for television?]. 40th anniversary ed. Tokyo: Asahi Shimbun Publishing, 2008.

Hakuhodo-DYMedia-Partners. *Sumātofon no Fukyū o Haikei ni, Keitai Netto Setsuzoku Jikan ga Sara ni Shinchō. Josei 20dai•30 Dai de Ōhaba Na Shinbi* [Background of the popularization of smartphones; Mobile internet connection time is further extended]. Hakuhodo DY Media Partners, Inc. Corporate Public Relations Group, June 10, 2013.

Hakuhodo Inc. *Seikatsu-Sha no Media Kankyō to Jōhō Ishiki* [Consumer media environment and information awareness]. Tokyo: Shōhishachō [Consumer affairs agency], 2021. https://www.caa.go.jp/policies/council/cepc/meeting_materials_4/assets/consumer_education_203_210129_02.pdf.

Hall, Stuart. *Encoding and Decoding in the Television Discourse*. Birmingham, UK: Centre for Cultural Studies, University of Birmingham, 1973.

Hamano, Satoshi. *Ākitekucha no Settaikei: Jōhō Kankyō wa Ikani Sekkeisarete Kita ka* [The ecosystem of architecture: How the information environment has been designed]. Tokyo: Chikuma Shobo, 2015.

Hambleton, Alexandra. "Reinforcing Identities? Non-Japanese Residents, Television and Cultural Nationalism in Japan." *Contemporary Japan* 23 (2011): 27–47.

Hannerz, Ulf. "Other Transnationals: Perspectives Gained from Studying Sideways." *Paideuma: Mitteilungen zur Kulturkunde* 44 (1998): 109–23.

Harrington, Stephen, Tim Highfield, and Axel Bruns. "More Than a Backchannel: Twitter and Television." *Participations* 10, no. 1 (2013): 405–9.

Hartley, John. "From Republic of Letters to Television Republic? Citizen Readers in the Era of Broadcast Television." In *Television after TV: Essays on a Medium in Transition*, edited by Lynn Spigel and Jan Olsson, 386–417. Durham, NC: Duke University Press, 2004.

Hatakeyama, Michiyoshi. "Watashi ga Jiyū Hōdō Kyōkai o Yameta Riyū" [Why I quit the Free Press Association]. *Furīransuraitā Hatakeyama Michiyoshi no Burogu* (blog), 2012. http://hatakezo.jugem.jp/?eid=44.

Hill, Annette. "Media Audiences and Reception Studies." In *Reception Studies and Audiovisual Translation*, edited by Elena Di Giovanni and Yves Gambier, 3–19. Amsterdam: John Benjamin, 2018.

Hill, Annette. "Push–Pull Dynamics: Producer and Audience Practices for Television Drama Format the Bridge." *Television and New Media* 17, no. 8 (2016): 754–68.

Holt, Kristoffer, Tine Ustad Figenschou, and Lena Frischlich. "Key Dimensions of Alternative News Media." *Digital Journalism* 7, no. 7 (2019): 860–69.

Holt, Kristoffer, and Michael Karlsson. "'Random Acts of Journalism?': How Citizen Journalists Tell the News in Sweden." *New Media and Society* 17, no. 11 (2015): 1795–810.

Honma, Ryū. *Dentsū to Genpatsu Hōdō: Kyodai Kōkoku-Nushi to Ōte Kōkoku-Dairiten ni Yoru Media Shihai no Shikumi* [Dentsu and nuclear coverage: How big advertisers and big advertising firms control the media]. Tokyo: Aki Shobo, 2013.

Hori, Jun. "Ima Koso Motomerareru Ōpun Jānarizumu" [Seeking open journalism]. Speech, GoHoo: Dai 2-kai Hōdō Hinshitsu Seminā, Tokyo, Japan, July 29, 2013.

Horie, Takafumi, and Takashi Uesugi. *Dakara Terebi ni Kirawareru* [Therefore we hate TV]. Tokyo: Daiwashobo, 2011.

Horkheimer, Max, and Theodor W. Adorno. *Dialectic of Enlightenment: Philosophical Fragments*. Translated by Edmund Jephcott. Edited by Gunzelin Schmid Noerr. Stanford, CA: Stanford University Press, 2002.

Ihlebæk, Karoline Andrea, and Arne H. Krumsvik. "Editorial Power and Public Participation in Online Newspapers." *Journalism: Theory, Practice and Criticism* 16, no. 4 (2015): 470–87.

Inai, Eiichirou. "Terebi wa Nan no Tame ni Aru no Ka?" [What is the purpose of TV?]. *Ayablog*. Updated October 9, 2013. http://ayablog.jp/archives/24260.

Ippan Shadanhōjin Dejitaru Hōsō Suishin Kyōkai (DPA). *Dejitaru Hōsō ga Yattanda! (Digital Broadcast is Here!)*. Tokyo, Japan: 2013.

Ivy, Marilyn. "Formations of Mass Culture." In *Postwar Japan as History*, edited by Andrew Gordon, 239–58. Berkeley: University of California Press, 1993.

Iwabuchi, Koichi. "'Ordinary Foreigners' Wanted: Multinationalization of Multicultural Questions in a Japanese TV Talk Show." In *Television, Japan, and Globalization*, edited by Mitsuhiro Yoshimoto, Eva Tsai, and JungBong Choi, 27–50. Ann Arbor: Center for Japanese Studies, University of Michigan, 2010.

Iwakami, Yasumi, Takashi Uesugi, Hajime Shiraishi, and Hitofumi Yanai. "Media Akutibizumu" [media activism]. Symposium, University of Tokyo, December 6, 2012.

Jenkins, Henry. *Convergence Culture: Where Old and New Media Collide*. New York: New York University Press, 2006.

Jenkins, Henry. *Textual Poachers: Television Fans and Participatory Culture*. 20th anniversary ed. New York: Routledge, 2013.

Kaigo, Muneo. "Internet Aggregators Constructing the Political Right Wing in Japan." *JeDEM—eJournal of eDemocracy and Open Government* 5, no. 1 (2013): 59–79.

Karlsson, Michael, and Kristoffer Holt. "Is Anyone out There? Assessing Swedish Citizen-Generated Community Journalism." *Journalism Practice* 8, no. 2 (2014): 164–80.

Kazi, Taha. "Religious Television and Contesting Piety in Karachi, Pakistan." *American Anthropologist* 120, no. 3 (2018): 523–34.

Kellner, Doug. "Critical Perspectives on Television from the Frankfurt School to Postmodernism." In *A Companion to Television*, edited by Janet Wasko, 29–50. Malden, MA: Blackwell Publishing, 2008.

Kelly, William W., ed. *Fanning the Flames: Fandoms and Consumer Culture in Contemporary Japan*. Albany: SUNY Press, 2003.

Kingston, Jeff, ed. *Press Freedom in Contemporary Japan*. Abingdon, UK: Routledge, 2017.

Kingston, Jeff. "Watchdog Journalism in Japan Rebounds but Still Compromised." *Journal of Asian Studies* 77, no. 4 (2018): 881–93. https://www.cambridge.org/core/product/identifier/S002191181800253X/type/journal_article.

Kitada, Akihiro. "Japan's Cynical Nationalism." In *Fandom Unbound: Otaku Culture in a Connected World*, edited by Ito Mizuko, Okabe Daisuke, and Tsuji Izumi, 68–84. New Haven, CT: Yale University Press, 2012.

Kitada, Akihiro. *Warau Nihon no "Nashonarizumu"* [Teasing "Nationalism" of Japan]. Tokyo: NHK Books, 2005.

Kitada, Akihiro, and Fabian Schäfer. "Media/Communication Studies and Cultural Studies in Japan (1920s–1990s): From 'Public Opinion' to the 'Public Sphere.'" In *Kommunikationswissenschaft Im Internationalen Vergleich: Transnationale Perspektiven*, edited by Stefanie Averbeck-Lietz, 409–36. Wiesbaden: Springer Fachmedien Wiesbaden, 2017.

Kitada, Akihiro, and Alex Zahlten. "An Assault on 'Meaning': On Nakai Masakazu's Concept of 'Mediation.'" *Review of Japanese Culture and Society* 22 (December 2010): 88–103.

Koh, Yoree. "Twitter CEO's Direct Message @Japanpm." *Wall Street Journal,* March 25, 2013. http://blogs.wsj.com/japanrealtime/2013/03/26/twitter-ceos-direct-message -japanpm/.

"Kokuseki chīkibetsu zairyū shikaku: Zairyū mokutekibetsu zairyū gaikokujin" [Statistics of foreign residents: Former statistics of registered foreigners]. Seifu Tōkei Pōtarusaito. Updated December 1, 2018. https://www.e-stat.go.jp/stat-search/file s?page=1&layout=datalist&toukei=00250012&tstat=000001018034&cycle=1&yea r=20180&month=24101212&tclass1=000001060399.

Konno, Tsutomu. "Kanōsei no Teiji ni Mukatte" [Toward the presentation of possibility]. *Geijutsu Kurabu,* July 1973, 91–113.

Krauss, Ellis S. "Changing Television News in Japan." *Journal of Asian Studies* 57, no. 3 (August 1, 1998): 663–92.

Krauss, Ellis S. "Portraying the State: NHK Television News and Politics," edited by Ellis S. Krauss and Susan J. Pharr, 89–130. Honolulu: University of Hawaiʻi Press, 1996.

Kurahashi, Kohei. "Netto Uyoku to Sankagata Bunka: Joho ni Taisuru Taido to Mediariterashi no Migi Senkai" [The internet right-wing and participatory culture: Attitudes toward information and media literacy's right turn]. In *Netto Uyoku to wa Nani ka?* [What is the internet right wing?], edited by Naoto Higuchi. Tokyo: Seikyusha, 2019.

Kyodo News. "Bujoku-zai Genbatsuka, Kaisei-Hō ga Seiritsu Netto Chūshō Taisaku de Chōeki Dōnyū" [Strict punishment and a revised law introduce imprisonment for measures against online harassment]. Yahoo.jp, June 13, 2022. https://news .yahoo.co.jp/articles/5d3f945c33c1796192f4d7bba3ad48137b19ee5d.

Lewis, Seth C., Kelly Kaufhold, and Dominic L. Lasorsa. "Thinking about Citizen Journalism: The Philosophical and Practical Challenges of User-Generated Content for Community Newspapers." *Journalism Practice* 4, no. 2 (2010): 163–79.

Lindner, Andrew M. "Editorial Gatekeeping in Citizen Journalism." *New Media and Society* 19, no. 8 (2017): 1177–93.

Livingstone, Sonia. "Active Audiences? The Debate Progresses but Is Far from Resolved." *Communication Theory* 25, no. 4 (2015): 439–46.

Los Angeles Times. "Japanese Journalist Rockets into Space." December 3, 1990. http:// articles.latimes.com/1990-12-03/news/mn-4314_1_space-station.

Lubarsky, Jared. "The Man Who Owns Ten O'Clock." *Japan Quarterly* 38, no. 3 (July 1, 1991): 313–19.

Luhmann, Niklas. *Art as a Social System.* Translated by Eva M. Knodt. Palo Alto, CA: Stanford University Press, 2000.

Lukács, Gabriella. "Dreamwork: Cell Phone Novelists, Labor, and Politics in Contemporary Japan." *Cultural Anthropology* 28, no. 1 (2013): 44–64.

Lukács, Gabriella. *Scripted Affects, Branded Selves: Television, Subjectivity, and Capitalism in 1990s Japan.* Durham, NC: Duke University Press, 2010.

Mahon, Maureen. "The Visible Evidence of Cultural Producers." *Annual Review of Anthropology* 29, no. 2000 (January 14, 2008): 467–92.

Mankekar, Purnima. *Screening Culture, Viewing Politics: An Ethnography of Television, Womanhood, and Nation in Postcolonial India*. Durham, NC: Duke University Press, 1999.

Manning, Paul, and Ilana Gershon. "Animating Interaction." *Hau: Journal of Ethnographic Theory* 3 (2013): 107–37.

Martin, Rick. "Japanese Television Network Claims over 1m Participants in Interactive TV Game." *The Bridge*, July 8, 2013. http://thebridge.jp/en/2013/07/teamlab-television.

Matza, Tomas. "Moscow's Echo: Technologies of the Self, Publics, and Politics on the Russian Talk Show." *Cultural Anthropology* 24, no. 3 (2009): 489–522.

Mazzarella, William. *Censorium: Cinema and the Open Edge of Mass Publicity*. Durham, NC: Duke University Press, 2013.

Mazzarella, William. *Shoveling Smoke: Advertising and Globalization in Contemporary India*. Durham, NC: Duke University Press, 2003.

McCurry, Justin. "Japan Upgrades Nuclear Crisis to Same Level as Chernobyl." *Guardian*, April 12, 2011. https://www.theguardian.com/world/2011/apr/12/japan-nuclear-crisis-chernobyl-severity-level1.

McKenna, Michael. *Real People and the Rise of Reality Television*. New York: Roman and Littlefield, 2015.

Metag, Julia, and Adrian Rauchfleisch. "Journalists' Use of Political Tweets: Functions for Journalistic Work and the Role of Perceived Influences." *Digital Journalism* 1, no. 18 (2016).

Ministry of Internal Affairs and Communications. *Omona Media no Riyōjikan to Kōisha-Ritsu* [Major media usage hours and actor rates]. Tokyo: Ministry of Internal Affairs and Communications, 2019. https://www.soumu.go.jp/johotsusin-tokei/whitepaper/ja/r01/html/nd232510.html.

Moeran, Brian. *A Japanese Advertising Agency: An Anthropology of Media and Markets*. Honolulu: University of Hawai'i Press, 1996.

Moll, Yasmin. "Television Is Not Radio: Theologies of Mediation in the Egyptian Islamic Revival." *Cultural Anthropology* 33, no. 2 (2018): 233–65.

Molyneux, Logan. "What Journalists Retweet: Opinion, Humor, and Brand Development on Twitter." *Journalism: Theory, Practice and Criticism* 16, no. 7 (2015): 920–35.

Morley, David. "Unanswered Questions in Audience Research." *Communication Review* 9, no. 2 (2006): 101–21.

Morofuji, Emi, and Yoko Watanabe. *Changes and Trends in Media Use: From the Results of the 2010 Japanese Time Use Survey*. Tokyo: NHK Broadcasting Culture Research Institute, 2011.

Motoki, Masahiko. "Naze Kisha Kurabu wa 'Seiken Bettari' Na no ka?" [Why are the reporters clubs so tight with the political administration?]. *President Online*, November 16, 2017. https://president.jp/articles/-/23625.

Muehlebach, Andrea, and Nitzan Shoshan. "Introduction." *Anthropological Quarterly* 85, no. 2 (2012): 317–43. http://muse.jhu.edu/content/crossref/journals/anthropological_quarterly/v085/85.2.muehlebach.html.

Mulgan, Aurelia George. "Media Muzzling under the Abe Administration." In *Press Freedom in Contemporary Japan*, edited by Jeff Kingston, 17–29. Abingdon, UK: Routledge, 2017.

Müller, Eggo. "Formatted Spaces of Participation: Interactive Television and the Changing Relationship between Production and Consumption." In *Digital Material: Tracing New Media in Everyday Life*, edited by Joost Raessens, Marianne van den Boomen, Sybille Lammes, Ann-Sophie Lehmann, and Mirko Tobias Schäfer, 49–63. Amsterdam: Amsterdam University Press, 2009.

Nakai, Masakazu. *Zenshū*. Edited by Osamu Kuno. 4 vols. Tokyo: Bijutsu Shuppan-sha, 1964–81.

Nakano, Koichi. "The Right-Wing Media and the Rise of Illiberal Politics in Japan." In *Press Freedom in Contemporary Japan*, edited by Jeff Kingston, 30–39. Abingdon, UK: Routledge, 2017.

Nakaoku, Miki. "Taimushifuto Shichō-Ritsu to Sōgō Shichō-Ritsu" [Time-shifted ratings and overall ratings]. *Dentsu*, May 26, 2017. https://dentsu-ho.com/articles/5159.

nao. "Terebi Kyoku Himei: 'Rokuga Chūshin No Hito Ga Ōsugi! Cm Mo Mite!'" [TV stations scream: "Too many people are recording television! Watch commercials too!"]. *Buppī sokuhō*, August 15, 2013. https://ameblo.jp/matomeark/entry-11463417453.html.

Narzary, Dharitri Chakravartty. "The Myths of Japanese Homogeneity." *China Report* 40, no. 3 (2004): 311–19.

Neikirk, Lee. "For Japan, TV Technology Is a High Priority." *USA Today*. Updated December 24, 2013. http://www.usatoday.com/story/tech/2013/12/23/reviewed-japan-8k-tv/4041099/.

NHK. "Terebi Hōsō Anibāsarī Supesharu 'TV—60 Shūnenkinen Shitsumon'" [TV broadcasting anniversary special "TV 60th Anniversary Question"]. Tokyo: NHK Tokyo, March 1, 2013, 50 min.

NHK Hōsō Bunka Kenkyūjo. "2013-Nen Kenkyū Happyō to Shinpojiumu—Jisshi Hōkoku" [2013 research presentation and symposium—implementation report]. Paper presented at the 2013-Nen Kenkyū Happyō to Shinpojiumu, Tokyo, March 13–15, 2013.

NicoNico. "2019 Dēta de Miru Nikoniko" [Niko Niko seen through its 2019 data]. Dwango, Inc. Updated December 26, 2019. https://site.nicovideo.jp/newyear2020/about/.

Nielsen. "Nielsen Expands Dynamic Ad Insertion Pilot with Leading Smart TV Platform and New Broadcast Partner." Nielsen, November 29, 2018. https://www.gracenote.com/nielsen-expands-dynamic-ad-insertion-pilot-with-leading-smart-tv-platform-and-new-broadcast-partner/.

Nihon Shinbun Kyōkai Henshū Iinkai. "Kisha Kurabu Ni Kansuru Nihon Shinbun Kyōkai Henshū Iinkai No Kenkai." [The views of the editorial committee of the Japan Newspaper Association regarding press clubs]. Updated March 9, 2006. https://www.pressnet.or.jp/statement/report/060309_15.html.

Nippon.com. "Shinbun Yomanai Kedo, Jōhō Toshite Shinraidekiru no wa Shinbun!?: Nippon Zaidan no '18-Sai Ishiki Chōsa'" [Young Japanese still trust TV and newspapers more than online media]. nippon.com. Updated November 12, 2019. https://www.nippon.com/ja/japan-data/h00577/.

Nippon Hōsō Kyōkai. "Sōsharumedia de Kawaru Arata Na Terebi no Shichō Sutairu 'Sōsharuterebi Awādo 2013'" [New style of TV changeable with social media "Social TV Award 2013]. News release, July 23, 2013. https://www.nhk.or.jp/pr/keiei/otherpress/pdf/20130723.pdf.

Nishida, Jiro. "Terebi to Sōsharumedia no Kashikoi Kankei: Kabushikigaisha Bideopuromōshon Komyunikēshon Direkutā Sakai Osamu-San" [The smart relationship between television and social media: Video Promotion, Inc. communication director Osamu Sakai]. IPG Interactive Program Guide. Updated March 1, 2013. http://www.ipg.co.jp/press/story/vol116.html.

O'Day, Robin. "Differentiating SEALDs from Freeters, and Precariats: The Politics of Youth Movements in Contemporary Japan." *Asia-Pacific Journal* 13, no. 37 (2015): 1–9. https://apjjf.org/-Robin-O_Day/4376.

Oi, Shinji, and Shinsuke Sako. *Journalists in Japan*. Worlds of Journalism Study, February 17, 2017. https://worldsofjournalism.org/country%20reports/.

Onecareer.jp. "(Gyōkai Kenkyū: Terebikyoku) Terebi Gyōkai Shibō-Sha Hikken, Kī-Kyoku 4-Sha (Fujiterebi, Nihonterebi, Terebiasahi, Tbs Terebi) no Jigyō Shafū no Chigai o Tettei Hikaku!" [(Industry Research: TV Stations) A must-see for TV industry aspirants, a thorough comparison of the differences in business and corporate culture of the four key stations (Fuji TV, NTV, TV Asahi, and TBS TV)!]. Onecareer.jp. Updated August 3, 2020. https://www.onecareer.jp/articles/222#c5.

Ōta, Tōru. "Producing (Post-) Trendy Japanese TV Dramas." Translated by Madori Nasu. In *Feeling Asian Modernities*, edited by Koichi Iwabuchi, 69–86. Hong Kong: Hong Kong University Press, 2004.

Our Planet-TV. "Kokkai Kisha Kaikan no Okujō Shiyō o Meguri, Saiban Teiso | Ourplanet-TV: Tokuteihieirikatsudōhōjin Awāpuranetto Tībī" [Concerning the use of the National Diet Press Association building's roof, court petition | Our Planet-TV: Nonprofit organization Our Planet-TV]. Our Planet-TV. Updated September 24, 2012. http://www.ourplanet-tv.org/?q=node/1447.

Painter, Andrew A. "Japanese Daytime Television, Popular, Culture, and Ideology." *Journal of Japanese Studies* 19, no. 2 (June 1, 1993): 295–325.

Parigi, Paolo, and Warner Henson. "Social Isolation in America." *Annual Review of Sociology* 40, no. 1 (2014): 153–71.

Parks, Lisa. "Flexible Microcasting: Gender, Generation, and Television-Internet Convergence." In *Television after TV: Essays on a Medium in Transition*, edited by Lynn Spigel and Jan Olsson, 133–62. Durham, NC: Duke University Press, 2004.

Perreault, Gregory P., and Patrick Ferrucci. "What Is Digital Journalism? Defining the Practice and Role of the Digital Journalist." *Digital Journalism* 8, no. 10 (2020): 1298–316.

Peterson, Mark Allen. "Getting to the Story: Unwriteable Discourse and Interpretive Practice in American Journalism." *Anthropological Quarterly* 74, no. 4 (2001): 201–11.

Pharr, Susan J. "Media as Trickster in Japan: A Comparative Perspective." In *Media and Politics in Japan*, edited by Susan J. Pharr and Ellis S. Krauss, 19–44. Honolulu: University of Hawai'i Press, 1996.

Postill, John. "Introduction: Theorising Media and Practice." In *Theorising Media and Practice*, edited by B. Bräuchler and John Postill. Oxford: Berghahn, 2010.

Postman, Neil. *Amusing Ourselves to Death: Public Discourse in the Age of Show Business*. 20th anniversary ed. New York: Penguin Books, 2005.

Putnam, Robert D. *Bowling Alone*. New York: Simon and Schuster, 2000.

Raibudoa Nyūsu. "Terebibangu no 'Gaitō Intabyū' ni Tabitabi Tōjō Suru Josei; Jitsuwa Tarento Ka" [Woman who often appears in TV "person on the street" interviews is really an actor?]. Livedoor. Updated July 7, 2014. http://news.livedoor.com/article/detail/9018629/.

Rancière, Jacques. *The Emancipated Spectator*. New York: Verso Books, 2014.

Rausch, Anthony. *Japan's Local Newspapers: Chihōshi and Revitalization Journalism*. London: Routledge, 2012.

Reporters without Borders. "Japan | RSF." Reporters without Borders, 2022. https://rsf.org/en/country/japan.

Reporters without Borders. "Japan: Tradition and Business Interests." Reporters without Borders, 2019. Accessed June 23, 2019. https://rsf.org/en/country/japan.

Reporters without Borders. "2014: Asia-Pacific | Rsf—Reporters Sans Frontières." 2014. Accessed September 10, 2020. https://web.archive.org/web/20220128155449/https://rsf.org/en/2014-asia-pacific.

Rodwell, Elizabeth A. "The Machine without the Ghost: Early Interactive Television in Japan." *Convergence: The International Journal of Research into New Media Technologies* 27, no. 5 (2021): 1376–92.

Rodwell, Elizabeth A. "Open Access, Closed Systems: Independent Online Journalism in Japan." *Information, Communication and Society* 26, no. 6 (2021): 1244–61.

Russell, Adrienne. *Journalism as Activism: Recoding Media Power*. Cambridge: Polity, 2016.

Sakai, Osamu. *Terebi wa Ikinokoreru ka? Eizō Media wa Atarashī Chihei E Mukau* [Can television survive? Video media moves toward new horizons]. Tokyo: Discover Twenty-One, 2011.

Sakai, Osamu. "Terebi wa Terebi o Hamidashite Iku: Terebi Hōsō 60-Shūnen NHK × Nittere 60 Ban Shōbu" [TV goes beyond TV: 60th anniversary of TV broadcasting, NHK × NTV 60th Battle]. *Kurieitibu Bijinesu-Ron* (blog), July 20, 2013. http://sakaiosamu.com/2013/0204080023/.

Sakamoto, Rumi. "'Koreans, Go Home!' Internet Nationalism in Contemporary Japan as a Digitally Mediated Subculture." *Asia-Pacific Journal* 9, no. 10 (2011): 1–21. https://apjjf.org/-Rumi-Sakamoto/3497/article.pdf.

Sankei News. "20% Dai . . . 3 Shū Renzoku de Zero 1/28-2/3" [20% base . . . zero for three consecutive weeks]. *Sankei News*. Updated February 6, 2013. Accessed June 12, 2023. https://web.archive.org/web/20130621235046/http://sankei.jp.msn.com/entertainments/news/130206/ent13020610070004-n1.htm.

Sas, Miryam. "The Culture Industries and Media Theory in Japan." In *Media Theory in Japan*, edited by Marc Steinberg and Alexander Zahlten, 217–46. Durham, NC: Duke University Press, 2017.

Sauter, Molly. "Is HQ Trivia the Future of TV?" *The Outline*, November 16, 2017. https://theoutline.com/post/2492/hq-trivia-interactive-tv-uncanny.

Schudson, Michael. *The Power of News*. Cambridge, MA: Harvard University Press, 1995.

Schultz, Tanjev. "Mass Media and the Concept of Interactivity: An Exploratory Study of Online Forums and Reader Email." *Media, Culture and Society* 22, no. 2 (2000): 205–21.

Seaver, Nick. "Captivating Algorithms: Recommender Systems as Traps." *Journal of Material Culture* 24, no. 4 (2019): 421–36.

Sekiguchi, Toko. "Japanese Politicians Bite Back against Media." *Wall Street Journal*. Updated July 5, 2013. http://blogs.wsj.com/japanrealtime/2013/07/05/japanese -politicians-bite-back-against-media/?mod=WSJBlog.

Senden Kaigi. "Jikeiretsu Dēta de Miru Korona to Media Sesshoku Shōhi Kōdō no Henka" [Changes in corona and media contact/consumption behavior as seen from time series data]. Senden Kaigi. Updated August 2020. https://mag.senden-kaigi.com/senden/202008/report/019313.php.

Shigenobu, May. *"Arabu no Haru" no Shōtai: Ōbei to Media ni Odorasareta Minshu-Ka Kakumei* [Unveiling the "Arab Spring": Democratic revolutions orchestrated by the West and the media]. Tokyo: Kadokawa Shoten, 2012.

Shiraishi, Hajime. *Bideokamera de Ikō* [Let's go with a video camera]. Tokyo: Nanatsumori Shokan, 2008.

Shiraishi, Hajime. *Media o Tsukuru: "Chīsa Na Koe" o Tsutaeru Tame ni* [Making media: To transmit "small voices"]. Tokyo: Iwanami Shoten, 2011.

Sieg, Linda. "Japanese Media Self-Censorship Grows in PM Abe's Reign." *Reuters*, February 24, 2015. https://www.reuters.com/article/idUSL4N0VX1TK20150224.

Snow, Nancy. "NHK, Abe and the World: Japan's Pressing Needs in the Path to 2020." *Asian Journal of Journalism and Media Studies* 2 (2019): 1–13. https://www.jstage .jst.go.jp/article/ajjms/2/0/2_2.0_15/_pdf/-char/ja.

Sontag, Susan. *Regarding the Pain of Others*. New York: Macmillan, 2003.

Stafford, Barbara Maria. *Echo Objects: The Cognitive Work of Images*. Chicago: University of Chicago Press, 2007.

Stevens, Carolyn S., and Shuhei Hosokawa. "So Close and yet So Far: Humanizing Celebrity in Japanese Music Variety Shows, 1960s–1990s." In *Asian Media Productions*, edited by Brian Moeran, 223–46. Honolulu: University of Hawai'i Press, 2001.

Stocker, Joel F. "Yoshimoto Kogyo and Manzai in Japan's Media Culture." In *Asian Media Productions*, edited by Brian Moeran, 247–69. New York: Routledge, 2001.

Stronach, Bruce. "Japanese Television." In *Handbook of Japanese Popular Culture*, edited by Richard Gid Powers, Hidetoshi Kato, and Bruce Stronach, 127–65. Westport, CT: Greenwood Press, 1989.

Tateno, Masaru, Alan R. Teo, Wataru Ukai, Junichiro Kanazawa, Ryoko Katsuki, Hiroaki Kubo, and Takahiro A. Kato. "Internet Addiction, Smartphone Addiction, and Hikikomori Trait in Japanese Young Adult: Social Isolation and Social Network." *Frontiers in Psychiatry* 10 (July 2019): 1–11.

Taylor, Jonathan. "Television 2.0: Futurecasting the Medium." *Variety*, April 24, 2000.

Tsuda, Daisuke. *Dōin no Kakumei-Sōsharumedia wa Nani o Kaeta no ka* [Mobilization revolution: What has social media changed?]. Tokyo: Chuko Shinsho, 2012.

Tucker, Joshua A., Yannis Theocharis, Margaret E. Roberts, and Pablo Barberá. "From Liberation to Turmoil: Social Media and Democracy." *Journal of Democracy* 28, no. 4 (2017): 46–59.

TVMANUNION. "Kigyō Rinen" [Our beliefs]. 2017. Accessed June 16, 2022. https://web.archive.org/web/20211025220618/https://www.tvu.co.jp/company/policy/.

Udupa, Sahana, Elonnai Hickok, Antonis Maronikolakis, Hinrich Schuetze, Laura Csuka, Axel Wisiorek, and Leah Nann. *AI, Extreme Speech and the Challenges of Online Content Moderation*. AI4 Dignity Project, LMU Munich, 2021.

Uesugi, Takashi. "About the Free Press Association of Japan (FPAJ)." Free Press Association of Japan (FPAJ). Updated February 4, 2012. Accessed June 7, 2023. https://web.archive.org/web/20121206052241/http://fpaj.jp/?page_id=15.

Uesugi, Takashi. *Kokka no Haji: Ichioku Sō Sen'nō-ka no Shinjitsu Tankō* [National shame: The truth about the brainwashing of 100 million people]. Tokyo: Bijinesu-sha, 2011.

"Uesugi Takashi, Iwakami Yasumi, Hatakeyama Michiyoshi: Rihito San-Shi no Hansei Mōdo ni Itaru Made" [Uesugi Takashi, Iwakami Yasumi, Hatakeyama Michiyoshi: 3 people in reflection mode]. Togetter, October 24, 2011. https://togetter.com/li/204811.

"Uesugi Takashi 122 [Sagishi]" [Uesugi Takashi 122 (scammer)]. 5chan. Updated March 13, 2021. https://egg.5ch.net/test/read.cgi/mass/1598062518/457-n.

Ujiie, Natsuhiko. "Terebi no Mirai Atogaki Toshite . . . Shinkan 'Dēta Saienteisuto'no Kansō" [The future of television: By means of an afterword, impressions of the new book *Data Scientist*]. *Ayablog*, September 9, 2013. http://ayablog.com/?p=487.

Ujiie, Natsuhiko. "Terebi no Mirai: Terebi wa Fuben de Jidai Okure no Sābisu Da" [The future of television: Television is an inconvenient, old-fashioned service]. *Ayablog*, May 24, 2013. http://ayablog.com/?p=471.

Ujiie, Natsuhiko. "Terebi o Minai ga Kahansū 'Otoko 20-Dai to Onna 10-Dai' no Shōgeki: NHK Chōsa de Wakatta Chijōha Hōsō no Owarinohajimari" [But I don't watch TV: The impact of the majority of "Males in Their 20s and Female Teens" and the beginning of the end of terrestrial broadcasting found by the NHK survey]. *Tokyo Keizai Shimbun*, June 2, 2021. https://toyokeizai.net/articles/-/431686.

Uricchio, William. "Television's Next Generation: Technology/Interface Culture/Flow." In *Television after TV: Essays on a Medium in Transition*, edited by Lynn Spigel and Jan Olsson, 163–82. Durham, NC: Duke University Press, 2004.

van Dijck, José. "Users Like You? Theorizing Agency in User-Generated Content." *Media, Culture and Society* 31, no. 1 (January 2009): 41–58.

Video Research Ltd. "Media Teiten Chōsa" [Media fixed point survey]. Media kankyō kenkyūsho. Tokyo: Media Kaiken, February 5, 2021. https://mekanken.com/mediasurveys/.

Video Research Ltd. "Sabisu" [Services]. Video Research Ltd., 2020. https://www
.videor.co.jp/service/.

Video Research Ltd. "Taimushifuto Shichō-Ritsu" [Time-shifted audience ratings].
Video Research Ltd., 2020. https://www.videor.co.jp/service/media-data/tstvrat-
ing.html.

Vis, Farida. "Twitter as a Reporting Tool for Breaking News." *Digital Journalism* 1,
no. 1 (2013): 27–47.

Warner, Michael. "Publics and Counterpublics." *Public Culture* 14, no. 1 (2002): 49–90.
http://muse.jhu.edu/journals/public_culture/v014/14.1warner.html.

Westney, D. Eleanor. "Mass Media as Business Organizations: A U.S.-Japan Comparison." In *Media and Politics in Japan,* edited by Susan J. Pharr and Ellis S. Krauss,
47–88. Honolulu: University of Hawai'i Press, 1996.

Wolferen, Karel van. *The Enigma of Japanese Power: People and Politics in a Stateless
Nation.* New York: Vintage Books, 1990.

Work-Data. "Nikoniko Dōga Riyōsha no Nenrei-Sō, Danjo-Hi Channeru Shūnyū"
[NicoNico Douga user age group, gender ratio, channel income]. Work-Data,
September 14, 2020. https://work-data.com/272.

Yahoo.jp. "Geneki Terebi Man 30 Nin ga Eranda 'Hontō ni Sugoi to Omou Terebi
Kyoku'" [Television stations 30 current TV employees think are really awesome].
Yahoo.jp. Updated March 23, 2021. Accessed July 19, 2021. https://friday.kodan-
sha.co.jp/article/169667.

Yamaguchi, Tomomi. "Xenophobia in Action: Ultranationalism, Hate Speech, and
the Internet in Japan." *Radical History Review* 2013, no. 117 (September 30, 2013):
98–118.

Yamakawa, Kushiro. "Kisha Kurabu wa Naze Nakunaranai ka." *Yamakawa Kushiro
Burogu* (blog), May 14, 2005. https://blog.goo.ne.jp/yamakawa21/e/0a608db1a47
178d375390f58bfe60b0a.

Yamamoto, Eiji. "Shibaitai wa Itsu Made Setai de Kataru no ka: Shichō-Ritsu to Iu
Yakkaina Shiromono" [How long will paper media talk in terms of households: A
troublesome thing called audience ratings]. *Media Border*, May 12, 2021. https://
mediaborder.publishers.fm/article/24117/?fbclid=IwAR2tPoWwftuWjfIDQ1ov6
e3Z-nlKOqVwUkRkx8u2LB6DPyWXG7Tt5xu_F_I.

"Yomiuri no Baka Kisha ni Buchi Kireru Uesugi-Shi to Iwakami-San" [Uesugi and
Iwakami flip out at stupid Yomiuri reporter]. nicovideo.jp. Updated October 20,
2011. https://www.nicovideo.jp/watch/sm15938686.

Yoshimi, Shunya. "Japanese Television: Early Development and Research." In *A
Companion to Television*, edited by Janet Wasko, 540–57. Malden, MA: Blackwell
Publishing, 2005.

Yoshimi, Shunya. "Television and Nationalism: Historical Change in the National Domestic TV Formation of Postwar Japan." *European Journal of Cultural Studies* 6, no. 4 (2003): 459–87. https://journals.sagepub.com/doi/
abs/10.1177/13675494030064002.

Yoshino, Yoshitaka. *Fujiterebi wa Naze Chōraku Shita no ka* [Why did Fuji TV decline?]. Tokyo: Shinchosha, 2016.

Yoshino, Yoshitaka. "Fuji wa, Naze 'Netto Enjō' no Hyōteki ni Naru no ka: 'Hanryū Gorioshi' wa Arienai no Da ga" [Why is Fuji the target of "online burning"? There is no such thing as "Korean Wave push"]. *Tokyo Keizai Shimbun*, September 6, 2016. https://toyokeizai.net/articles/-/134071?page=3.

Ytre-Arne, Brita, and Ranjana Das. "An Agenda in the Interest of Audiences: Facing the Challenges of Intrusive Media Technologies." *Television and New Media* 20, no. 2 (2018): 184–98.

INDEX

Page numbers in italics refer to figures.

GoHoo (Misinformation), 65–66, 68, 71, 73–74, 75–76, 87, 88
Gracenote, 38–39, 138
Gramsci, Antonio, 103, 111–12
Gripsrud, Jostein, 53, 59
guest experts, 99–103, *101*, 104–5
Gusterson, Hugh, 19
Gyao (pay service), 31

Habermas, Jürgen, 93, 109
Hagimoto Haruhiko, 2, 56
Hakuhodo (advertising company), 7, 14, 33–35
Hall, Stuart, 136–37
Hamano Satoshi, 77
Hannerz, Ulf, 20
Hanzawa Naoki (TV show), 44, 136
happiness, 29–33
Hartley, John, 136–37
Hatakeyama Michiyoshi, 84
Heisei era (1989–2019), 32
Hiro (pseud.), 116–19, 123
Honma, Ryū, 33–34
Hori Jun, 88
Horkheimer, Max, 8, 41, 42
Hōsō Bunka Kenkyūjo (Broadcast Culture Research Group) (NHK), 29–30
Hosokawa Shuhei, 98
Howe, Cymene, 41, 145n50
Hulu, 31, 156n2
hypernormalization, 145n50

ii (like) buttons, 26–28, 41, 43
Inai Eiichirou, 112
independent media start-ups: insider/outsider divergence and, 15–18, 129; interactivity and, 73–80, *79*; media activism and, 66–68, 71–76; neutrality and, 80–85; origins and rise of, 64–68, *66*; right-wing groups (*netto uyoku*) and, 76–80, 82–84, 85–88. *See also* GoHoo (Misinformation); Independent Web Journal (IWJ)
Independent Web Journal (IWJ): citizen journalism and, 111–12, *112*, 115, 125–27; cocreation and, 130; insider/outsider divergence and, 129; interactivity and, 74–75; live streaming and, 74–75; media activism and, 71, 74–76; microphones and, 117; power and, 131; press

conferences and, 74–76, 115, 116; right-wing groups (*netto uyoku*) and, 80, 87; significance of, 3
interactive game shows: American television and, 5–6; *Arashi feat. You* (TV show) and, 89–91, 92–94, 95, 105, 129; *Bloody Tube* (TV show) and, 1–2, 91, 95–97, *96*, 129; *The Last Award* (TV show) and, 91, 99–103, *101*, 104–5, 137–38; *QB47* (*Kokumin-sō sanka kuizu shō! QB47*) (TV show) and, 91, 95
interactive television in Japan: advertising and, 35–40; barriers to, 131–37; collective viewing (*cha no ma*) and, 2, 104–6; ethnographic fieldwork on, 4, 18–21; Frankfurt School theory and, 40–43; game shows and (*see* interactive game shows); guest experts and, 99–103; news shows and, 54–55; *60 Ban Shōbu* (60-year battle) (TV show) and, 25–29, *27*, 40, 41, 43, 91, 102–3, 129, 138–39 (see also *Compass, The* [TV show]); origins and rise of, 2–10, 15–18, 91; "pushing buttons" metaphor and, 21–23; sense of national belonging and communitas and, 90–97, 104–7, 137–38; *tarento* (TV celebrities) in, 26, 91, 95, 97–99
interactivity in Japanese mass media: cocreation and, 130; concept of, 5–6; ethnographic fieldwork on, 4, 18–21; insider/outsider divergence and, 4, 15–18, 129; publics and, 5–6, 133–34; "pushing buttons" metaphor and, 21–23; television as barrier to, 131–37. *See also* interactive television in Japan; journalism in Japan
internet, 6–10, 12–13, 44–45, 134–35. *See also* live streaming; social media
intimacy: advertising and, 139; citizen journalism and, 110, 119; interactive television and, 106–7; live streaming and, 51–52, 54–55; *tarento* (TV celebrities) and, 98–99
iTunes, 31
Iwabuchi, Koichi, 99
Iwakami Yasumi, 74, 75, 81–82

Japan Atomic Energy Headquarters, 70
Japan Newspaper and Magazine Associations, 86–87

Jenkins, Henry, 16–17, 98, 137
Jinrōrian (TV show), 60
journalism as activism, 66. *See also* media
activism
journalism in Japan: characteristics of,
68–71; ethnographic fieldwork on, 4,
18–21; Fukushima nuclear plant disaster (2011) and, 3–5, 10–12, 31, 33–34, 66,
69–70, 134; insider/outsider divergence
and, 4, 15–18, 129; neutrality (*chūritsu*)
and, 56–57, 80–85, 113, 135; objectivity (*kyakukansei*) and, 57, 73–80, 113;
"pushing buttons" metaphor and,
21–23; social media and, 140. *See also*
citizen journalism; *Compass, The* (TV
show); independent media start-ups;
kisha kurabu (reporter's club) system;
press conferences
journalism in the United States, 65–66, 68,
71–72

Kanai Nobutaka, 145n49
Kaori (pseud.), 74–75, 110, 114, 117–18, 121–23
kashikari (lend-and-borrow) system, 34–35
Kennedy, John F., 47–48
kisha kurabu (reporter's club) system: Fukushima nuclear plant disaster (2011)
and, 11, 69–70; independent media
start-ups and, 16, 87–88; press conferences and, 64, 65, 67–68, 75, 76, 78,
79–80, 81–82, 83, 86–87; Shiraishi on,
109; social media and, 140
Kitada Akihiro, 52–53, 56, 77, 92, 156n62
Kokka no Haji (National shame) (Uesugi), 85
komentoforō (subtitling), 119
Konno Tsutomu, 2, 3, 56, 130–31
Kume Hiroshi, 54

lapel mics (*taipin-gata*), 117
Last Award, The (TV show), 91, 99–103, *101*,
105, 137–38
Liberal Democratic Party (LDP), 11, 34, 65, 86
Line (Korean chat app), 31
Lippmann, Walter, 158n29
live streaming: Independent Web Journal
(IWJ) and, 74–75; intimacy and, 51–52,
54–55; ratings and, 26; right-wing
groups (*netto uyoku*) and, 76. *See also*
NicoNico (live streaming platform)

Lost in Translation (Coppola, 2003), 3
loyalty cards, 37, 96
Luhmann, Niklas, 62
Lukács, Gabriella, 36

Mahon, Maureen, 20
Mainichi Shinbun (newspaper), 145n49
male gaze, 96
Mankekar, Purnima, 37–38
Manning, Paul, 85
Mariko (pseud.), 67, 73, 82
Marxian media theory, 40–41
Massive Interactive Entertainment System
(MIES), 2
masukotto kyara (mascots), 1–2
Mazzarella, William, 34, 59, 104
McLuhan, Marshall, 20, 40, 56
media activism, 66–68, 71–76
Memon, Bashir, 69
Michiko Ishizu, 142
microphones, 116–17
Mitsuko (pseud.), 110, 114, 116–18, 121–23
Moeran, Brian, 34, 36
Morse, Margaret, 53
Muraki Yoshihiko, 2, 56

Nader, Laura, 20
Nakai Masakazu, 158n30
Nandemo Yarimashō (TV show), 6
Naohiro (pseud.), 42
National Diet Press Club, 72
national identity and nationalism, 90–97,
104–7, 127–28, 137–38
Netflix, 31, 156n2
neutrality (*chūritsu*), 56–57, 80–85, 113, 135
Newslog (online newspaper), 85
news shows, 54–55, 136. See also *Compass,
The* (TV show)
News Station (news talk show), 54
New York Times (newspaper), 33, 68
NHK (Nippon Hōsō Kyōkai): *Cool Japan*
(TV show) and, 157n15; decline in
viewership and, 135; early interactive
TV programs and, 91; 8K broadcast-
ing and, 132; Fukushima nuclear plant
disaster (2011) and, 10–12; Hōsō Bunka
Kenkyūjo (Broadcast Culture Research
Group) and, 29–30; *kisha kurabu* (re-
porter's club) system and, 70; QB47

nuclear plant disaster (2011) and, 34;
News Station (news talk show) and, 54;
reputation of, 146n51; Shiraishi and,
109, 125
TV Man Union (Terebiman Yunion, TVU),
2–3, 56, 130–31, 147n6
TV Tokyo, 91, 157n15
Twenty-One (American TV show), 5
Twitter: *The Compass* (TV show) and, 47–
49, 61; Fukushima nuclear plant disaster
(2011) and, 12; independent media start-
ups and, 74, 81; news shows and, 136
2chan (forum), 77, 78–79, 84, 85–86
2channeru (2Channel) (website), 155n45

Uesugi Takashi, 3, 67, 72–73, 77–78, 80,
81–85, 109. *See also* Independent Web
Journal (IWJ)
Ujiie Natsuhiko, 10, 16, 135
United States: audience-crafted content in,
102; broadcast model in, 20–21; interactive game shows in, 5–6; journalism in, 65–66, 68, 71–72; lateralism
and, 41–42; VOD (video on demand)
services in, 21, 31, 38, 91
Uricchio, William, 58
UStream, 64–65, 74–75

Variety (magazine), 50

variety program (*waidō shō*) format, 6, 14,
91, 94, 97–99, 127
Video Research Ltd. (ratings aggregator),
26, 33, 35, 39–40, 149n50
VOD (video on demand) services, 21, 31,
38, 53, 91, 138. *See also* NicoNico (live
streaming platform)

Warner, Michael, 140–41
Westney, Eleanor, 14
Wolferen, Karel van, 35
World Press Freedom Index, 69

Yamagami Tetsuya, 145n38
Yamaguchi, Tomomi, 76
Yamamoto Eiji, 32–33, 39
Yanai Hitofumi, 68, 87, 88
Yomiuri Shinbun (newspaper), 13, 81–85
"You Are Just the Present" (manifesto), 2
You wa Nani Shi ni Nippon e? (Why did
you come to Japan?) (TV show),
157n15
YouTube, 6–7, 51–52, 81, 88, 150n2
Yurchak, Alexi, 145n50

Zahlten, Alex, 56
zenkoku (the whole country), 90–91,
93–94. *See also* national identity and
nationalism